SYSTEMIC CHANGE IN THE JAPANESE AND GERMAN ECONOMIES

Should Japan and Germany strive to rearrange their institutional structures to make them more similar to Anglo-American standards? Where will systemic change lead? This book offers fresh insights by collecting Japanese and German contributions to this scholarly discussion both from theoretical and empirical viewpoints. A major conclusion of several papers is that the forces of differentiation are frequently underestimated. Important thematic issues include: contingency, path dependence and complementarity. Examinations of economic globalisation and rapidity of technological change pose questions about the nature of socio-economic system analysis in the future.

Werner Pascha is Professor of East Asian Economic Studies and Deputy Director of the Institute of East Asian Studies, Duisburg University, Germany.

English-language Series of the Institute of Asian Affairs, Hamburg

VERBUND STIFTUNG
DEUTSCHES ÜBERSEE-INSTITUT

The Institute of Asian Affairs forms, together with the Institute of Comparative
Overseas Studies, the Institute of African Affairs, the Institute for
Ibero-American Studies and the German Oriental Institute, the Foundation
German Overseas Institute in Hamburg.

The objective of the Institute of Asian Affairs is to promote research on
contemporary political, economic and social developments in Asian countries.
In so doing, the Institute endeavours to encourage the expression of various
opinions. The reader should note, however, that the views expressed are those of
the authors and not necessarily those of the Institute of Asian Affairs.

SYSTEMIC CHANGE IN THE JAPANESE AND GERMAN ECONOMIES

Convergence and differentiation as a dual challenge

Edited by Werner Pascha

LONDON AND NEW YORK

First published 2004 by RoutledgeCurzon,
2 Park Square, Milton Park, Abingdon, Oxon OX14 4RN

Simultaneously published in the USA and Canada
by RoutledgeCurzon
29 West 35th Street, New York, NY 10001

RoutledgeCurzon is an imprint of the Taylor & Francis Group

Publisher's Note
This book has been prepared from camera-ready copy provided by the
author.

Printed and bound in Great Britain by TJ International Ltd, Padstow,
Cornwall

British Library Cataloguing in Publication Data
A catalogue record for this book is available from the British Library

Library of Congress Cataloging in Publication Data
A catalog record for this book has been requested

ISBN 0–700–71634–3

Contents

TABLES AND FIGURES

TABLES

FIGURES

CONTRIBUTORS

Patricia Boling is Associate Professor of Political Science at Purdue University, West Lafayette, Ind., USA

Friederike Bosse is in the Department for International Markets of the German Federation of Industries (BDI), Berlin, Germany

Ivan Botskor is Director of Japaninfo Publishing, Ulm, Germany

Günter Heiduk is Professor of International Economics at Duisburg-Essen University, Duisburg, Germany

Martin Hemmert is Associate Professor of International Business at Korea University, Seoul, Republic of Korea

Carsten Herrmann-Pillath is Professor of Economics at Witten-Herdecke University, Germany

Uwe Hunger is a Senior Associate in Political Science at Münster University, Germany

Jun Imai is a Research Associate in Industrial Sociology at Duisburg-Essen University, Duisburg, Germany

Seiichi Kawasaki is Professor of Economics at the School of Informatics and Sciences of Nagoya University, Japan

Yveline Lecler is Professor of Economics at Lyon 2 University, France

Anja Osiander is an Associate in Japanese Studies at Dresden Technical University, Germany

Werner Pascha is Professor of East Asian Economic Studies at Duisburg-Essen University, Duisburg, Germany

Nicole Pohl is Assistant Professor of Economics at Franklin & Marshall College, Lancaster, Pa., USA

Beate Reszat is Head of Research on International Finance and Monetary Relations at HWWA Institute for Economic Research, Hamburg, Germany

Carsten Schreiter is in the Ministry of Economics of the State of Hesse, Wiesbaden, Germany

Karen A. Shire is Professor of Comparative Sociology at Duisburg-Essen University, Duisburg, Germany

Cornelia Storz is Professor of Japanese Economic Studies at Marburg University, Germany

Ulrich Teichler is Professor for Education Research at Kassel University, Germany

Mark Tilton is Associate Professor of Political Science at Purdue University, West Lafayette, Ind., USA

Franz Waldenberger is Professor of Japanese Economic Studies at Munich University, Germany

Christian Wey is Professor of Network Economics and IC at Berlin Technical University and a department head at the German Institute for Economic Research (DIW), Berlin, Germany

Kiichiro Yagi is Professor of Economics at Kyoto University, Japan

ACKNOWLEDGEMENTS

The contributions to this book are based on papers originally prepared for an international conference on "Japan and Germany in a globalizing economic environment: Saving institutional strengths or radically converging on international standards?", held at Duisburg University, Germany, on April 13–14, 2000. The conference was part of the "Japan in Germany" events of 1999–2000, supported by the Economics Ministry of Northrine-Westphalia (NRW), the Economic Promotion Agency of NRW, the Japanese Chamber of Industry and Commerce in Germany, the Japanese Club and the City of Düsseldorf, the Friedrich Ebert Foundation and the German-Japanese Society of the Lower Rhine at Düsseldorf. Their support as well as the dedicated assistance of Duisburg University staff is gratefully acknowledged. The editor would also like to thank Dr. Werner Draguhn and Dr. Brunhild Staiger of the Institute of Asian Affairs, Hamburg, for their continuous support and encouragement. Without it, this book would not have been possible.

The basic idea for the conference as well as for the book was originally developed together with Professor Reimut Jochimsen (1933–1999), whose untimely death deeply affected us all. Reimut Jochimsen was one of those fortunate few who combined a distinguished career in academia and in politics, while keeping a strong interest in public, non-governmental affairs. At various stages in his life, he was a full professor of economics in Kiel, federal under-secretary of state for education, minister for science and later for economic affairs in NRW, Germany's most populous state (Land), president of the regional central bank branch and member of the influential Central Bank Council of the German Bundesbank. Based in Düsseldorf, the center of Japanese business activities on the European continent, he was an active go-between for the Japanese guests and their German hosts. Among other functions in this context, he served as president of the German-Japanese Society of the Lower Rhine. His ideas, his contributions and the sheer pleasure of his company are truly missed, and this book is dedicated to his memory.

Duisburg, January 2003   Werner Pascha

Section A:

The Contribution of Theory to Convergence

1

SYSTEMIC CHANGE, CONVERGENCE, AND INSTITUTIONAL CHOICE – AN INTRODUCTION AND A SUMMARY

Werner Pascha

1.1 THE PROBLEM

Among the major advanced economies, both Japan and Germany have experienced a disappointing growth performance in recent years. This holds in particular when looking at the latter 1990s and when comparing these two countries with the USA or the UK (cf. chart 1).

Table 1 Real GDP growth of selected countries
(percentage change at annual rate)

	1970–80	1980–90	1990–00	2001	2002
France	3,3	2,4	1,8	1,8	1,2
Germany[1]	2,7	2,2	1,6	0,6	0,2
Japan	4,4	4,1	1,3	0,4	0,3
United Kingdom	1,9	2,7	2,3	2,1	1,8
United States	3,2	3,2	3,2	0,3	2,4

[1] from 1970–80 and 1980–90 for western Germany
Source: OECD data

Several explanations have been proposed to explain the lacklustre growth performance. Factors mentioned for Japan include:

- the prolonged adjustment to the bubble of the late '80s,
- an inadequate macroeconomic management (monetary and fiscal policy),
- difficulties of switching from a catching-up type to a frontier economy,
- the inaptitude of the political system and of the senior bureaucracy.

As for Germany, the following factors, among others, are often stressed:

- the adjustment problems following the unification boom, including the huge fiscal transfers to the new federal states (Länder),

16

- overly strict and complicated regulation,
- the inflexibility of the labour market,
- difficulties of the political system like the clumsy federalist decision making process.

Not only are there different explanations, but they are also on different levels of analysis. On the most straightforward level, failure is simply understood as being due to wrong decisions and moral or intellectual defects of decision makers involved. As for Germany, setting the exchange level of East German Mark for West German DM 1:1 (for many types of transaction), was sometimes considered a fatal economic mistake of the German unification process, haunting the country ever since. In Japan's case, trying for too long to sit out the post-bubble bust of the early '90s without enforcing a massive financial clean up is a similar argument for explaining prolonged trouble.

On a similar level, we find "bad luck"-types of argument. For instance, just when Japan had grown by 3.6 % in 1996, the government made the mistake of raising the taxes somewhat too early – followed by the outbreak of the Asian Crisis, which deepened the drawback of early 1997. In Germany's case, it was just too bad that the markets in post-communist Central and Eastern Europe broke down during the '90s and that interest rates in the Euro Zone were too high for the low inflation and low growth environment in Germany.

In another line of arguments, certain features of the German and Japanese economies are held responsible for malfunction. In Germany's case, the power of trade unions would be a candidate for such arguments, in Japan's case, the system of incremental process improvement in the industrial sector, which might inhibit radical technological innovation.

Such explanatory attempts are somewhat unsatisfactory, because in all cases mentioned one critical question remains unanswered: why would the economy not adjust? In the real world, outside of ideological fairy tales, the presence of policy mistakes, unwelcome developments and characteristics not fitting the new challenges are part of the normal course of events. Nobody can expect otherwise. So why should the German and Japanese economies not have been able to react properly to the challenges they had to face?

1.2 INTRODUCTION TO THE ISSUES ANALYSED

In the following book, economists and other social scientists close to socio-economic themes follow one particular type of argument, namely that change in Japan and Germany was and is inhibited by systemic features of the two economies. Due to the institutional fabric and the interrelatedness of the institutional arrangements, change may be too slow, lead into the wrong direction or be undesirable in the first place.

Table 2 Major institutional arrangements in Japan, Germany, and the USA according to standard images

		Japan	Germany	USA
Financial system	Major allocation mechanism	Credit-based	Credit-based	Capital market-based
	Regulation	(Formerly) strict separation	Universal banks	(Lenient) separation
Corporate governance	Major mechanism	*Keiretsu* business groups, main banks, government guidance	Strong banks and insurers; *Hausbank* system	Active shareholders, investment funds, etc.
Labour/industrial relations	Allocation mechanism	Internal labour market	External and internal labour market	External labour market
	Job mobility	Low	Medium	High
	Wages and Promotion	Seniority-based	Intermediate, collective bargaining	Market evaluation
	Industrial Relations	Enterprise unions	Industry unions, statutory workers' council (Betriebsrat), codetermination	(Weaker) craft/industry unionism

While this is certainly not the only approach that might be taken, it does account for some peculiar properties of Japan and Germany since the 1990s at first glance:

- Decisions and decision makers are not simply – and naively – understood as wrong or bad. Rather, it is discussed that even while individual courses of action may have been understandable, the systemic boundaries and effects led to outcomes that nobody might have wanted in the first place.

- It is striking that the slump in Japan and in Germany has been rather prolonged. This seems to suggest that the problem is not a short-term issue. Rather, a certain stickiness seems to be involved which leads to "wrong" courses of action. It is thus natural to turn to the institutional level, which is characterized and even defined by the persistence of certain behavioural patterns.[1]

- Germany and Japan on the one and the USA and the UK on the other hand can indeed be grouped according to similarities of their institutional frameworks. This holds, for instance, when corporate governance, the financial system, and the labour system are taken into consideration (cf. chart 2). One may then conjecture that such peculiarities might indeed be important for the problems of systemic adjustment and low economic performance.

Another important concept besides systemic change, which guides the following contributions, is the (possible) convergence of economic systems. If indeed economic systems can be grouped in ideal or real types, one can ask whether "change" actually means the transfer to a different type altogether, involving not only one institution or sub-system, but the whole institutional arrangement. Following the discussion of the 1990s, the overarching question can be posed whether Japan's and Germany's system might be expected to converge towards the Anglo-American type of economic system. Alternatively, one might ask whether the pressures of economic globalisation will eventually lead towards a convergence on global standards (which may – or may not – be similar to what one already finds in some economies). Another distinction should be introduced at this stage (cf. chart 3): First of all, there can be different views on whether economic systems should move towards a global benchmark which possesses best-practice characteristics, or whether they should not (normative analysis). Secondly, there can be

---

[1] It is tempting to discuss these issues with the terminology of institutional economics. In the most famous contribution to institutional change and its relation to economic performance in recent years, Nobel Prize winner Douglass C. North defines institutions as "the rules of the game in a society or, more formally, ... [as] the humanly devised constraints that shape human interaction" (North 1990: 3). Several concepts used in this introduction and throughout the book, like path dependence or principal–agent issues, draw heavily on institutional economics.

diverging views on whether such systems will (have to) change and will be able to change or not, irrespective of whether such a change is considered desirable or not (positivist analysis).

Table 3 Different scenarios for convergence

Positivist level Normative level	Institutions *will/can* change	Institutions *will not/cannot* change
Institutions *should* change	Convergence towards best-practice standards	Secular decline of non-adjusting economies
Institutions *should not* change	Convergence as a "trap of globalism"	Parallel development and competition of different systems

In the course of the book, it will turn out that things are not that simple. Some of the issues underlying the following contributions can be highlighted as contingency (1), path dependence (2), and complementarity (3).

(1) Setting up and running an institution obviously has pronounced effects on the costs (and benefits) generated. It is fair to assume that if different institutional solutions can be observed, this will often be due to different trade-offs between the various cost (or, respectively, benefit) categories. Put differently, the choice of systemic structures may be considered contingent upon the peculiar cost-benefit trade-offs.

Arguably, the most consequential trade-offs to reckon with are those between governance and allocation costs. Different institutional arrangements can, to some extent, be interpreted as various approaches to find a sensible balance between governance and allocation effects.

For instance, discussing the corporate governance structures of Japan, Germany, the USA and the UK, one frequently finds assertions that the first two make use of rather complex network structures among firms, whereas the latter more often rely on markets. Markets are a highly regarded institution to solve allocation problems (as long as some conditions are fulfilled), whereas complex networks can serve the purpose of improving governance, because deep relations between the relevant parties make it easier to monitor effort and sincerity. Neglecting set-up and switchover costs, there are two major issues to be considered when choosing an arrangement: the ease to run such a system, and the character of real world problems to be solved. If it is too troublesome to run a network, because actors do not agree on a world view or are too selfish, this raises the relative merits of relying on markets and what they can do for allocation, some governance problems notwithstanding. If, on the other hand, allocation is not a serious issue, concentrating on governance is more important and fruitful; this could be the case when a late-comer economy knows rather well where and how to allocate capital and labour.

Sometimes, it is argued that the dynamics of technological change and the advent of generic technologies raise the benefits of network-type governance modes. The increasing number of alliances is cited as evidence. However, networks only work when they can be enforced. Once the prerequisites for such enforcement are endangered, other modes gain relative merit. For instance, as soon as partners can easily exit their networks, the potential gains of networks become questionable. In these cases, and globalisation might be considered as such a development, markets and hierarchies with their more clearly spelt-out explicit contracts could gain ground. Moreover, the more choices there are, the more market-oriented solutions will unfold their advantages, unless one finds a way to keep networks "open".

(2) We should now give up the assumption that switchover from one system to another is unproblematic. The path-dependence of institutions as stabilised behavioural patterns means that there is an inbuilt inertia. Consequently, slow incremental change will be more likely than revolutionary turn-arounds. This issue can be exemplified with respect to the labour market. There is a general impression that this institutional arrangement is quite different in Japan and the USA, while Germany is often considered rather close to the Japanese case (cf. chart 2). Whereas labour in Japan is often associated with lifetime employment, reliance on internal labour markets, underdeveloped external labour markets, and seniority-based wage structure and promotion, the US labour market shows a higher labour mobility, well-developed external markets and performance-related pay. In the convergence debate, it is frequently discussed whether either of the systems will have to give way, and Japan's labour system is often thought to be headed for change. Irrespective of whether any of the systems is more efficient, we can look at the individuals and their choices. If the external labour market dominates the economy, the firm or individual will also tend to prefer it: If one loses one's job, one can easily look around for the next best employment, and the firm also has few incentives to invest in fixed personnel, when it can easily turn to external markets. On the other hand, when internal labour markets dominate the economy, the individual will also tend to seek stable employment, because he has few chances to find something else; also, the firm will take care of its long-term personnel, because it cannot rely on external labour markets to flexibly fill gaps.

Suppose that A is the solution realised in the USA and B the one in Japan. What are the chances that B converges towards A? Clearly, when a few firms and individuals deviate from the B pattern, the system has a tendency to swing back towards B, because it will be difficult to find jobs and promising job seekers on the (small) external labour market. Only when the deviation reaches a certain limit will there be a permanent change, with the system gravitating towards A. Consequently, we find a strong inbuilt inertia. When change exceeds a certain limit, the system can shift to a totally different point with remarkably strong adjustment – not only driven by the activity of the first deviators, but also particularly through reactions from those who have so far strongly clung to the former equilibrium.

We have so far assumed that all solutions are equally able to solve the allocation problem of labour. Life will usually be more complicated, though. There are three interesting cases:

- External factors may directly influence the cost and benefit profile of various institutional arrangements for labour markets. For instance, when the population is rapidly aging, a seniority-based pay system will become increasingly, possibly unbearably, expensive.

- Another aspect is that the profile of various arrangements depends on the state of institutional arrangements in other parts of the economy. We will return to this institutional complementarity below.

- Finally, there is an additional inertia, because institutional arrangements cannot only be understood in functional terms, but also as sources of rents and quasi-rents for interested actors who have few incentives to allow the status quo to be changed. Under the condition of inertia derived above, rent-seeking interests have ample chance to organise themselves and to entrench their extraction strategy. As for the Japanese labour market, for instance, it has been frequently suggested that lack of exit and voice options for the employed has led them to be easily pushed around by the management.

As a final note on path-dependence, it should be noted that there is an unfortunate possibility in policy-oriented discussions to embrace the fashionable concept of path-dependence to avoid change and adjustment. It is disturbing that the tendency towards inertia may be drawn attention to, not because of well-established causal relations, but because of the self-interest and disinformation activities of rent-seekers. There is a danger that the role played by referring to "uniqueness" in the apologetic Nihonron literature is taken over by the notion of path-dependence in the more fashionable arguments, based on institutional theories.

(3) The co-evolution of complementary institutions can be understood as a process quite similar to the establishment of a single institution through path-dependence. One can show this with respect to institutional arrangements like the labour market and corporate governance. (Note that even a single institutional arrangement can be understood as a closely-knit co-evolution of several institutions.) Within corporate governance, let us concentrate on the role of cross-shareholding, which has been of widespread importance in Japan. Lifelong employment and cross-shareholding are mutually complementary: only when shareholding has a high degree of stability, will it be safe for management to consider employment as fixed and not to respond to short-term difficulties by laying off employees.

What do these findings tell us about the chances for change in an economy characterised by a complementarity of its institutions? When cross-shareholding is reduced through the competitive pressure from globalising financial markets, the effect on labour relations may at first be minimal. When (almost) all companies engage in cross-shareholdings and "Japan-type" labour conditions, they will be reluctant to reduce cross-shareholdings even in the case of pressure from the financial markets, because the cross-shareholdings save them from the pressure of business fluctuations and thus from giving up lifetime employment. When the downward pressure on cross-shareholdings becomes even stronger, there will be a significant move towards opening the labour market, as investors expect short-term results and managers feel forced to give up employment stability. In that case, a gestalt change of the complete labour-cum-corporate governance system can happen. When we associate this with the "Anglo-American" approach to industrial relations, we might indeed find convergence – but after overcoming the very strong inertia of complementarity.

Two points should be noted in this context. Firstly, the complementarity is usually mutual; i.e. not only the labour system is supported by the strength (or absence) of cross-shareholdings, but also the other way round. Secondly, we have so far assumed that actors are well informed about what costs and benefits they may encounter in different institutional settings. However, we have to take into account that an appraisal of the pros and cons of a single institution critically depends on its environment, namely on other institutions which will often have a complementary character. This means that institutions do not possess an "absolute value" independent of the institutional framework they are embedded in. There is no Archimedean point from which to evaluate institutions. They may have (had) beneficial effects in one (national) system, but would lead to disaster when introduced into another system, with its different net of mutual complementarities.

The relativity of institutional solutions with regard to real world challenges has important repercussions for the probability of convergence. While a challenge (like "economic globalisation") may be similar for a vast number of institutional systems, the sensible responses can be quite different. The systemic complementarities can be expected to be extremely difficult to quantify. Because importing an institution – which has been successful elsewhere – is thus associated with considerable uncertainty, there may be a considerable – and quite rational – bias against rashly converging. Even in the case of successful convergence, when the net positive effect of a certain "successful" institution in country A is considered to be known, the net positive effect in country B will usually be lower, because it will normally be less complementary to B's institutional arrangements. This appraisal might change when B's complete institutional setting is under review for reform, but this would give rise to even more risks and uncertainties.

"Choosing" an institutional setting obviously refers to government activity. When discussing institutional complementarities, it is thus necessary to spend considerable effort on appraising the impact of the state and its regulatory activities. When discussing capital markets and corporate governance, for instance, a key question for appraising different organisational responses is in which regulatory environment they are employed. For simplicity, one may distinguish neoclassical and relational regulation (see Dietl 1998: 23), which are actually nothing but institutional arrangements that may, or may not be consistently applied. Neoclassical regulation aims at allocative efficiency, which it wants to pursue by eliminating market imperfections as much as possible. For instance, takeovers are discriminated against, because they may lead to more concentrated market structures. Relational regulation is interested in governance efficiency and tries to accomplish enhanced corporate governance through incentive compatibility between principals and agents, for instance. Relational regulation has no bias against takeovers, because they may solve some typical governance problems. (The reader may note that this distinction mirrors the earlier distinction of reducing allocation vs. governance costs through institutional choice. Before, we looked at the matter from the point of view of private actors, whereas here we assume the perspective of the state regulator).

A key question is how – and which kind of – information is used in the various regulatory environments. For instance, the use of insider knowledge has little positive value in a neoclassical world. Rather, some actors may turn away from the capital market because of their frustration with others realising insider rents. Therefore, neoclassical regulators usually try to set up measures against insider trading. In relational regulation, insider trading may actually serve a positive function, because insider rents constitute an incentive for banks and other agents to engage in costly monitoring activities and thus gain valuable insider information.

Both regulatory environments have their characteristic strengths and weaknesses. Institutional and organisational responses of private actors, like the role played by investment trusts, holding companies, financial keiretsu (corporate groups), etc., can be understood as attempts to get along with the peculiar market imperfections. They perform an important role within the respective regulatory environments and are, as discussed before, contingent upon them.

We now give up another assumption, which we so far have implicitly made, namely that institutions are universal throughout a (national) system. In Dietl's (1998) framework introduced above, an important feature is to distinguish between young, medium, and mature industries, because their information characteristics are quite different. In young, immature industries the unpredictability and instability of technological developments prevents insiders from acquiring important information. In mature industries, insiders have more chances to successfully evaluate risks and opportunities. Given neoclassical regulation, immature industries may thus often be governed through capital markets, whereas in maturing and mature industries, holding companies and multidivisional organisations may more often be found. (The argument is somewhat more complicated because of the role of investment plasticity, i.e. the range of choices available to the firm that is to be controlled, but this aspect is left out here for simplicity.)

It is thus conceivable that different industries or sectors develop quite different approaches to upcoming challenges, like the globalisation of financial markets. This argument cannot only be applied to industrial branches, but also to other markets and institutional arrangements. As for the labour market, for example, it is already textbook knowledge that Japan is not universally characterised by lifetime employment and seniority wages. In small and medium enterprises (SMEs), only a small number of regular employees are usually covered by such a system. When we discussed the complementarity of cross-shareholdings and the "Japan-type" labour system above, we have left out of consideration that (at least) in the SME sector, non-permanent and non-seniority-based labour arrangements can be quite compatible with a "Japanese" environment.

Even within industries, the approaches taken by different firms to position themselves among their competitors may be quite diverse. There may be leaders concentrating on technological advance, others stressing a massive expansion to serve a growing market and still others occupying small niches. These strategies will have different degrees of complementarity with peculiar institutional solutions for labour, corporate governance or innovation. Assuming that a general tendency towards deregulation enlarges the range of institutional arrangements for economic actors, it is conceivable that the real issue is not whether the economic institutions in all national systems become alike, but what choice there is and whether certain patterns or regularities can be expected and indeed observed. In this respect, globalisation may have a strong supporting effect: as borders are getting less important for determining which institutions (labour, finance, innovation) to use, actors can choose their own mix out of an enlarged pool of potential institutional arrangements, making it ever more difficult to speak of "national systems" and of convergence or divergence on that level. Rather, one may want to look for clusters of peculiar institutional arrangements or companies in different countries employing similar strategies, embedding themselves in their "own" set of supporting institutions.

As for the underlying sources of institutional change, North (1990: 84) rather plainly mentions changes in relative prices and in tastes. Of course, there may be some endogenous sources of change, but it seems reasonable to conjecture that the ultimate source of major shifts will usually be exogenous. They may have all kinds of backgrounds, a new military technology, a new religion or a major natural disaster, and one can do little but take them at face value.

Economic globalisation, and the globalisation of financial markets in particular, is usually seen as the possible source of a sea change of institutional rearrangements all over the globe. Its potential impact is considered so strong, because it changes such a large number of relative prices in an economy exposed to increased global interaction. Apart, changes in tastes may be experienced on an unprecedented scale, as cultural artefacts and underlying values and attitudes race around the world through such media as the Internet, influencing people everywhere and simultaneously.

Globalisation thus does not have an impact on only one or a small number of institutional arrangements, but strongly influences all of the major institutional arrangements of an economy: capital markets, corporate governance, labour, innovation, government policy/regulation, education. This is a necessary condition – albeit not a satisfying condition – for overcoming the inertia of complementary institutional arrangements.

1.3 SUMMARY OF THE CONTRIBUTIONS

How do the contributors of the present volume tackle these issues? Firstly, we will give an overview of the individual papers. Afterwards, we will relate them to the overarching topics discussed above.

While systemic change in Japan and Germany is an important empirical issue, theoretical points should not be overlooked. Yagi, Hermann-Pillath and Kawasaki look at contributions particularly relevant in a Japanese-German context.

Yagi points out the intellectual undercurrents of the Japanese post-war system, which is usually associated with economic planning, state intervention, and industrial policy. In particular, he takes a close look at three leading economists and their background, Arisawa, Tohata, and Nakayama. Yagi finds that already by the late 1960s, the "intellectual hegemony"of the school of "managed" economic policy had ended. In her comment, Osiander deals with the relevance of the developmentalist intellectual tradition. She notes that the turn taken by the Japanese post-war economy seems to have been quite different from what some of its leading masterminds had envisioned.

Hermann-Pillath surveys the contribution of a variety of economic theories to explain convergence and/or divergence of economic systems. He argues from an institutional and evolutionary background, looking at the dynamics of systems and the patterns of change. Such an approach tries to avoid the dangers of oversimplifying neoclassical research and its obsession with equilibrium-based modelling. He finds that the openness of developments, the need for "metainstitutional frameworks" to allow for discoveries, among others, makes the convergence of institutions quite unlikely. Rather, divergence may be a precondition for comparative advantage and a convergence of economic performance. As a discussant, Schreiter agrees with many points while asking for more spelled-out "pattern predictions" (F. A. Hayek) in the presence of innovation and openness. Using Hayek's term, Schreiter refers to the Austrian-British Nobel Prize winner who influenced many German academics: skepticism about clear-cut, deterministic expectations of historical change is widespread.

Kawasaki's contribution represents the so-called "comparative institutional analysis" (CIA) school, which has made a major impact in Japan. The school looks at the complementarity of institutional structures and analyses the functionality of systemic relations. Kawasaki takes the development of Japanese computer network systems as a case in point. While this is an empirical application, the author emphasises the basic approach of CIA. In what is quite typical of CIA reasoning, he stresses the role of different types and framings of information processing for distinguishing business models in computer industry. As compared to the A ("American") model, the J ("Japanese") model is based on horizontal information sharing, and has advantages when utilising and improving known technology. Japanese firms had problems to react appropriately to an emerging N ("network") type of new IT industries, lacking the flexibility of government, bureaucracy and firms to appropriately transcend the old J-type.

The following three contributions take up major forces, which are frequently thought to put severe strain on the economic systems of Japan and Germany, namely (international) finance (Reszat), technology (Hemmert), and corporate governance (Waldenberger).

Reszat treats the development of international financial centers and proposes a research concept to study Tokyo's chances of being the major center in the Asia-Pacific time zone. She chooses an evolutionary-institutional approach and stresses the importance of the spatial self-organisation of the market-driven international financial system for locational "decisions". At the same time, path-dependence and lock-in represent other factors determining the prospects of Tokyo as an international center. Heiduk and Pohl underline the necessity of careful modelling to grasp the complex evolving relationships among such factors. They remind us not to overlook the individual actors, when they act and react to the stimuli they encounter at a peculiar time and place.

Hemmert takes a comparative look at the technology and innovation management in German and Japanese firms, introducing the reader to a survey recently undertaken. Companies in both countries use "follower" strategies and are not particularly known for breakthrough innovations. However, there are also systemic differences, for instance in their internal organisation of research and development (R&D), which are related to, among others, human resources and the organisation of manufacturing industry. While changes are noticeable and mutual benchmarking is important, Hemmert doubts whether a case for uniform global standards can be made. The internationalisation of R&D, a major positive force in recent years, is actually driven by and utilises institutional diversity. Discussing the paper, Botskor stresses the role of the wider socio-economic environment for systemic change, and the critical role of education in particular.

Waldenberger also undertakes a comparative analysis of Japan and Germany, focussing on corporate governance issues. He introduces both as being characterised by relational systems of governance, as compared to market-based systems. They are insider-oriented and have arisen in the catch-up phase of both late-developing economies, functioning in the absence of well-developed external markets for labour and capital. As for the future, Waldenberger notes the importance of change in an environment characterised by rapid developments and uncertainty. Such change will take time, though, and, consequently, it will allow firms to choose among various governance structures.

In the following section, three important channels of bringing about systemic change are concentrated upon, namely the purchasing system for Japanese business networks, which is often considered an important agent of change, the role of international standards in forcing convergence upon economies, and the need of changing the employment system in both Germany and Japan.

Lecler takes a close look at the purchasing system of Japanese companies both at home and abroad. Based upon surveys and two case studies for two, rather different industries – electric/electronic appliances as well as cars –, she finds considerable evidence for convergence. Subcontractors in Japan have to change considerably to adjust, weakening the traditional relational principles that characterised Japanese production networks until recently. Moreover, due to various forces Japanese multinationals investing abroad are not able to reproduce the "old ways", with Southeast Asia as a region of choice for such attempts. In her comments, Bosse voices some doubt whether the convergence with Western modes will ever be complete. While indeed there may be more open and expanded purchasing networks, much will depend on the firm strategies, and some asymmetric power relations are likely to remain.

Storz is interested to understand how Japanese and German enterprises introduce the ISO 9000 standard, which deals with product and work organisation. While such a standard should indeed be expected to be global at first glance, she concludes that one standard is actually not one standard. The reason is that it has to be interpreted, implemented and communicated, and is thus dependent on pre-existing long-term (or generalised) relationships as well as differences between appearance and "true", informal behavioural patterns. Adaptation is thus culture-specific and does not lead to uniform convergence. Wey basically agrees with Storz and offers some additional insight into the industrial economics aspects of the subject. As ISO 9000 is a minimum quality standard, it may be put to work in different "dialects". Hopefully, these can be compatible and offer positive network effects.

In their paper on the employment system in Japan and Germany, Shire and Imai remind us that both countries are not only confronted with the pressure from the markets and from liberalisation, but also from work transformations which cover, among others, new types of workers and new industries. Looking at changes away from the old, rather successful type of a "functional flexibility"-approach based on continuous employment, training deployment in a range of tasks, the authors notice that this change is not simply market oriented. Rather, for new types of labour like organisational professionals, both Germany and Japan often turn to traditional solutions (guest workers in Germany, peripheral, albeit educated women in Japan), showing a considerable degree of continuity. Discussing these findings, Hunger stresses the role of cultural history and political institutions in explaining the slow speed of change. Eventually, the forces gain momentum from the margin, though, and both countries may have to give up their status as non-immigrant countries, for instance.

Tilton and Boling look at different issues of market rigidities in Japan and Germany, discussing industrial issues (telecommunication, steel) as well as labour markets and the impact on childbearing and the future workforce. They note serious shortcomings. In telecommunication, both countries were laggards in the '90s, in Japan's case due to high, regulated prices for telecom services and in Germany's case due to codetermination. In the long run, weaknesses in the labour market and in associated childcare policies may be even more critical. The gender regimes of both countries – for different reasons – inhibit women and families to raise children and supply an adequate future labour force. Shrinking populations are dangerous, and it is an open question how the socio-economic systems can find appropriate policy schemes to get along with them.

Another key policy arena for long-term development is education. Teichler reports findings from a recent survey among ten thousand graduates in Europe and Japan. As for the Japanese graduates, the task of adapting to an international and globalising work environment seems to be particularly challenging, at least if compared with their European counterparts. However, Teichler notes that many US graduates, while not included in the survey, may have been even less exposed to internationalisation so far.

1.4 COMMON THREADS, COMMON FINDINGS?

It would seem quite preposterous to try to draw firm conclusions from the various contributions in this volume. Where will systemic change lead Japan and Germany? What can, what should the countries try to do? Will there be "convergence" towards Western, global, or Anglo-American modes of organising the economy or not? The reader will hardly be surprised to learn that there are no simple answers in the book. The editor is confident, though, that this should not keep any interested reader from diving further into the following pages. Why? As happens so often, posing topical questions like the one concerning convergence will not lead to "plain vanilla" answers, but rather to more advanced and adequate ways of looking at real-world issues.

With these considerations in mind, we can try to pull some of the strings together, making use of the concepts introduced above and hopefully not doing injustice to the authors by oversimplying their arguments. One overarching impression is that most contributors are skeptical about a straightforward tendency towards "convergence". No author subscribes to an explicitly normative position about the issues studied, but there are some arguments that point to the positive, often underestimated side effects of divergence. Hermmann-Pillath notes that diversity can be understood as constituting important comparative (institutional) advantages, and Hemmert remarks that the benefits of international cooperation in innovation are actually based on the idea that there are differences that can be exploited. With respect to the contingency issue, Lecler's paper is particularly interesting, because it shows the limits of transferring certain institutional sets abroad. We can learn from Storz that one should not always take certain arrangements at face value and expect them to be the same all over the world; this does not even hold for seemingly well-defined constructs like an ISO standard.

Path-dependence plays a role in almost all papers, most explicitly in Reszat's. Tilton/Boling warn us that sticking to a certain path may have significant opportunity costs, which may not be visible at first sight. Yagi points out the importance of mental models for framing our view of systems and their paths – even long after a certain viewpoint may have ceased to be a major intellectual force. Complementarity is another concept to which many authors refer or which they implicitly use. Waldenberger argues most explicitly along those lines, remarking that complementarity on a national level may become less important when sectoral or even actor-specific institutional sets become possible. Teichler's paper is important, because his discussion of the role of eduction shows that one cannot only deal with economic institutions in a narrow sense.

A final issue stressed by almost all contributors is the all-encompassing power of forces influencing the socio-economic systems and their paths of change. Economic globalisation and the rapidity of technological change make their impact felt in almost any field. Shire/Imai concentrate on these effects in their paper on labour relations, and Kawasaki shows how new computer network systems can alter the whole playing field for enterprises working in that sector. The consequences for "systemic change" are so far-reaching and delicate at the same time that it is questionable wether it will make much sense in the future to pose this issue along national demarcation lines. Rather, it will be interesting to study diversity, how it comes about, how it can be fostered, and how it flourishes. Industries, regions, strategic clusters of firms may be more important for such phenomena than national border lines – at least for scholars studying these issues.

REFERENCES

Dietl, Helmut, *Capital markets and corporate governance in Japan, Germany and the United States*. London 1998.

North, Douglass C., *Institutions, Institutional Change and Economic Performance*. Cambridge et al. 1990.

2

JAPANESE THEORY OF INDUSTRIALIZATION/ MODERNIZATION: BETWEEN LIBERALISM AND DEVELOPMENTALISM

Kiichiro Yagi

After a decade of economic stagnation, it is now in vogue among economists to say that the economic system of Japan suffers from an "institutional fatigue". This expression, however, connotes that the unique institutional arrangement of Japanese economy had once an age when it functioned well. The precise diagnosis and prescript against this "fatigue" differs in each case, particularly by the range of the time that the observer adopts. Debates on the origin of the post-war economic regime in the wartime economy are also related to this problem (Noguchi 1995, Okazaki and Okuno 1993). In this case beside the protection and control of the partitioned industries (*gyokai*) by the government, the closed long-term relations in the employment, supplier-customer relation (*keiretsu*), and main bank system are the main targets of the criticism. Further, the literature that applies the concept of "developmentalism" to the industrialization of Japan (Murakami 1992 (1996), Yagi 1997b) seem to have nearly one century's time span for their considerations. In this case, an active role of the government in the economic development that is not always justified by the orthodox Western liberal economics emerges in the front of consideration. From this viewpoint, also the Meiji-government that promoted industrialization by establishing not only basic institutions but also model plants falls in the group of developmentalist state along with the Shôwa-government.

2.1 NATIONALISTIC RESPONSE OF A MEIJI LIBERAL

What I now discuss in this paper is the intellectual background of Japanese economic policy that was prevalent up to the end of high-growth era. As Bao (1994) put it, "The practice of managed economy was not only influenced by foreign economic ideas, but also supported by the long tradition of state intervention in Japanese economic thinking after the Meiji Restoration"(Bao 1994: 116).

However, in using such series of words as "managed economy", "state intervention" and "developmentalism", one has to avoid the misconception that economic liberalism was essentially foreign to the economic thought of modern Japan. On the contrary, it was the Western economic liberalism that awakened modern Japanese who had been long accustomed to live passively under feudal control. One of the most important origins of Japanese developmentalism was the practical response of Japanese liberals who realized the gap between Western advanced nations and their own nation. The first forerunner of this direction was Fukuzawa Yukichi (1835–1901), the champion of Meiji enlightenment and a great liberal, himself. Deeply impressed by primary textbooks in political economy, Fukuzawa stressed the independence of individuals and advocated a new moral on the principle of reciprocity that was open to the free competition. But he soon realized that a predetermined harmony would not appear spontaneously in such a situation as in the international relations where the discrepancy between the strong and the weak nations, the advanced and the delayed nations existed.

In contrast to a dogmatic liberal such as Taguchi Ukichi (1855–1905), Fukuzawa supported the residential restriction of foreign merchants in Japan and suggested a protective policy in the international trade.[1] In the *An Outline of a Theory of Civilization (Bunmeiron no gairyaku)* he declared "Independence of the nation is the purpose. Our present civilization is the means to attain it"(Fukuzawa 1958–64: 209). He did not defer to the nationalism by regarding the demand of nation itself as a "public cause". From the viewpoint of the human race as a whole, it was only a "private cause" of a late-starting nation.

> "What I expressed by 'our present civilization' is not the true civilization. My intention is to establish first independence of our nation, leaving the rest for the task of the second step, and to expect future progress. So long as we limit our discussion in this range, the national independence is by itself the civilization. Without civilization, we cannot maintain our national independence" (ibid.: 209f.).

To Fukuzawa, it was just this quest for the independence of the nation that could encourage Japanese to avoid servility and to demand equality in their transactions with Westerners.

Instead of the predetermined natural law of the economic harmony, a natural course of the development of the "civilization" emerged as the main subject of the *Outline*. He discerned the essence and the appearance of the "civilization" and defined the former as the "progress of the intelligence and virtue of the people" (ibid.: 40). He contended that in order to catch up the advanced nations Japanese had to begin with "difficult tasks" of acquiring

---

[1] Kumagai (1998) describes the contrast of the two Meiji liberals. On Fukuzawa's attitude to economics and liberalism, see also Sugiyama (1994) and Yagi (1999).

the sense of independence before indulging themselves in the attraction of Western products. It was his conviction that the "civilization" was the universal course of development among nations, so long as they did not lose the sense of independence.

Fukuzawa's recasting of the Western liberal economics reminds us of Friedrich List's criticism against the "cosmopolitan" economics of A. Smith and J. B. Say. "The strategic view of the economy" (Bao 1997: 24) is common to the understanding of the economy of both scholars. As List wrote, "It was the lesson of the history that all nations that could not have the mighty business class in an appropriate period declined" (List 1841). Fukuzawa strove to create the "middle class" who could lead Japanese economy on the base of their intellectual forces by his school, Keio Gijuku, and by his publication. In his prospect, the growth of the "middle class" would bring the balance of power in the relations between government and the private sector. Under the principle of the division of labour, the government was entrusted to make legislation and to form policies for the sake of nation, and the private sector would support it by their cooperation and initiatives.

We have so far summarized the pragmatic economic thinking of Fukuzawa. By his theory of "civilization", Fukuzawa provided the then Japanese with the perspective that would conciliate the antagonism between liberalism and interventionism with a time span. It is interesting that this trait survived for a century in Japan and molded the economic policy in her post-1945 industrial state.

2.2 CONSENSUS AMONG ECONOMISTS IN 1945

In the history of Japanese economic policy, the years immediately after 1945 were marked by the active participation of economists in policy making. On the very next day to the Emperor's broadcasting of the surrender, a group of economists gathered in a room of the Foreign Ministry. This gathering, the Special Research Committee of the Foreign Ministry, consisted of ca. twenty economists and economic experts including Marxian economists as well as non-Marxian economists.[2] The following summary of the general conditions and current economic policy issues that was proposed for the

---

[2]Its main members were: Arisawa Hiromi, Aki Koichi, Inaba Hidezo, Ishikawa Ichiro, Inoue Harunaru, Uno Kozo, Ouchi Hyoue, Ohno Kazuo, Kameyama Naoto, Kishimoto Seijiro, Kondo Yasuo, Taura Teizo, Tatumi Yoshitomo, Tuchiya kiyoshi, Tohata Seiichi, Tomooka Hisao, Nakayama Ichiro, Yamanaka Tokutaro, Yamada Moritaro, Wakimura Yoshitaro. In addition Morita Yuzo, Sasaki Yoshitake, Nakayama Shiro, Ishikawa Akio, Sugiyama Tomogoro, Sugihara Arata, Tsuru Shigeto, Seki Morisaburo, Satoh Kensuke, Ichikawa Yasujiro, Mukaiyama Mikio, and Ohhara Hisayuki joined the discussion. Final report was written by its general secretaries, Ohkita saburo, Gotoh Yonosuke, Oda Hiroshi, and Namiki Shokichi (Arisawa 1989: 49–50).

discussion could show the consensus of the economists at that time to discuss the future of Japanese economy.

Three General Basic Conditions

1. The organic combination of the world economy would increase and world-wide division of labour would develop. However, it was admitted that the world economy would be divided into the Soviet bloc and the Anglo-American bloc, and Japanese economy was to be based on the latter.
2. Planning and organization of the management of the economy. Scientific coordination of the consumption and production that could correspond to the progress from the manufacture to the modern mass production system.
3. Socialization of the economy. Socialization and cooperation of the production and consumption.

Three Current Economic Policy Issues

1. Prevention of unemployment
2. Increase in production
3. Self-sustaining normal balance of the trade[3]

Politicians and bureaucrats who lost the frame of orientation were willing to listen to the opinion of economists. After a series of intensive discussions this committee published its final report, *The Basic Problems of the Economic Reconstruction (Nihon keizai saiken no kihon mondai)* in early 1946 and dissolved. In the same year, Ishibashi Tanzan was nominated as the finance minister of the Yoshida cabinet, Tsuru Shigeto displayed his leadership at the Economic Stabilizing Bureau (*Keizai antei honbu*), Yamada Moritaro sat at the table of the Land Reform Committee, and Ouchi Hyoue's words on the public finance were respected.

However, most of them lost influence on the economic policy after the "Dodge Line" and the "reverse course" around 1950. In this period when the agricultural and labor reforms came to the end, the ministerial bureaucracy regained its power. The Economic Stabilizing Bureau that was the citadel of the non-bureaucrat economists was downgraded by Yoshida's antipathy to the idea of economic planning. From the few economists whose influence survived after 1950, we will deal with three economists all of whom served on the Special Committee of 1945–46: Arisawa Hiromi (1896–1988), Nakayama Ichiro (1898–1981), and Tohata Seiichi (1899–1983). They were often called *gosanke* (the trio: three large clans in the Edo period that have the rank of advisory status to the Tokugawa Shogunate), since they continuously occupied important positions in various administrative and advisory committees.

---

[3]Extracted from Ohkita Saburo's presentation in his discourse with Arisawa (Arisawa 1989: 7).

2.3 SOCIALIZATION AND DUAL STRUCTURE: ARISAWA HIROMI

It was Arisawa that took the initiative of the Special Committee. Among the items cited above, the concept of "socialization" and "planning", in particular, showed his influence on the discussion of the committee.

In the economic history of post-war Japan, Arisawa's name appears often as the advocate of the "priority production" of coal and steel that resurrected the Japanese economy. But in his view, this concept was coupled with the concept of the socialization that he had kept in mind since his study abroad. In the preface to *Inflation and Socialization* (*Infureeshon to shakaika*) that was published in the autumn of 1948, Arisawa added his following recollections:

"I arrived Berlin in the early spring of 1926. At that time, the world economy was in the period of relative stability. German economy that muddled through two years' stabilization crisis following the catastrophic inflation was moving gradually to prosperity.

The politico-economical process of the German Republic then was quiet in a sense and no serious problems were on the surface. As post-war issues such as the democratic revolution, socialization movement, inflation, and reparation were solved for the present, the track for the German economy was fixed already. In 1925, the German Communist Party determined its New Directions in September, and the National League of German Industry proclaimed the Program of German Industry. After some delay, the Socialdemocratic Party adopted its Keele Program at the plenary congress in May 1927. Both of the labor parties and associations of capitalists prepared for developing their movements with new directions under the changed situation.

Taking Dr. Alexander Konradi, the historian who had once worked at the archive of the SPD as a tutor, I at once began the research of the politico-economical process of the republic. Naturally, I had to study the process since the cease fire in detail. Why had the socialization movement that had once been enthusiastically demanded by the mass and seemed irresistible, disappeared like a bubble? In Hilferding's words, why had the revolution turned out to be a mere wage struggle? Crisis and catastrophe attacked German capitalism repeatedly and its life came sometimes nearly to an end. Still it revived like a phoenix out of the ashes. Studying the process I was caught by a melancholy. Dr. Konradi told me cool, 'The matter was over in the confusion and errors'.

At that time I had never dreamt that my own nation would follow the same destiny after two decades. I found myself in the midst of the same situation and problems that I studied twenty years ago in Berlin. The international environment of Japan was totally different from the German case. The economic distress was severer. From this very reason I thought that the reconstruction of Japanese economy and the solution of the inflation should be based on the socialization and that the radical democratization should not be reduced to the wage struggle. After the lapse of twenty-two months from the end of the war, I have to think that the history has repeated twice. Dr. Konradi's words appear now again on my mouth.

The course of the reconstruction of the Japanese economy was about to fix its direction. Now it cannot be changed by anyone. A period in the postwar is about to be over. We will face a new situation and new problems in the coming stage. Therefore, the direction of our movement must change. We have to reflect deeply what we have to do in the new stage" (Arisawa 1948: 1–3).

This was written soon after the failure of the nationalization plan of the coalmines in 1947. This was the promise that Socialists made at the second election and won the largest mandate in the Diet. The original plan admitted workers' participation in every stage of the management of the nationalized mines. However, the Katayama's coalition cabinet could only pass a mutilated bill in the Diet, that was destined to be repealed in a few years. Arisawa was not a neutral observer in this matter, because he was the head of the Special Working Committee for the Coalmining that was established in November 1946 and proposed the "priority production" to the then Yoshida cabinet. In his journal article written in January 1946 where Arisawa published his idea of strategic role of the promotion of coalmining in the resurrection of the "reproduction process" of Japanese economy, he also envisaged the "transformation" from capitalism to socialism in the worker-led reconstruction process of the industry: "What does it mean that we have the unemployed with working will and the workers who could not eat despite of their work? They move rapidly to the conscious political sabotage of labor. Its meaning is clear: The refusal of the work under the capitalist production. Thus the transitional period contains 'transformational period'" (Arisawa 1948: 31–32).

Arisawa belonged to a group of those Marxian economists, rono-ha, who were critical to the Russian-oriented Communist Party Japan. After his arrest in 1938, he was expelled from his chair of statistics at the University of Tokyo and survived the war years by participating several research projects including that of the Showa Research Association (Showa Kenkyukai)[4] and the Colonel Akimal's Secret Military Forces Research.[5] In the four books he could publish under his own name before his arrest, Planning Industrial Mobilization (Sangyo doin keikaku) (1934), Japan under the Managed Economy (Keizai toseika no riron) (1937), War and Economy (Senso to keizai) (1937), and The Industrial Control of Japan (Nihon kogyo tosei-ron) (1937), he developed his theory of the managed economy that was based on the Marxian as well as German monopoly theories. In the introduction of the direct control of the investment of the cartelized industry, he recognized the element that changed the nature of cartel as a concentration of capital interest. In his view the managed economy involved an anti-capitalistic element that transferred the control of production from capitalists' hands to the government.[6]

---

[4]Sakai (1992), p. 139. On this research association see also Fletcher III (1982) and Yagi (1997a).

[5]Arisawa was the head of its section on American and British economies. Coincidently Nakayama also worked as the head of its Japanese section. This research team dissolved secretly after the Military declined the conclusion that the expansion of war was beyond the capacity of Japanese economy. All the related materials had to be brought into the fire.

[6]Almost all economists in the elder generation saw an inevitable tendency in the monopolization of industries. In Arisawa's case, the concept of 'socialization' was the only feasible alternative to capitalist nature of the monopolization.

In 1939 Arisawa collaborated secretly in drafting the "economic new order" of the economic department of the Showa Research Association. This department called for the separation between ownership and management and the reorganization of capitalist firms into cooperative production units. This coincides with Arisawa's theory of the managed economy that the production-oriented socialization could overcome the vested interest of monopoly capitals. It is a delicate question whether he favored bureaucratic command economy as was conceived by the "new bureaucrats". Nakamura (1974) compared the original concept of the reform of the Showa Research Organization with the "economic new order" that was designed by the "new bureaucrats". The former stressed the "control from inside" based on the production principle, while the latter aimed an extensive mobilization that could serve the demand of the military.

Ironically enough, Arisawa participated in a similar discussion behind the closed door once more after a quarter of the century. When the Ministry of Trade and Industry established the Council of Investigation into Industrial Structure in 1961 to prepare the trade liberalization, Arisawa assumed the head of the Subcommittee on Industrial Order. It was reported that the original plan of the Ministry that was strongly oriented to a bureaucratic control was severely criticized by Arisawa and other members and was modified into "the collaboration system of the government and the private" (Ohyama 1996: 123–129). But members of the Subcommittee shared with the bureaucrats of the Ministry the view of mitigating the monopoly regulation in order to build strong firms that could cope with the international competition.

The term of "socialization" seems to have disappeared from his writing after the collapse of the Katayama cabinet and the "Dodge Line". Instead he emerged as the supporter of modernization of industry. In the economic policy debate in the fifties, his name appears again in combination with the theory of "dual structure" of Japanese economy. The origin of this theory was also traced back to his research in the Japanese industry in the 1930s. He found the sharp contrast and subtle inter-relations of the large-sized industry and the small- and medium-sized industry. In his finding, Japanese industry attained already the stage where efficient large-sized plants occupied her production centre. The reason of the survival of immense numbers of inefficient small-sized industry lay in the abundance of cheap labor (Arisawa 1937). In this sense, the gap between both was a structural problem that has also the aspect of labor problem. In his analysis of the controlled economy, Arisawa maintained that the organization of the small- and medium-sized industry could contribute in increasing the efficiency and rationality as well as independence against the monopoly power of the large capital. Such a structural gap is also to be seen between the modern industrial sector and the agriculture sector that reserved huge amounts of under-employed labor forces. From this viewpoint the employment problem could not be solved without the solution of these structural productivity gaps. The term, "dual structure", was used in the *Economic White Paper* of 1957. In this White Paper, a prospect to solve the "dual structure" by a continuous economic growth was provided.

He also played an important role in the "energy revolution" in Japan. Though he was deeply involved in the coalmining since the postwar years, he realized the necessity of the transition to petroleum and endeavored to persuade coal miners to adopt the rationalization scheme. The move to the imported petroleum was all the more advantageous to reduce the high manufacturing cost of Japanese industry that hindered the export of Japanese products in those years. When the rationalization bill passed the Diet in 1962, Arisawa looked after the last protest march of miners organized by the Union of Coal Miners that had once the reputation of the strongest labor union in Japan. In the 1960s he further supported the use of nuclear energy as a member of the Energy Committee of the Government. Up to this point, the viewpoint of efficiency has totally replaced that of "socialization".

2.4 MODERNIZATION AND INDUSTRIALIZATION[7]

Nakayama's major was one of the pioneers of mathematical economics in Japan. His *Pure Economics* (*Junsui keizai-gaku*) (1933) was the standard book with which a generation of Japanese economists learned the essence of the general equilibrium theory. In postwar years, Nakayama served long as a learned member of the Central Labor Relations Committee and was its chairman when the Labor Dispute of the Miike Mine broke out in 1960. His recommendation put the end to one of the severest disputes in postwar industrial relations. Tohata was an agricultural economist who introduced the modernization principle against the traditional approach that stressed the strenuous work of small farmers. In the postwar years, he served as director of National Research Institute of Agricultural Economics and the Institute of Developing Economies besides many activities in the various administration councils. At the same time when Nakayama was dealing with the Miike labor dispute, Tohata was in charge of the report of the structural policy in agriculture, which became the core of the Basic Law of Agriculture of 1961.

Two economists whose majors made a good contrast studied in Germany in the same period under the same teacher. First Nakayama came to Bonn in 1927, following the suggestion of his mentor, Fukuda Tokuzo (1874–1930) to study under Joseph Schumpeter (1883–1950). However he had to wait one

---

[7]In this part I owe much from the collaboration in a joint research into Japanese economics after 1945. The result was published in Japanese as Ikeo (1999) and is going to appear in English as Ikeo (2000). Cf. Ikeo (1998, 1999), Minoguchi (1999a), and Nishizawa (1999) on Nakayama's economics, and Minoguchi (1999b) on Tohata.

year before Schumpeter came back from his stay at Harvard University. Then Tohata joined Nakayama in the next year to attend Schumpeter's seminar. They admired Schumpeter up to the end of their life and translated most of Schumpeter's works into Japanese.

Tohata Seiichi

It was Tohata's *Development Process of Agriculture in Japan* (*Nihon nogyo no tenkai katei*)(1936) that the Schumpeter's concepts of the "entrepreneur" and "economic development" as a creative response to the changing environment were applied to Japanese reality. In this book Tohata regarded small farmers and landowners in Japanese agriculture as "passive subjects" and asked who was the true "mover" of the agricultural development. He found the answer in the market-creative function of the manufacturer of agricultural products and organizational function of the government. Manufactures of non-rice products introduced innovations in agriculture via the market, especially in fruits and field crops. The government that established experimental stations and helped agricultural associations was also the subject that exerted "entrepreneurship" in agriculture. The reason that enormous mass of small rice producers remained "passive subjects" lay in their lack of marketing experience under the tenant system as well as in the relative scarcity of land and capital in relation to the rural population. This situation made Japanese agriculture far behind other manufacturing industry and created its backwardness in the national economy. In his postwar research he organized several times the joint research into the underemployment or excess-population that made the marginal productivity of the labor in the agricultural sector considerably lower than the wage level in the manufacturing industry.

Paradoxically enough, Tohata viewed the modernizing factor of the agriculture in relation to the wartime-managed economy.[8]

"The current task of the control of agriculture can be expressed in another way, i.e. the path of the small farming in the age of a rapid heavy industrialization of the nation. The problem is the more urgent than in the case of gradual industrialization. The problem emerged in the front as the conscious process of planned change, not as a spontaneous economic process. The prospering heavy industry deprives the agriculture of considerable amount of its population by the increase in employment externally. In this sense, the decrease in the relative share of the agricultural population is inevitable. So long as the domestic agriculture has to maintain its production volume, the increase in the labor productivity must be realized. The demand of the agricultural instruments that are needed for this increase creates the market for heavy industry. Further, the increase of the cattle in agriculture, that is also the means of the increase in labor productivity, has economic support from

---

[8]Tohata envisaged the possibility of the development of entrepreneurial activity in the concept of the separation of management and ownership under the economic reform plan of the Showa Research Association; see Yagi (1997a).

the changing demand of food in the heavily industrialized nation. These interrelations are seen usually at least. The economic construction that Japan is now performing under the war, too, goes along this direction. If it be true, we can conclude that the present agricultural control is creating a new bright dimension." (Published originally in 1942.) (Tohata 1947: 157).

The shrinkage of industrial production in the postwar years temporarily reversed this move of population. However, the parasite landowner and the natural rent that had so far distanced tenant farmers from the market vanished. The price-supporting system of main products provided Japanese farmers with the safety net and the expansion of agricultural financing supplemented the lack of capital. These were the preconditions for the modernization of agriculture. The only one remaining, and the most essential problem for the development of entrepreneurship in agriculture was the size of cultivated land. So, Tohata advocated the structural policy for agriculture through the promotion of selective expansion. Though this was the main policy recommendation of the Investigation Council of Basic Problems of Agriculture of 1960, the Ministry of Agriculture modified it with its protectionist position in the legislation and implementation of the agricultural policy under the Fundamental Law of Agriculture (1961). Intended selective expansion, too, was not fulfilled due to the increase in the price of land.

Nakayama Ichiro

Nakayama was one of few economists that engaged in the postwar economic policy with the background of modern theory. Though economists of later generations might wonder how his economic theory and his public activity is related, we should remember that he succeeded a socio-economical perspective from his mentors, Fukuda and Schumpeter. As for the recognition of structural gap and backwardness of Japanese economy, his was not so far from that of Arisawa. However, Nakayama and Arisawa showed a contrast in stressing either trade or domestic development in the years around the recovery of independence. Nakayama described tendencies and development of international trade and found the solution of the problem of population in the growth of industry via the promotion of trade. Arisawa was inclined to stress the full use of the domestic resource from his anxiety of the revival of the damping on the base of cheap labor as well as the limitation of the international market. If we consider the international relations then that hindered Japan from trade with China and the Soviet Union, his anxiety is to some extent understandable. But in this debate it was Nakayama that was proven to be more deep-sighted.[9]

[9] Despite this divide in this dispute, Nakayama and Arisawa shared the same view of promotion of fusion to build up the competitive firms in the age of trade liberalization. Nakayama was the chairman of the Council of Investigation into Industrial Structure under the MITI in the early 1960s.

Nakayama's engagement in labour politics in the postwar period reminds us of his mentor, Fukuda's welfare economics that integrated the class struggle in the making of social policy.[10] Fukuda's focus on the living right as well seems to correspond Nakayama's favor to the criterion of "living cost" (*seikatsu kyu*) in the wage negotiation. Nakayama avoided Marxian flavored term "class struggle" and insisted to use "industrial relations" (*roushi kankei*). He further recognized in the enterprise union of postwar Japan a favourable condition to attain the consensus of both parties. In his view both unions and managements are equal partners in wage negotiations, while in daily operation both have a common aim of the increase in productivity that in turn would make the source of higher income. Though Nakayama's judgment in the labor dispute was sometimes regarded as pro-labor, he would not admit the shop floor union activity that might bring confusion in the production plans. His proposal of the settlement of the Miike labor dispute gave virtually an end to the shop floor militancy in the private sector union movement.

It was Nakayama who combined the American origin movement of productivity improvement with the promotion of joint labor-management consultation. When its Japanese headquarter was established, he chaired its regular committee for the joint consultation. In 1959 he argued that a doubling of the salary could be realized on the ground of the increased labor productivity. The Ikeda Cabinet that endeavored to dissipate the political tension that had been caused by the revision of the Security Treaty with USA in 1960 adopted this "dream" in its new economic plan.

2.5 OVERVIEW IN THE EARLY 1960s

In the following paragraphs that Nakayama wrote after his leave from the Central Labor Relations, we can read the balance sheet of the Japanese industrialization that was reflected in the eyes of a leading economist.

"The industrialization of Japan could make a rapid progress by bravely using traits of its traditional society. On the other hand, however, rapid industrialization gradually undermined the traditional society on which it stood. Though the postwar social appeared to have added a great change to this situation, the essential trend was nonetheless effected. This reform rather spurred the advance of industrialization newly, by eliminating the remaining traits of the old society. What expresses the influence of the industrialization that has shaken the basis of the society most manifest is the problem of dis-equilibrium that was especially strongly felt in postwar years. The contradiction between the level of production and that of living, the economic gap between industry and agriculture, and the existence of the dual structure – these are the phenomena that accompanied the rapid industrialization for a long time. They became foci of the problems of postwar Japanese economy due to the change of the view of the society. ... The fact of dis-equilibrium existed earlier, thus

[10]See Inoue and Yagi (1998) about Fukuda's welfare economics.

asserting that growth was enabled on the basis of the dis-equilibrium. But so long as the value judgment of a traditional society prevailed without change, this fact was not fully brought into consciousness as the problem to solve. This consciousness of the problem itself signifies that the traditional society was considerably changed not only in its institutions, but also in the criterion of value judgment. This is a result of the democracy in the postwar years.

The problem is how we can have the social structure that fits to the high level of industrialization. For this task, many efforts have been made in postwar Japan. That the dual structure was the necessary measure for the correction of the distortion from the rapid growth, has been at the focus of discussions from the beginning, and several years have passed since the White Paper on Economy dealt with it. That the solution of the income gap was adopted as one of the main goals in the present income doubling plan is, together with the introduction of the minimum wage and extension of the social security, runs on the same line as the measure to eliminate the gap between the production level and the living level. ...

From the viewpoint of the construction of a society that fits the high level of industrialization, these measures have great significance. If various contradictions are the ultimate sources of the social tensions, the measure to ease the social tension and to attain social stability as the basis of industrialization must be first directed to the elimination of these objective contradictions. It is admitted that the elimination of these contradictions, thus the stabilization of the economic society from the structural viewpoint provides us with important conditions to fill the vacancy of the lost traits of tradition.

However, this is not enough. The ultimate support of the social structure is, needless to say, human morality, which is not reconstructed after the destruction of the traits of traditional society. The postwar democracy supplied a new ground for the reconstruction. But democracy itself is the institutional arrangement to attain political decisions. In Japan's case, it had indeed a great effect in eliminating old obstacles against growth, but it does not mean the completion of the reconstruction. The vacancy of a society that was born with the rapid industrialization still remains. That the logic of the industrialization itself is indifferent to the morality may bring forth a tragedy to the society" (Nakayama, *Collected Works*, (1972–73) vol. 15, pp. 21–22).

In the early 1960s when Nakayama wrote these paragraphs, Japanese economy was passing the turning point in the labour market. Riding the wave of economic prosperity, industry and commerce in the metropolitan area absorbed the latent labor forces so far conserved in the traditional self- and family-employed sectors. The wage increased about 10 percent every year.

Arisawa's hidden dream of "socialization" was replaced by the export-oriented oligarchy of big business. Tohata's vision of selective expansion was dissipated by the intensification of renter's interest of farmers and politics of protectionism. Nakayama's productivity oriented corporatism seemed to have survived a decade more. However, after the oil crisis, unionism lost its concentration to countervail the hegemony of the management.

The basic concept of economic policy of the gosanke was challenged by a younger generation of economists.[11] It was the great fusion in the steel and iron industry (1968) that provoked this criticism. While the fusion represented the consensus of bureaucrats and economists of the senior generation,

---

[11] Its most aggressive representative was Komiya Ryutaro. See details in Noguchi (1999).

a group of younger modern economists made their objection in an impressive proclamation. This marked the end of the intellectual hegemony of the 'managed' economic policy in the postwar period. After three decades it is now rather difficult to understand the historical significance of the economic policy in the two decades after 1945.

REFERENCES

Arisawa, Hiromi, *Planning Industrial Mobilization* [Sangyo doin keikaku]. Tokyo 1934.

Arisawa, Hiromi, *Japan under the Managed Economy* [Keizai toseika no nihon]. Tokyo 1937a.

Arisawa, Hiromi, *War and Economy* [Senso to keizai]. Tokyo 1937b.

Arisawa, Hiromi, *The Industrial Control in Japan* [Nihon kogyo toseiron]. Tokyo 1937c.

Arisawa, Hiromi, 'An Inevitable Thin' [Fukahiteki na mono], first published in *Sekai*, March 1946, cited from Arisawa (1948).

Arisawa, Hiromi, *Inflation and Socialization* [Infureeshon to shakaika]. Tokyo 1948.

Arisawa, Hiromi, *Talking on the Postwar Economy – Evidences for the History of the Showa Era* [Sengo keizai wo kataru – Showa-shu heno shogen]. Tokyo 1989.

Bao, Gao, 'Arisawa Hiromi and His Theory for a Managed Economy', in *Journal of Japanese Studies* (1994), pp. 115–153.

Bao, Gao, *Economic Ideology and Japanese Industrial Policy – Developmentalism from 1931 to 1965*. Cambridge 1997.

Fletcher III, William Miles, *The Search for a New Order – Intellectuals and Fascism in Prewar Japan*. Chapel Hill NC 1982.

Fukuzawa, Yukichi (1868) 'Sequel to the Situation of the West' [Seiyo jijo gaihen], in *Fukuzawa* (1958–64): Vol. 1.

Fukuzawa, Yukichi, 'An Outline of a Theory of Civilization' [Bunmeiron no gairyaku], in *Fukuzawa* (1958–64): Vol. 4.

Fukuzawa, Yukichi, *Collected Works of Fukuzawa Yukichi* [Fukuzawa Yukichi zenshu], ed. by Keio-Gijuku, 21 vols. Tokyo 1958–64.

Ikeo, Aiko (ed.), *Economic Development in Twentieth Century East Asia*. London 1997.

Ikeo, Aiko, 'Economic Development and Economic Thought after World War II: non-Marxian economists on development, trade and industry', in *Sugihara/Tanaka* (eds.) 1998.

Ikeo, Aiko (ed.), *Japanese Economics and Economists after 1945*. London (forthcoming).

Ikeo, Aiko (ed.), *Nihon no keizaigaku to keizaigakusha – sengo no kenkyu kankyou to seisaku keisei*. Tokyo 1999. English edition: Ikeo ed. (2000).

Inoue, Takutoshi, Kiichiro Yagi, 'Two inquirers on the divide: Tokuzo Fukuda and Hajime Kawakami', in *Sugihara/Tanaka* 1998.

Kenneth B. Pyle, 'Advantages of Followership: German Economics and Japanese Bureaucrats, 1890–1925', in *Journal of Japanese Studies*, 1974, pp. 127–164.

Kumagai, Jiro, 'Enlightenment and economic thought in Meiji Japan: Yukichi Fukuzawa and Ukichi Taguchi', in *Sugihara/Tanaka* 1998.

List, Friedrich, *Das nationale System der politischen Oekonomie*. Stuttgart 1841.

Minoguchi, Takeo, 'Nakayama Ichiro and Japanese Economy' [Nakayama Ichiro to nihon keizai], 1999a, in *Ikeo* 1999, pp. 252–266.

Minoguchi, Takeo, 'Tohata Seiichi and Japanese Agriculture' [Tohata Seiichi to nihon no nogyo], 1999b, in *Ikeo* 1999, pp. 290–304.

Murakami, Yasusuke, *An Anticlassical Political-economic Analysis: a Vision for the Next Century*, translated with introduction by Kozo Yamamura, Stanford Univ. Press, 1996.

Murakami, Yasusuke, *Hankoten no keizaigaku*, 2 vols. Tokyo 1992. English edition: Murakami 1996.

Nakamura, Takafusa, 'Ryu Shintaro and the Managed Economy' [Ryu Shintaro to tosei keizai], in *Rekishi to Jinbutsu*, April 1974, pp. 66–74.

Nakayama, Ichiro, 'Industrialization and Democratization of Japan' [Nihon no kogyoka to minshuka], 1961, in *Nakayama* 1972–73, Vol. 15.

Nakayama, Ichiro, *Collected Works* [Nakayama Ichiro Zenshu], 18 + 1 vols. Tokyo 1972–73.

Nishizawa, Tamotsu, 'Nakayama Ichiro and the Stabilization in Industrial Relations' [Nakayama Ichiro to roshi-kankei no anteika], in: *Ikeo* 1999, pp. 276–290.

Noguchi, Asahi, 'Trade Liberalization and the "Structural Industrial Policy"' [Taigai jiyuuka to 'sangyo kozo seisaku'], in: *Ikeo* 1999, pp. 305–335.

Noguchi, Yukio, *The 1940 Regime* [1940 nen taisei]. Tokyo 1995.

Ohyama, Kosuke, *Political Economy of the Administrative Guidance* [Gyosei shido no seijikeizaigaku]. Tokyo 1996.

Okazaki, Tetsuji, Masahiro Okuno, *Origins of Modern Japanese Economic Systems*. Tokyo 1993.

Sakai, Saburo, *Showa Research Association* [Showa kenkyu-kai]. Tokyo 1992.

Sugihara, Shiro, Toshihiro Tanaka (eds.), *Economic Thought and Modernization in Japan*. Cheltenham UK 1998.

Sugiyama, Chuhei, *Origins of Economic Thought in Modern Japan*. London 1994.

Tohata, Seiichi, *Development Process of Japanese Agriculture* [Nihon nogyo no tenkai-katei]. Tokyo 1936.

Tohata, Seiichi, *Landowners and Farmers over Land* [Nochi o meguru jinushi to nomin]. Tokyo 1947.

Tohata, Seiichi, *Founders of Japanese Capitalism – Various Economic Subjects* [Nihon shihonshugi no keiseisha – samazama na keizai shutai], Iwanami-Shinsho 1964.

Yagi, Kiichiro, 'Economic Reform Plans in the Japanese Wartime Economy – the case of Shintaro Ryu and Kei Shibata', 1997a, in *Ikeo* 1997.

Yagi, Kiichiro, *Intensive and Extensive Mobilization in Japanese Economy – an Interpretation of Japanese Capitalism with Historical Perspective*, paper presented to the 5th annual SEEP conference, Marienrode near Hannover, 29 October – 1 November 1997, 1997b.

Yagi, Kiichiro, *Social Economics of Modern Japan* [Kindai nihon no shakai-keizaigaku]. Tokyo 1999a.

Yagi, Kiichiro, 'Economics in the Academic Institutions after 1945 (Keizaigaku no gakujutsu taisei)', 1999b, in *Ikeo* 1999, pp. 65–103.

Discussant: Anja Osiander

Developmentalism and liberalism are not necessarily opposites. Liberalism is an ideal. Developmentalism can be a means to approach it. This is what I take to be the core message of Professor Yagi's paper.

As Professor Yagi has shown, this understanding of developmentalism has been used time and again by economists who found their nations to be "underdeveloped" compared to other nations. The German economist Friedrich List used it in a treatise on political economy for Germany back in 1841. Some fifty years later, Fukuzawa Yukichi, perhaps the most famous Japanese intellectual during the Meiji era, expressed a similar argument in his writings on how to raise the Japanese society to a state of enlightenment and civilization as he conceived it. Similarly, in the years after 1945, when Japanese economists were faced with the task of drafting solutions for various key problems in the efforts to rebuild the Japanese economy and to put in on track towards stable growth and prosperity, the argument again was put to use.

Professor Yagi gives three examples of Japanese economists who used the concept of developmentalism in order to bring the Japanese economy closer to the ideal of a fully liberalized, self-regulating economy.

The first example given by Professor Yagi is that of Tohata Seiichi. Tohata was particularly concerned with the question of how to increase productivity in farming. His ideal was borrowed from Schumpeter. He envisaged the farmer as an entrepreneur. With farmers acting as entrepreneurs, the market mechanism would work efficiently even in agriculture and would ensure high productivity. However, historically tenants in Japan were not accustomed to act as entrepreneurs. Moreover, they did not own enough land to produce substantially beyond their own needs. They also lacked capital for investment in machinery and the like.

In this situation, Tohata saw a positive role for state intervention in three respects: A) The state supported experiment stations for technological innovations in farming. B) The state also supported farmers' associations. C) During the war, the state strongly promoted the build-up of heavy industries. Thus, the state accelerated structural changes which forced the farming sector to increase its productivity.

Yagi's second example is that of Nakayama Ichirô. Before the Pacific war, Nakayama had been one of the leading scholars in Japan with regard to neoclassical theories of a general equilibrium. Yet he, too, was strongly influenced by Shumpeter's ideas. As chairman of an important advisory council to the Ministry of International Trade and Industry, he synthesized liberalism with pragmatism. He promoted an active industrial policy in which the state would encourage cooperation of companies. The goal was to improve their capacity to compete internationally in an era of trade deregulation.

Nakayama was also influential in framing a liberal view of industrial relations. According to him, management and workers share a common interest in increasing the productivity of the company. Thus, he supported the system of enterprise unions. His ideas helped to create a legitimate place for union activities within a framework of industrial relations in Japan which, by the time of the 1960s had turned predominantly liberal.

The third example presented by Professor Yagi is that of Arisawa Hiromi. His case is somewhat different since he was not a liberal. Rather, his thinking was strongly influenced by the ideas of Marx and Hilferding. Arisawa foresaw a general trend towards the monopolization of economic power in any market economy. In order to counter this trend, he favored the socialization of key industries. However, this reform concept lost its influence in Japanese politics within three years after the war had ended. Arisawa was among the first to admit this fact.

Arisawa therefore favored developmentalist ideas as a second best option for a reality in which, unfortunately, liberal ideas of economic order dominated economic policy in Japan. He became very influential with his theory of the dual structure of the Japanese economy, and he supported government policies which would help to close the productivity gap between large-sized industry vis-à-vis small- and medium-sized industry. Arisawa also favored state guidance in the transition from coal to petroleum as the primary source of energy for the Japanese economy.

This is, in brief, the summary of Professor Yagi's findings. Now, what can we learn from this historical evidence – especially when discussing the prospects of the economic order in Japan and Germany today?

There are three conclusions which I would like to draw from Professor Yagi's presentation. The first conclusion will stress a trend towards the convergence of the economic order – though it is a convergence of a very particular kind. The second conclusion will stress exactly the opposite: it will argue for a trend against convergence. And my final comment is meant as an encouragement for debate as well as for some caution in our conclusions.

The first point which I would like to raise has to do with the intellectual embeddedness of economic thinking. Professor Yagi presents the ideas of the most influential economists in Japan in the 20 years after 1945. As he shows very convincingly, their ideas were not generated out of the blue, nor did they come about as some genuinely Japanese way of thinking. All three

48

of these economists had studied in Germany, and these studies provided them with their basic intellectual framework.

Nowadays, students from all over the world go to the USA to study economics. Moreover, when I studied economics at a German university some ten years ago, we used US textbooks or German textbooks that were based on the ideas of US economists. In other words: It is the intellectual environment of the leading departments of economics at US universities which today shapes discussions on the proper economic order world-wide.

What is this intellectual environment like? The schism that used to divide Marxist and liberalist economists has vanished, as has the schism between Keynesianism and monetarism. For the past 20 years, supply-side oriented economics have been dominating scholarly debates in the USA. And, by now, the impact of this intellectual trend can be felt in economic policy all over the globe. Here, you can indeed see a strong trend towards convergence. However, it is a convergence brought about by intellectual history, not by market forces.

The second point which I would like to raise could be called the issue of pragmatism. What struck me most about Professor Yagi's findings is that one must carefully distinguish between liberalism as an ideal and liberalism as an ideology. In the same vein, we should also carefully distinguish between globalization as an ideal and globalization as an ideology.

You can be in favor of the ideal of globalization and liberalism and still advocate non-liberal policies – precisely because you think that the economy is not ready yet for a globalized liberal order. This logic has been used by Friedrich List when he talked about Germany as a late-comer to international trade among industrialized nations. The same logic led Nakayama Ichiro and Arisawa Hiromi to advocate collusion among Japanese companies in order to cope with international competition and with a strategic shift in energy supply. The reason for this has always been the concept of "catching up" with other national economies which appear to be better positioned to profit from a liberal arrangement of economic exchanges. Today, in the age of "globalization", this logic resonates as appealingly as ever.

Thus, if it is possible to interpolate any trend from the historical evidence presented by Professor Yagi, then we should not be surprised to witness the advent of non-liberal devices in economic policies in Germany and Japan. The devices will likely be justified as a means to strengthen certain parts of the economy to make them more competitive in a global economy. The instruments will be chosen according to the political and economic situation prevailing in Japan and Germany respectively at the time. Thus, they are highly likely to differ from each other. In such a scenario, then, we will witness no convergence of rules and practices.

The picture becomes slightly more complicated when we extend the scenario to include the potential influence of interest group agents on economic policy. There may be some agents advocating the endorsement of practices which are becoming the universal standard in global exchanges. There may be others calling for rules which may differ from these new global rules. The outcome then will depend on the relative weight of the voice of certain protagonists in the political process.

Even in the extended scenario, though, there appears to be some bias in the logic which works against convergence. For proponents of idiosyncratic rules may retain the upper hand no matter how the economy actually performs. If the economy manages to perform well even with idiosyncratic rules, proponents of an adjustment to global standards will find it more difficult to show that convergence is necessary. If the economy does not perform well, proponents of idiosyncratic rules can make an even stronger case for a developmentalist perspective. They may argue that it is necessary to forestall the adjustment to some globalized standards so that their respective constituencies may attain a better position before the economy enters the world of globally standardized exchanges. Developmentalism will sound more convincing as a guide for economic policy as long as it is coined as a plea for pragmatism.

The third point which I would like to raise has to do with the irony of history. The ideas of Arisawa, Nakayama and Tohata strongly influenced the evolution of the postwar economic order in Japan. And yet, even their ideas did not prevail. They were overtaken by other events and other ideas. Eventually, the evolution of the Japanese economy proceeded along a course which was quite different from what its leading architects had envisaged. Therefore, when trying to forecast the effects of globalization on the economy in Japan and Germany, we should bear in mind a strong caveat. No matter how cleverly we manage to analyze the evidence, things may still turn out differently from what we think.

3

THE EVOLUTIONARY PERSPECTIVE ON INSTITUTIONAL DIVERGENCE AND COMPETITIVE ADVANTAGE

Carsten Herrmann-Pillath

3.1 THE ISSUE: DOES CONVERGENCE OF ECONOMIC PERFORMANCE NECESSARILY PRESUPPOSE CONVERGENCE OF INSTITUTIONS?

Since the demise of socialism and the breakdown of the so-called "Asian model of capitalism" many observers are inclined to believe that all economic systems will eventually converge toward a specific set of optimal or "best practice" institutions. This general mood notwithstanding, there are also many complaints about the actual implementation of institutional regimes recommended as being "optimal" by international organizations like the IMF, and there are still "renegade states" like Mahathir's Malaysia where deviant policies are pursued intentionally. Even if international organizations are not empowered to impose such a set of institutions, international negotiations within the framework of the WTO also follow the implicitly given idea that there is such a standard for reference. Yet, precisely those international negotiations demonstrate that there is still widespread disagreement about the appropriate institutions and controversy over the sovereign right of national governments to set up and maintain "deviant" institutions. This problem has become even more salient since in international negotiations the additional demand has been raised that national governments should also actively impose "best practice" even if the domestic market gives rise to seemingly deviant institutions spontaneously, that is without active government intervention. With this kind of an "educational" encroachment on sovereign rights under the umbrella of a global convergence of competition policies (WTO 1997), the issue of institutional convergence deserves some foundational theoretical consideration.

In this paper I wish to review some theoretical arguments about whether to expect institutional convergence to emerge from history, or not. These arguments go back to the ongoing controversy between "neoclassical" and

51

"evolutionary" thinking in economics, and I wish to demonstrate that an evolutionary view entails a dissenting position to the belief that we live in an economic world of institutional convergence. I will counter the latter claim with the evolutionary argument that institutional divergence is one of the most important determinants of dynamic competitive advantages in the global economy.

The question has to be put more exactly in terms of the relation between institutional convergence and convergence of economic performance: Nobody disputes the observation and perhaps even the expectation that there is and always will be a great variety of deviant institutions all over the globe. Yet, the "best practice" reasoning adds the presumption that deviance from the optimal set will necessarily entail a loss of efficiency and hence, in the long run, will result in a disadvantage as compared to the economies adopting the optimal institutional setting and which are therefore operating at the productivity frontier. So we have to ask whether, in the long run, institutional convergence toward the optimal institutional pattern is a precondition for convergence of economic performance.[1]

The simplest answer to that question is provided by Neoclassical Institutionalism, e.g. (Eggertsson 1990), where the link with long-run growth theory is also explicit. Neoclassical growth theory is the most straightforward explanation for the convergence of economic performance (measured as income per capita) across countries, e.g. (Sala-i-Martin, 1996). The implicit precondition, of course, is that the allocation of resources takes place within the institutional setting of (almost) perfectly competitive markets with certain structural similarities, so that we may directly conclude that convergence to that institutional pattern must at least take place simultaneously with the convergence of levels of income. Convergence in the neoclassical growth model also requires the similarity of certain structural parameters (like the savings rate) which may also reflect institutional patterns, so that, all in all, the neoclassical model at least implicitly implies complete and perfect institutional convergence across countries, if convergence of performance is to be achieved. This perspective underlies the myriad of recommendations given to the developing countries in the recent decades, namely first "to get the prices right" and then to watch the growth machine running smoothly. Obviously, this idea is a close relative to another idea implicit in neoclassical growth theory, namely that technological knowledge

---

[1] This approach, for example, is the bread and butter of comparative analysis of transition economies. Researchers try to identify measures of performance and measures of progress in the transition to the market economy. The correlation is tested by statistical or even econometric methods. See e.g. for the national level, Melo/Gelb (1997) or Melo/Ofer (1999), for the subnational. In the mid-nineties, the famous Krugman debate over the alleged institutional deficiency of the "Asian model" directly referred to the concept of productivity frontier because data on growth accounting were interpreted as reflections of institutional regimes (for a survey of the problems involved, see Rodrik 1998).

and hence the production function are identical all over the world, and that knowledge diffuses quickly across the globe.

Of course, there cannot be any dispute about plain assertions like modern market economies presuppose a stable legal framework for private property rights. The problem of institutional convergence can be only posed in a meaningful way on the more concrete and specific level of institutional analysis like concerning liability laws, regulations on corporate governance or social policies. As the WTO process testifies, here we find ample ground for institutional diversity and conflict, as well as strong claims for an ever increasing reach of the forces of convergence. As a quick look demonstrates, these problems have nothing to do with the idealized setting of perfectly competitive markets. Simply said, the interaction between market- and non-market determinants of the economic process comes to the fore, as well as the question how the problem of "missing markets" and market imperfections are solved by means of particular institutional measures in different market economies. It is in this area where there is much leeway for institutional divergence, even if we were to believe that in the market sector there would be strong forces of convergence toward the competitive ideal type.

Basically speaking, there are two general reasonings in favour of convergence.

First, as already mentioned, allegedly there is a determinate relation between the attainable level of economic performance and a particular set of institutions. For example, there is the argument that the Anglo-American model of corporate governance is more efficient than the Japanese one, and the proof of the pudding might be the long infirmity of the Japanese economy after the "burst of the bubble", as compared to the capability of the American economy to relaunch its growth performance.

Second, international trade and capital movements impose competitive pressure towards convergence of institutions, unless a country were ready to give up certain advantages of the international division of labour, and hence, efficiency gains. This argument includes the aforementioned activities to negotiate a common institutional framework. Different from the first argument, convergence need not encompass the entire institutional set-up, because the degrees of freedom depend on the strength and direction of the competitive pressures.[2]

---

[2] Hoekman/Kostecki 1995: 247–251 survey the actual needs for convergence resulting from competition in international trade. However, there are serious difficulties in determining the relation between "needs" and "feasibility", unless there would be a cost-benefit-analysis of convergence at hand. At the same time, we have to distinguish between convergence as a result of competition and convergence as presumed precondition for "fair competition". Regarding the latter point, we note that there is also the rather blunt opposing view that there are no "neutral" institutions which do not affect competitiveness in some way so that any step towards "levelling the institutional playing field" would always need to arrive at complete convergence (i.e. perfect harmo-

The second argument, however, raises an important question: What happens if peculiar institutional properties of a particular economy determine its international competitiveness? In that case, institutional divergence could be a precondition for convergence of economic performance, just as the dynamic competitive process cannot take place within a group of "representative firms", but requires unique characteristics of innovators. Institutions would be part and parcel of sustainable competitive advantages specific to certain locations and countries, and not simply the "neutral setting" of the economic process. Hence, the argument referring to globalization as a force of convergence would be turned upside down, if only institutional divergence provides the foundation for sustainable competitive advantages. Following the literature on sustainability of competitive advantages,[3] we would even conclude that precisely those institutional peculiarities would foster sustainability that cannot be imitated easily, probably that even cannot be easily recognized, for example, because of a strong tacit dimension. Obviously, this kind of perception underlied much of the discourse about "Japaneseness" of the phenomenal rise of the Japanese economy in the 20th century. Hence it seems to be worthwhile to check the theoretical validity of this view.

The paper consists of two main parts. Firstly, we review some of the most important theoretical approaches to the problem of institutional convergence. Secondly, we try to demonstrate that sustainable competitive advantages indeed rest upon differences in the non-market context of market processes which cannot be eroded by institutional competition in the context of globalization of markets. Hence, this general argument will not change if there is an explicit adoption of certain formal institutions. To the contrary, we confront the neoclassical view on convergence, which necessarily assumes that competition will also lead toward institutional convergence, with the evolutionary view that competition will always trigger off institutional divergence leading to the creation of new competitive advantages. We will adopt a theoretical perspective with foundational intent. This contrasts with the current literature on "harmonization" and convergence which is mostly policy-oriented in nature striving at insights that can be used to guide pragmatic action, for example, in the WTO context.

nization). Of course, this triggers the backlash that convergence cannot be a reasonable objective of policy initiatives. On this general point see, e.g. (Leebron 1996: 73).

[3] The resource based view of the firm claims that competitiveness of firms can only rest upon certain resources that are unique to the firm, like special technological knowledge that is not accessible to competitors, see Barney (1991). This argument has been extended to entire economies by Porter's (Porter 1990: 73ff.) classic who argued that ordinary factor endowments cannot be the foundation of competitive advantages, but only so-called specific advances factors. On the ongoing controversy over the "competitive advantage" versus the "comparative advantage" point of view, see, for example, (Hunt/Morgan 1995).

3.2 STEPS TOWARD AN EVOLUTIONARY VIEW ON CONVERGENCE

Subsequently we provide a summary overview on some approaches to the problem of convergence that focus on different aspects of institutional change. The sequence of the arguments suggests that there is a systematic development toward an evolutionary view, which is done here for sake of demonstrating an implicit logic of theoretical progress. However, most of the scholars we mention do not count themselves as evolutionary economists, and the sequence does not reflect a temporal sequence of actual contributions.[4]

3.2.1 "Getting the prices right" versus learning to compete

The classical dispute about convergence can be found in the analytical treatment of development problems. Here we also find a clear reference to an evolutionary argument: Beginning with the 19th century economist Friedrich List, scholars have argued recurrently that the catching-up process requires another institutional regime than the final state of the developed economies. We confront both views in Figures one and two.

Figure 1 Neoclassical institutionalism

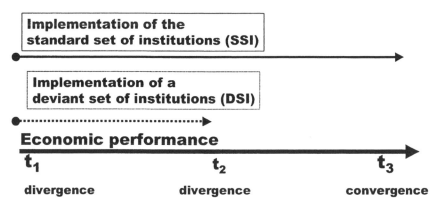

Economic performance

t_1 t_2 t_3

divergence   divergence   convergence

Source: Author.

Neoclassical institutionalism sticks to the hypothesis that there is one particular set of institutions (with varieties, of course, yet staying within clear boundaries) that should be implemented just from the beginning and

---

[4]For example, Krugman would fiercely deny being classified as an "evolutionary economist", and indeed his general theoretical framework is non-evolutionary, namely equilibrium theories on monopolistic competition. Yet, his treatment of certain frequency-dependent processes refers to evolutionary mechanisms.

that provides the proper framework for a continuous process of growth. If a "deviant institutional set" is adopted, the economy will eventually run into a trap of divergent economic performance, so that catching-up will not be possible. In that case, an institutional "big bang" becomes unavoidable in order to pull the economy out of the otherwise self-sustaining suboptimal state (because, for example, maintenance of proper institutions requires a certain endowment with human capital that cannot be accumulated on the low level of income). This provides legitimacy to outside intervention and advice, as for example, in the case of IMF conditionality.

Figure 2 Development economics

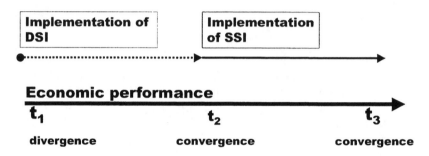

Source: Author.

The counterargument rests upon the consideration of the time needed for learning how to compete, given an initial backlog. The original List approach focused on the foreign trade regime; however, this is only one example for the general point that in order to be able to catch up, the institutional set-up is assumed to have to be different from the regime of mature market economies. There are many variants of this argument. I only wish to mention one recent justification of "big push" policies promoted by the government that has been provided by "New Growth Theory".[5] This is a deviant institutional regime because the "big push" either presupposes a distorted price system that leads to the appropriate reallocation of resources into the capital goods sector or a coordinating activity of the government that synchronizes the private investment decisions. The major reason for that kind of deviance is the existence of positive externalities in capital formation, real and/or human. Positive externalities introduce a particular dynamics of the growth process so that critical mass phenomena and multiple equilibria emerge. Since the market-guided optimization calculus of economic agents does not take the externalities into consideration, the

---

[5]The "big push" model is summarized by Krugman 1995: 8–23. My presentation is more general because the original formalization only stresses pecuniary externalities dependent on market size, whilst technological externalities may work in the same direction, of course.

underdeveloped economy may fail to cross the threshold value after which the growth process heads toward convergence. Hence, there have to be two different institutional states, the deviant one prevailing until the threshold is reached, and the standard one after crossing the threshold level of minimum economic performance.

This class of possible explanations (and justifications) of divergence, however, has the assumption in common that in the final state there will be institutional convergence. A typical criticism puts the finger on the problem how the regime switch can be orchestrated, given the difficulties to identify the threshold value ex ante and given the fact that the deviant regime will nurture special interest groups that resist institutional change in later stages of development. However, if indeed multiple equilibria are a defining feature of the growth process, the link between convergence of institutions and convergence of economic performance would be broken in any case because the former is no longer a necessary condition of the latter.

At a closer look, the "New Growth Theory" argument provides a first hint at a possible evolutionary alternative: What happens if the required positive externalities are supported by other means of behavioral coordination than government intervention? For example, if along Weberian lines there is a general societal norm to be thrifty and to invest in the formation of real wealth for future generations, the effect on capital formation might drive the economy beyond the threshold level of investment without any need for government intervention. People would behave as altruists producing the public good of externalities, precisely because they believe in following their egoistic preferences to achieve some future apparent good. Since there is no necessary link between economic performance and the adoption of certain values and beliefs, there is no reason that belief systems that do not support this kind of behavior will automatically vanish.[6] Just the other way round, certain beliefs may even support a low-level development trap, like those focusing on other-worldly spiritual achievements.

3.2.2 Informal institutions and cultural change

The aforementioned argument introduces cultural differences among different economic systems. There is another class of approaches to convergence which starts out from the fact that neoclassical institutionalism only

---

[6]This kind of reasoning underlies much of the literature on the link between savings behavior and growth in East Asia, arguing that Confucian values have contributed to high rates of accumulation, which is very similar to the Weberian point on Calvinist frugality and responsibility to accumulate wealth in the real world. However, the Confucian story is also linked with the debate about the failure of China to industrialize endogeneously because of the skewed distribution of income which favoured landed elites who invested in non-productive assets in the context of the Confucian value system, like ancestral temples. The latter story provided the legitimacy for violent government intervention and forced accumulation, hence an economic as well as cultural "big push".

refers to formal institutions that are being implemented and protected by the government. This is tantamount to the conviction that norms, values and informal institutions prevalent in society either do not stay in conflict with the standard set of institutions or will adapt quickly and smoothly after these have been implemented. At least, whether there is a conflict or not depends on the appropriate incentives set by the government when creating the standard set (Mummert 1999). However, since government itself is an institution this consideration does not resolve the basic question how both kinds of institutions relate to each other.

Figure 3 (New) Institutional economics

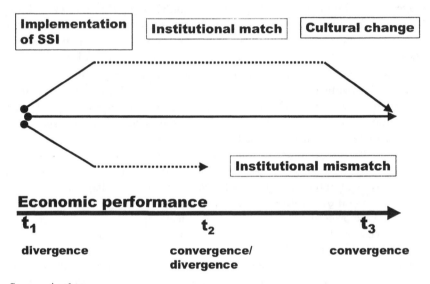

Source: Author.

Amongst others, North (1990) has therefore argued forcefully that one should distinguish analytically between formal and informal institutions, with the latter allowing to grasp fuzzy concepts like "culture". Convergence of formal institutions by fiat does not automatically imply that informal institutions will also converge. Depending on the assumptions on adaptability of informal institutions, the problem of "institutional match" results. If informal institutions do not match the standard set of formal institutions, and if they do not adapt smoothly, there is the scenario that a deviant regime will emerge out of the interaction even if at the beginning the standard set has been adopted. Divergence of economic performance is the necessary result. This leads to one scenario where mismatch between existing informal institutions and imposed formal institutions actually prevents the betterment of economic performance from occurring. Some authors therefore conclude that formal institutions need to be adapted to the informal institutions so that this effect can be avoided (e.g. Leipold, 2000). However, this begs the question whether and when the formal institutions must prevail in the long run.

Indeed, deviance can stay within certain limits so that the growth mechanism is not impaired, perhaps even supported, if there is preadaptation of certain informal institutions to the standard set within the scope of functionally equivalent solutions (e.g. different kinds of corporate governance under the general regime of private property rights). In that case, final convergence of institutions will take place as a process of cultural change, namely a slow adaptation of the informal institutions to the standard set, after a somewhat long period of deviance caused by the impact of informal on formal institutions. This is a strong claim indeed because the idea of convergence would now also include values and social norms, that is to say, the idea of a globally uniform civilization is implicitly present.[7]

Another version of the story would refer to the New Growth Theory argument presented above. In that case, informal institutions would be autonomous with regard to formal institutions, but would affect the macroeconomic process via their impact on economic decisions taken within the setting of formal institutions. That is, even if there were no direct conflict between formal and informal institutions, we would reach the conclusion that cultural convergence is a precondition for convergence of performance. That position seems to underly the many attempts at discovering "quasi Protestantism" in countries achieving the take-off, obviously committing the logical fallacy that a similar consequence entails similar antecedent conditions.

The major difficulty of this approach lies in the empirical proof of the pudding. Reference to informal institutions opens up the Pandora box of investigating into social norms, cultural standards and world views, which presupposes the use of analytical devices and theories that transcend standard economics by far.[8] Therefore, economists mostly rely on intelligent

---

[7]For example, in Hayami's (1998) account of the Japanese experience we find the argument that after World War II Japan returned to "prototypically" Japanese institutions after firstly having adopted an Anglo-Saxon institutional regime. In that Japanese prototype there is a strong role for community-and group-based mechanisms for coordination and information processing, features stressed in almost all accounts of the "Japaneseness" of Japan's economy, as, for example, Iwata (1992). Especially after the Asian crisis, many observers believe that Japan now needs to reshuffle its socioeconomic fabric and will converge to more universal institutions. This would be tantamount to cultural convergence after 50 years of divergence within certain limits. This was previewed by many commentators on the Japanese model, like Haitani (1990).

[8]In recent theoretical approaches on institutional change this is sometimes blurred, as for example in Greif's (1994) much-quoted analysis of medieval long-distance trade in the Mediterranean. In spite of an analytical tractability of the historical data by means of game theory, this kind of efficiency explanation does only cover up proximate causes stabilizing the institutional regularities in question. Greif clearly shows that the ultimate explanation needs to go back to exogenous cultural standards and social structures which are no longer amenable to economic analysis but need to be understood by anthropological and sociological methods. Dopfer (1985) argues that this mix of

stories like the many explanations offered for the rise of Japan out of her feudal tradition persisting in the modern institutions that were introduced in the late 19th century (for a recent account, see Okazaki/Okuno-Fujiwara 1998). This, of course, only scratches the surface of a fully-fledged cultural investigation, which, for example, would have to scrutinize values, behavioral standards and beliefs that actually provide the foundation of institutional resilience (see, for instance, Ikegami's, 1995, magisterial work). However, as we realize immediately from Figure 3, there is still no rejection of the basic presumption that convergence of institutions is a prerequisite for long-run convergence of economic performance. The only difference is that during convergence a long period of deviance might be necessary to accomplish cultural change and to avoid institutional mismatch.

3.2.3 Endogenous policy theory and Panglossian convergence

The next class of theories related to the issue of convergence treats policies as endogenous. There is a bridge to our former subsection because implementation of formal institutions, of course, presupposes an agent capable of doing this task. Mostly, this will be the government which is a formal institution of its own. This entails the question whether governmental behavior also reflects an interaction between formal and informal institutions, the latter being labeled by political science as "political culture", e.g. (Thompson/Ellis/Wildawsky 1990). Under these more complex circumstances, serious doubts may arise whether government can really be capable to free itself from the entire maze of informal institutions pervading the market as well as the government. Instead, we could imagine a complex interaction between efforts of changing formal institutions and concomitant evolutionary changes of informal institutions in both the market and the government.[9]

Endogenous policy theory, however, does not directly address this issue but starts out from political economy considerations. Right from the outset, this has to be distinguished neatly from mere interest group analysis or Public Choice approaches, because endogenous policy analysis eventually attempts an encompassing definition of "optimality of institutions" by treating the costs of the political process as endogenous. Therefore, the standard of reference is no longer allocative efficiency but viability of the entire institutional regime, because the isolated assessment of economic institutions according to efficiency standards can no longer be applied in order to

---

methods can be systematicized within a "nomothetic apporoach" that treats historical phenomena as theoretical entities.

[9]In Herrmann-Pillath (1998) I have therefore proposed to approach the transformation of economic systems as a process of "institutional self-organization".

identify exogenous political determinants detrimental to efficiency.[10] We can imagine the case that the standard set of institutions is implemented; however from the endogenous policy perspective this set does not prove to be viable and will finally change into a deviant set. Post-Soviet Russia comes to mind where shock therapy failed because of a misfit between economic policies and the prevailing political, perhaps also cultural context (cf. Shleifer 1997).

Figure 4 Endogenous policy theory

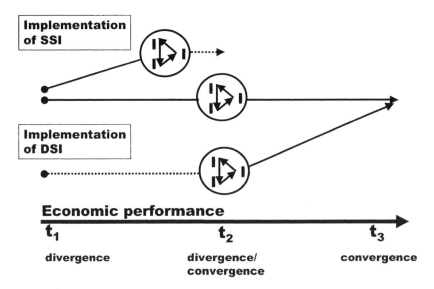

Source: Author.

The crucial point of this argument rests upon the proper analysis of the mutual interaction between interests in institutional change, capability and willingness to influence policies, and the resulting intervention affecting interests, so that circular causation results (see the triangular interaction between the three "I's" Interest, Influence, Intervention in Figure 4). The only ingredient we have to add is the problem how to establish a governance structure for that process and how to make mutual commitments possible (for example, between politicians and the electorate). In other words, whereas standard institutional analysis focuses on the issue of governance in the economic process, endogenous policy adds the dimension of governance in the political process, and puts both into the general framework

---

[10]This discussion is proceeding especially in the context of international trade theory, where Bhagwati, amongst others, has identified a "determinacy paradox" fundamentally affecting the economist's advice to politicians, see O'Flaherty/Bhagwati (1997). The concept of "viability" is closely related to North's (1990) concept of "adaptive efficiency". Penz (1999) develops a general theoretic approach to that idea.

of economic theory, trying to understand the complex interactions in that kind of a multi-level governance structure.

Dixit (1996), for example, proposes to distinguish between economic transaction costs and political transaction costs as standards of efficiency applied to the economic and the political institutions, respectively. If the political transaction costs of introducing and maintaining certain economic institutions prove to be excessive, depending on the given structure of the political system, economic institutions are not viable, and total efficiency will be impaired, even if the standard set is implemented.[11] In other words, the optimal set of institutions might be different from the viable one, and could only be achieved by changing the political system in a way such that the endogenous policy process will then generate the optimal set endogeneously.

Evidently, this approach raises the very difficult issue whether convergence of economic institutions is dependent on the convergence of political institutions, because different political institutions will presumably match with different economic institutions.[12] Hard core neoclassical institutionalists will immediately jump on that train and identify a certain model of democratic government as the optimal one. However, changing political systems seems to be a process of much higher complexity and intricacy than changing particular economic institutions.[13] We do not wish to delve into that pool of alligators and confine ourselves to the observation that under these circumstances endogenous policy analysis faces the serious dilemma of Dr. Pangloss: on the one hand, there is still the clear belief that convergence of economic performance rests upon convergence of institutions, but on the other hand every set of institutions can be proven to be efficient if there is the observation of stability in the past, since we may explain this as an outward reflection of the trade-off between economic and political efficiency, hence as being the optimal solution in terms of total efficiency.[14]

---

[11] One simple approach to measure that trade-off could be Rodrik's (Rodrik 1996: 28) "political cost-benefit ratio" that compares the welfare gains of a policy reform with the total amount of rents to be redistributed among the affected parties. The latter might be closely related to the political transaction costs because resistance to change will increase, the higher that amount.

[12] For example, the implementation of government interventions like time-limited protection will work out very different in a political system that is dominated by a strong and highly qualified bureaucracy, as compared to democratic-populist systems where incumbents need to follow short-term interests of voters. Such an argument can be found in Amsden's (1991) account of the East Asian model.

[13] Therefore, major societal crises may be necessary to change the politico-economic system, like defeat in war in the case of the "miracle economies" Japan and Germany after World War II. These cases also include an inportant role of exogenous intervention by the US government. This is an argument well-known from Olson's analysis of the rise and decline of nations.

[14] One of the independent theories of institutional change, the French regulation school, also faces this difficulty, because unless a "grande crise" explodes, viability of the institutional structure allows no general statement about desirability, that is, there is no

That means, there is always a sort of "convergence" in the sense of staying in the most optimal possible state of the world.

This concept of optimality, however, does not preclude the possibility that the different "efficient" systems will display a divergent economic performance in terms of level of income per capita. Therefore, the endogenous policy approach raises the important issue of how to measure welfare in cardinal terms independent from GDP data. There is a need to assess certain political aspects of the general social systems, like perhaps crime rates and the intensity of social conflicts. As is well known from the long debate over alternative measures of GDP, this is an issue that is very difficult to resolve.

3.2.4 Diversity of techno-economic paradigms and competitiveness

So far, we have only considered approaches that assume the possibility of divergence over a certain period of time, with that period left unspecified, however. To my best knowledge, one of the rare theoretical positions explicitly assuming that convergence of economic performance is linked with divergence of institutions is that related to the idea of techno-economic paradigms. This literature is highly diversified, but one common perspective seems to be that the issue of convergence is treated in the context of global competition. Here the question arises whether institutional divergence might provide the base for competitive advantages of locations. If this is linked with a generalized competence theory approach to the firm, institutional diversity would result into absolute advantages of certain countries, locations and firms, which statistically would be reflected in the measurement of total factor productivity, and which cannot be grasped by standard theories of international trade like the relative factor endowments approach.[15] A careful consideration of those arguments shows that the level of disaggregation is lower than in the approaches that we touched upon so far. The idea of techno-economic paradigms refers to specific patterns of social structures, political institutions and economic organization, especially in terms of corporate organization. There is also a spatial disaggregation involved when technology is understood as a concrete artefact in space-time. In that sense, typical examples like the analysis of the "British decline" (as surveyed by Kirby 1992) or the confrontation between American "Fordism" and Japanese "Toyotism" (Coriat/Dosi 1998) attract the criticism of an

standard for evaluation at hand. See my discussion in Herrmann-Pillath 2000: chapter 7.

[15] For an exemplary treatment of this approach see Dosi et al. (1990). On a theoretical level, it is important to stress the role of absolute advantage here, which simply means that certain patterns of technologies and institutions become singular determinants of competitiveness, with no other factors staying in a substitutive relation (cf. MacDonald/Markusen 1985).

overdrawn generalization, as far as national characteristics are concerned. Yet, a foremost example is the analysis of industrial clusters that are embedded into national and local contexts, with the former being dominant e.g. in the legal framework, and the latter being salient in government-enterprise interactions related to R&D. As the much-debated example of supplier networks and competition policy demonstrates, these disaggregated patterns certainly do affect the convergence issue as, for example, in WTO treatment of non-tariff barriers to trade.

Figure 5 Techno-economic paradigms and institutional speciation

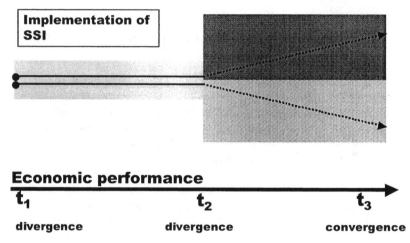

Source: Author.

The major empirical claim of the techno-economic paradigm approach rests upon the assumption that certain technologies as knowledge structures are contingent on particular institutional contexts, so that the standard understanding of comparative advantage can be linked with the specific institutional differences (Cimoli/Dosi 1995). This idea has been put into the systematic framework of "national innovation systems", even ending up with the hypothesis of a "systemic entrepreneurship" along Schumpeterian lines (Ebner 1999). However, there are considerable problems with generating testable hypotheses because of the complexity of the interactions supposed to take place, and because of the problems to disentangle technology and context empirically. Nonetheless, there are serious empirical arguments supporting such kinds of interaction. Again, the most salient example is Japan, where the argument has been proposed by Dyer (1996, 1997) amongst others, that the peculiar network relations underlying supplier-producer interaction enable the firms to lower transaction costs whilst supporting the formation of highly specific assets which lead to higher productive efficiency, i.e. cost advantages resulting in competitive advantages. This is especially valid for complex products, which need a very close coordination across the downstream and upstream firms, so that one can observe strong Japanese competitive advantages in these industries, whereas in other industries this is not as salient. Since this coordinative capability finally rests upon the maintenance of values of loyalty and interpersonal bonding (hence, a special set of informal institutions, see section 2.2), the networks are being perceived as barriers to entry by outsiders. Indeed, breaking up the special supplier-producer relations in Japan has always been a major issue in international trade policy conflicts involving Japan (for a survey, see Kotabe/Wheiler 1996). Applying competition policies to change these relations would mean, of course, that institutional convergence is imposed by government intervention.

3.2.5 Institutional competition and institutional learning

With the foregoing approach we have already entered the field of evolutionary thinking in the narrow meaning of the term: Here, variety is not only regarded as a necessary feature of reality, but also as a necessary condition for any kind of change and development in the economy. This change of perspective is completed if we turn to the general idea of institutional competition, which is more or less a fully elaborated version of the competitive advantage thinking without assigning technology to the core position. Furthermore, the idea of institutional competition integrates many of the aforementioned approaches because there is an explicit consideration of the economic agents who change and maintain certain institutions within particular competitive environments. These environments impose specific constraints, like, for example, the challenges posed by a particular natural environment (e.g. arid zones) or special political conditions like the endemic threat of war.[16]

Furthermore, we add the explicit consideration of the institutional framework governing the interaction between institutional change in different economies. Although this seems to be a newly emerging phenomenon in history, as far as explicit contractual relations are concerned, we can identify metainstitutions also in earlier times if we follow the distinction between formal and informal institutions (for example, the political rituals governing the relations between empires and peripheral peoples). The original model of this approach has been proposed with Hayek's concept of group selection (for a survey, see e.g. Radnitzky 1987). We assume that competitive pressures lead to selective retention and diffusion of certain institutional patterns, the latter being determined either by the forces weeding

---

[16] Economic historians have put much emphasis on these complex determinants, like Jones (1988) who explicitly applies a competitive paradigm on long-run change of institutions. For the impact of "ecological" factors on institutional change, see White (1987) and Herrmann-Pillath (2000: chapter 3).

out bad solutions or by imitative learning on the part of the agents (cf. Weede 1993). Whether this will eventually lead toward convergence, is a matter of experience, unless there is the proof that for every competitive environment imaginable, the optimal set of institutions would be the same. On the other hand, the current process of integrating the world economy seems to demonstrate the hierarchical nature of the convergence issue. We may suppose that there is convergence on the metainstitutional level (e.g. of WTO rules), and at the same time divergence on the institutional level may persist. Whether divergence will be sustained or not, depends on whether economic agents impose relevant constraints on the metainstitutional level. This in turn depends on certain perceptions and theories about institutional competition, which may be disputable among the groups involved (as, for example, when applying the idea of "levelling the playing field" on social standards) (cf. Bhagwati/Hudec 1996).

Figure 6 Institutional competition and evolving meta-institutions

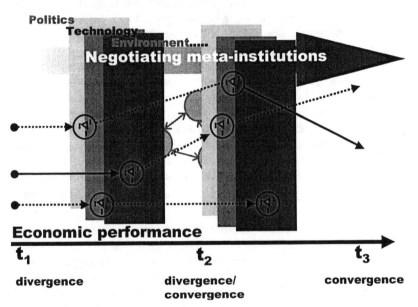

Source: Author.

From the normative perspective, the main difference between the evolutionary and the neoclassical interpretation of institutional competition results in the former introducing the concept of institutional learning, whereas the latter only analyzes the allocative consequences of institutions mediated via incentives and the resulting actions of economic agents. The phenomenon of institutional learning implies that the metainstitutional framework must be designed according to the general aim to enable the economic agents to discover better institutions, depending on their context, and depending on the internalization of possible external effects of those institutions in negotiations with economic agents acting within different institutional settings.

One example might be helpful to clarify that distinction. This is the question whether the rule of origin should apply in international trade. From the neoclassical perspective, mutual recognition of product regulations will be sufficient to reach optimal outcomes in terms of learning. The evolutionary approach focuses on the question whether rules of origin enable the economic agents to learn about the optimal regulations with highest efficacy. We could argue that just the opposite rule might be the better alternative, namely obliging every producer to stick to the domestic regulations worldwide, and at the same time to subject every imported good to domestic regulations (cf. Bhagwati 1996: 32ff.). This metainstitutional setting will speed up learning processes in every country affected, because consumers in foreign countries learn about the different regulations more explicitly, and because affected export interests will raise voices in the domestic political process. Domestic firms will either try to influence home government to remove certain fetters to competitive strategies in target markets, or they will try to reap advantages in target markets by making the quality effects of their domestic regulations explicit via special marketing efforts. Presumably, this process will work with higher learning efficacy than the opposite process where domestic consumers have to learn to distinguish among different countries of origin, and where indirect demand signals drive the foreign producers to learn about alternative regulations, and where there is only an indirect impact on government policies. Hence, whereas the neoclassical view emphasizes the possibly negative role of divergent domestic regulations as impediments to trade, the evolutionary view argues that institutional divergence is a necessary condition for institutional learning.[17]

3.2.6 Some comparative conclusions

We have considered some possible approaches to convergence. Most of them are not mutually exclusive. In particular, the institutional competition approach can integrate all the other perspectives aside from that of neoclassical institutionalism. If we connect the approaches, outcomes in terms of hypotheses can be even more diversified. For example, we could link the Northian view with New Growth Theory, such that dysfunctional outcomes of certain informal institutions that do not match the standard set might be

---

[17]Kerber (1998) also stresses that the idea of institutional competition will necessarily stay in conflict with the demand for zero non-tariff barriers to trade because trade impediments will always result from institutional divergence which is a necessary prerequisite of competition. There is also another approach to the problem of rules of origin taken by Gerken (1999) who argues that the rule of origin violates certain basic rights of import-competing producers for equal and just treatment, as far as product standards are concerned.

even multiplied because the threshold value of performance is not reached that triggers endogenous growth. Learning the wrong technologies, which do not fit the existing institutions, might lead to other kinds of institutional mismatch. The experience of developing countries seems to be rich with illustrations.

However, such wealth of observations notwithstanding, the whole issue of convergence is haunted by empirical underspecification, a problem that we have touched repeatedly. Let us summarize some of the issues.

- *What is the relevant time horizon?* Unless the time is specified when the final assessment is done of the relation between convergence of performance and convergence of institutions, we cannot falsify any of the approaches. In particular, neoclassical institutionalism can never be falsified by the simultaneous observation of divergent institutions and convergent performance. This is why events like the Asian crisis play such a powerful effect on the convergence debate (as quasi-"experimentum crucis"). Observers interpret them as "falsifications" of theories that claim that divergence is an optimal state. Yet, methodologically the convergence issue seems to be highly problematic and may be left in the realm of economic metaphysics, because such a conclusion indeed has to assume that there will be no further history after the event (as implied in Fukuyama's famous phrase).

- *What is the relevant level of aggregation?* The relation between different classes of institutions is very difficult to conceptualize in a systematic taxonomy. Aside from mere platitudes that the market economy relies on private property, matters cannot be handled easily if the very broad grey area of goods and services with some degree of publicness and externalities is touched upon. The relation between the many governmental restrictions of utilizing private property and the general concept is by no means straightforward to specify, as, for example, regarding liability rules (limited liability treats private losses as public goods, etc.). Hence, convergence may only make sense on a highly aggregate and abstract level; however just there the idea loses bite.

- *What is the distinction between institutions and rules, norms and values?* At a closer look, neoclassical institutionalism is contingent on the assumption of rational man, meaning that there is no difference across human beings as far as the behavioral response to institutions is concerned (the infamous "representative agent"). Convergence of institutions based on efficiency considerations presupposes identical mechanisms of compliance and motivation. The problem with this assumption is, of course, that there is still a heated debate about the anthropological foundations of the standard approach to rationality, and no conclusive empirical result so far attained. Therefore, we move between the Scylla of adopting the unproven belief into universally rational man or the Charybdis of arbitrary degrees of freedom depending on our particular construction of cultural specificity. Yet, one point has to be noted: If there are indeed economically relevant differences across cultures and behavior, the one-to-one relation between convergence of performance and convergence of institutions is definitively broken up.

- *What is the prime mover of institutional change?* The different approaches assign the role of the prime mover to different forces, respectively, like technology or the political process. The problem is that if we argue realistically that there is no prime mover but a complex interaction of different determinants, it is almost impossible to design a theory, not to speak of some serious empirical testing using accessible data. Neoclassical institutionalism simply sets this issue aside by adopting a pure normative stance toward convergence: its proponents straightforwardly tell you, if you wish to be rich, converge! The other extreme, evolutionary thinking, leaves even the normative dimension open and tells you: if you wish to be rich, believe it!

- *How to measure convergence?* The last issue that I wish to mention is the problem how to measure convergence in both dimensions of performance and institutions. Something in common to almost all approaches is to measure convergence of economic performance by means of GDP data. There are important philosophical dimensions of this problem, yet we need to acknowledge that performance indicators testing institutional aspects are strongly distorted if non-market goods are excluded, like government services or household production. If institutions in the market sector do affect behaviour in the non-market sector, GDP cannot be the only relevant measure for assessing economic performance. Even more difficult is the assessment of institutional convergence proper. Behind that lurks the very intricate issue of measuring institutional integration and defining very clearly the conceptual distinction between institutions and other kinds of rules. Take only the Northian dichotomy of formal and informal institutions. Convergence of informal institutions is almost impossible to observe unequivocally, and if informal institutions affect the workings of formal institutions, this is also valid for the latter.

Let us now try to reach somewhat more specific conclusions out of the obvious conundrum of convergence. Hence, we continue with our preliminary elaboration of an evolutionary approach, trying to escape from the Panglossian fallacy, and trying to draw together the different threads of the approaches that we have considered so far.

3.3 INDETERMINACY OF INSTITUTIONAL CHANGE, INSTITUTIONAL DIVERSITY AND COMPETETIVE ADVANTAGE

In the final paragraphs of the last section we have argued that measurement of convergence is very difficult. As I have argued elsewhere (Herrmann-Pillath 2000b), there is even a fundamental impossibility theorem on measurement of convergence. In simple words, if we were to believe that institutional competition would lead toward convergence, the actions of the economic agents triggering off that convergence can only follow the incentives and the information created within the market process. However, if performance is also influenced by non-market determinants, there cannot be an unequivocal reflection of any encompassing standard of optimality in the institutional competition within the market. This is true by definition for the entire set of public goods in the most general sense, that contributes to the working of the market. Hence, global competition cannot necessarily result in convergence of non-market dimensions of institutions. Yet, if those non-market dimensions influence institutional change in the economy, there are also impediments to convergence in the market-dimensions. That means, unless we are able to refer to a general standard of optimality encompassing both the market and the non-market aspects of the economic process, we cannot argue that institutional convergence is necessarily concomitant to convergence of performance. Hence, we may say that there is a general indeterminacy of measuring institutional change; since measurement has to be endogenous to channel institutional change into the supposed state of optimality. This indeterminacy will always generate diversity and path-dependencies. In the recent literature, this is reflected in some results demonstrating firstly, that there can be multiple equilibria of combinations between market structure and institutions that cannot be distinguished by the implied standard of efficiency, and secondly, that the diversity of institutions might be a precondition for specialization according to absolute advantages that result from specialization of production functions. Both observations support the view that globalization cannot lead to convergence of institutional determinants of competitive advantage, even if we observed convergence of economic performance. That is, convergence of performance allows institutional divergence, because precisely this divergence creates competitive advantages underlying the global division of labour.

3.3.1 Social capital, networks and multiple equilibria

It is now widely acknowledged that the costs of maintaining and implementing formal institutions depend on the existing set of informal institutions and on the stock of social capital.[18] Social capital is generated partly outside the economy, for example in ethnic groups obeying certain religious norms. Hence, the market depends on "free lunches" generated as unintended effects of non-market behavior (for a survey see Platteau 1994). There are complex mutual externalities between formal institutions and non-market behavior, which are very difficult to assess empirically, and which entail a causal complexity of the process of institutional change that turns the idea of necessary convergence into a mere vision.

For example, the interaction between social structures generating trust in the society might cause externalities on other processes in both the positive and the negative direction (on the ambiguity of social capital in general, see Woolcock 1998). One example can be found in the current debate about business networks and reciprocity versus anonymous competitive markets (Kranton 1996). Networks are based on trust-generating ascriptive ties and lead to higher efficiency of exchange by lowering transaction costs, yet at the same time this can reduce the level of trust outside those networks, that is, the anonymous market. The latter is becoming populated with individuals who are not trustworthy, just because the network attracts the trustworthy. This causes the members of the networks to stick to their kind, which introduces market imperfections and hence a loss of allocative efficiency which trades-off with the gain in transactional efficiency.[19] Yet, simply asserting that the market will prevail if trust is generated by another mechanism, in particular the juridical system, is no solution as long as that system is treated as exogenous (e.g. Kali 1999). The networked system might even prevent an efficient juridical system from emerging because ex ante there is no need to invest in its construction. Hence, the only way to imagine institutional change would be an outright change of the entire institutional setting, yet this is a completely unrealistic proposition. Another example for this kind of interaction between economic institutions and social capital is increased labour market mobility, because this might contribute to higher efficiency of allocation, yet the increased social entropy might trigger off the unravelling of spatially confined social fabrics and a destruction of social capital. Since social capital cannot be measured exactly in pecuniary terms (there is a missing market), total efficiency cannot be assessed.

---

[18]The World Bank even has begun to apply measures of social capital in its credit business, see Krishna/Shrader (1999). Although the concept is a disputed one in economic terms, the intellectual background does not seem to be so. For an extensive discussion see the volume edited by Dasgupta/Serageldin (1999).

[19]That result is heavily dependent on the modelling assumptions. One example is Rauch/Casella (1998) where the network characteristics operate like lower tariffs as compared to the rest of the world so that networking results in effects formally equivalent to the trade-off between trade creation and trade diversion in the creation of free trade areas. Efficiency gains depend on whether trade creation effects are stronger than trade diversion effects.

As we see, since there are complex relations between market- and non-market aspects of institutions, we cannot expect that institutional change will only reflect the impact of market signals. Rather we have to note that there is even a feedback from non-market processes to market signals which gives rise to pronounced phenomena of path-dependence. Convergence cannot be but a chance result of that process. Formally, this can be modelled as a frequency-dependent process where multiple equilibria emerge: For example, there can be two societies with networked markets and with legally-ordered markets respectively, the intermediate mix of both being unstable, and the final state being dependent on the initial frequency of the respective behavioral types in the population. Both may coexist as equally viable institutional regimes, provided that a workable metainstitutional framework will emerge minimizing conflicts between the systems. This has been demonstrated in Greif's (1993, 1994) analysis of the Mediterranean long-distance trade in the Middle ages, where two different institutional regimes emerged out of a "collectivist" cultural background of Arab Jews and the "individualist" setting in Genoa, the former relying on informal mechanisms of trust and reputation, and the latter on formal contractual standards.[20]

If there are multiple equilibria, there is no way to select between different institutional regimes by means of an economic criterion of efficiency. This is also evident from the comparison of network structures in East Asia by Feenstra and collaborators (Feenstra et al. 1997a, 1997b, 1999). They assume a monopolistic vertical market system where price is higher than marginal costs, so that there is an incentive for vertical integration if internal marginal cost pricing can be applied after integration. However, there is a circular causality because integration increases the monopolization of markets, leading to an increase in prices. This circular causality gives rise to multiple equilibria featuring, for example, Korean chaebol type structures as well as Taiwanese SME networks. Both are efficient solutions with internal marginal cost pricing, yet there is also a different kind of specialization according to competitive advantages, with the Korean ideal type featuring less product variety and higher quality than the Taiwanese. So institutional divergence is a result from global competition actually stabilizing certain non-market determinants of the equilibria, like government intervention in the Korean case, or social capital of family firms in the Taiwanese case.

---

[20] In his comments on Greif, Kali (1999) makes the point that Greif does not offer a criterion for assessing the comparative efficiency of networks and formal contractual relations. In the Maghribi trader case, Kali believes that the eventual disappearance of those trading groups after the Middle Ages can be regarded as a proof of lower efficiency. This is an institutional competition argument; however, as we have seen, there is no compelling reason why only economic determinants might have led to the decline of the Maghribis, and, furthermore, the argument in fact refers to viability, not efficiency, since there was obviously a tremendous change of the environment in that long period.

Since we cannot assess these factors independently, there is no way to solve the indeterminacy problem.

3.3.2 Coordination of production and competitive advantage

The Feenstra analysis of networks points at a more fundamental issue, namely that many arguments on institutional convergence assume that a clear distinction can be made between productive efficiency and institutional efficiency, so that there is no direct impact of institutional differences on productive efficiency aside from the impact on market structures. This reflects the more fundamental issue that the assumption might not be valid that is implicit to the New Institutional Economics, that there is a separation between production costs and transaction cost possible. From that perspective, institutions and organizations are centered around the problem of behavioral coordination resulting from opportunism and bounded rationality, and there is no place for the reasoning presented above in section 2.4 that there might be a direct link between technology (or, in broader terms, knowledge) and institutions.[21] To the contrary, if there are processes of learning and knowledge accumulation taking place among economic agents, the institutions governing their interaction cannot be exclusively assessed in terms of transaction efficiency because there is a separate impact on the coordination of production in the narrow meaning, e.g. (Langlois/Foss 1999). Hence, depending on technology, the criteria for institutional efficiency may diverge, because there is a complex interaction between transaction and production.

In the last decade, some economists began to use a new type of production function with the formal property of modularity (Milgrom/Roberts 1990). Modular production functions are ideally suited to reflect the complex phenomena of coordination that take place in modern industrial systems. For example, a supermodular production function means that marginal productivity of one input depends positively on the marginal productivity of the other inputs, so that total output is determined by the weakest link.[22] Hence, in order to maximize productive efficiency, the level of input quality must be very high for every input. If the production function

---

[21] Cf. Williamson (1999) who discusses the conflict between transaction cost and competence theories of the firm. The term "competence" is more general than "technology", but the basic point remains the same, because competences refer to particular kinds of knowledge, including, of course, technological know-how, explicit as well as tacit.

[22] More generally, this refers to complementarities among inputs, a property that can be modelled by different ways. Kremer (1993) uses a conventional production function which, however, includes a multiplicative term reflecting quality in terms of probabilities of failure. This leads to similar results as for the case of modular production functions, as far as complementarities are concerned. Modular production functions are an empirical application of modular functions in general which are not susceptible to

is submodular, there is exactly the opposite relation. That means, total output is almost exclusively dependent on the input with the highest quality ("star") whilst the quality of other inputs has only marginal importance or, in other words, increasing their quality will entail a waste of resources. This is a clear example for the irrelevance of transaction costs for institutional choice of governance mechanisms, because the organization of the coordination of inputs directly affects production costs and efficiency of production.[23]

Obviously, production functions with different degrees of modularity have far-reaching implications for the institutional framework both with regard to the organization of the production process and to the input markets. Supermodular production functions imply that enterprise organization needs elaborated systems of quality control and strong incentives for workers to follow quality standards. At the same time, the education system has to guarantee a high average level of education. If the production process is complex and is concomitant to a high rate of accumulation of tacit knowledge, we arrive at the vision of an institutional set up where labour mobility is low, enterprise organization is open to participation of labour, and the education system is geared towards ideals of equal opportunity. With submodular production functions, such an institutional set-up would simply entail a waste of resources. Instead, the economy will develop hierarchical control modes of corporate organization, a bipolar education system, and a fluid labour market. This description exactly matches the seminal analysis of the "J-Firm" and the "A-Firm" by Aoki (1988), only adding a more exact formal treatment of the underlying production processes. [24]

These considerations show that the idea of institutional convergence is indeed systematically dependent on the mechanism of convergence implicit to the neoclassical production function, so that we are full circle back to the considerations in our first section. If we have to model reality with other production functions, there are serious reasons why institutional

---

differentiation. Formally, a supermodular function has the property: $f(x) + f(x') < f(\min(x, x')) + f(\max(x, x'))$.

[23]This point can be even strengthened if the impact of quality uncertainty is included in the analysis, see Kremer (1993). Institutions might emerge to reduce quality uncertainty without any relation with behavioral uncertainty (cheating, opportunism, etc.). This argument is well recognized in management science, where, for example, market volatility is a source of uncertainty that is not linked with behavioral categories, yet also determines institutional choice, see Sutcliffe/Zaheer (1998).

[24]This argument has very interesting implications for the US debate on the impact of globalization on wages for low-skilled US labour. Within mainstream research, the important observation has been made that empirical tests cannot distinguish neatly between the impact of goods prices on factor prices on the one hand and the impact of non-neutral technological change on the other hand (Hanson/Slaughter 1999). Submodular production functions imply that wages for low-skilled labour will decline with an increasing specialization of the US economy on that kind of production, which has nothing to do with competition of low-cost labour in other countries.

convergence might even block convergence of economic performance because the different production systems require different institutional settings. If locations with different production functions compete against each other, convergence of output will not lead toward convergence of institutions (Grossman/Maggi 1998). Locations with supermodular functions and locations with submodular functions will manifest almost opposing systems of enterprise organization, labour market regulation and education, amongst others. However, in the context of globalization both will be viable because there are gains from trade resulting from institutional specialization as a precondition for product specialization.

On the other hand, since in reality we can only reasonably assume that different countries have different mixes of production functions, we conclude that convergence cannot but be a chance event. Taking the education system as an example, if there are two sectors in the economy with sub- and supermodular production functions, somehow there must also be a split in the education system. How this actually works will depend on historical accidence. Therefore, again we reach the conclusion that non-economic factors will play a decisive role for institutional change, because, for example, the shape of education systems is determined by the broader context of societal and political development, eventually supporting patterns of modular specialization in the world economy which feeds back to institutional divergence.

3.4 CONCLUDING THOUGHTS

The last example raises the issue whether convergence would be even detrimental to efficiency in any case. So far, the nation state is one of the pillars of institutional diversity in the world economy. That diversity can be a stable solution if diversity provides the basis for absolute competitive advantages in global competition. Let us imagine abolishing the nation state and achieving full integration in one step. We could think of a scenario where certain absolute advantages of divergent institutions get lost because of pressures toward convergence (on the following, see Aoki 1996). This becomes obvious if, for example, we assume endogenous technology. Imagine the merger of a large economy specializing on submodular production processes and relying on a highly competitive market system with a small economy specializing on supermodular processes embedded in networks. Mixing both will weaken the latter system because of increased social entropy, higher mobility of factors, and more problems of quality assessment. Factor remunerations will undergo changes if standards of quality are difficult to unify. The final result can be that the supermodular industrial system dependent on a certain institutional framework cannot be maintained and will vanish. There will be convergence of institutions as well as convergence of performance, however, with a lower level of performance than that achievable with institutional divergence and international division of labour. This is a remarkable result because if the total system would maintain positive growth rates, we would never be able to realize the loss of welfare resulting from a lack of institutional divergence: together with Dr. Pangloss, we would seem to live in the best of all possible worlds, because we cannot know the alternative without actually moving toward a divergent institutional regime.

Hence we may conclude that even if we observe convergence to happen during globalization, there is no immediate conclusion possible as regards the welfare and efficiency aspects. We may even suspect that convergence entails loss of the advantages of diversity, although not being able to prove this.

Yet, there is another problem connected with globalization which might render the whole idea of convergence across countries meaningless. So far, we have assumed that institutions refer to territories of states. However, if for example there is a match between institutions and technology, there is another possibility. Institutions might be linked with corporate organizations, networked markets within and across branches of industry, or with regional and global socio-economic associations. That means, institutions can be denationalized, becoming transformed from national constitutions into charters of global institutional clubs (for a related idea in the more narrow field of standards, see Casella 1996). This idea is somewhat implicit to the more familiar notion of locational competition. In that case, institutions are still linked to national territories; however, free movement of capital implies that companies select the institutions that match their requirements in an optimal way. Some people would argue that this is the climax of convergence. Yet, in fact this is by no means a necessary result and will be strongly influenced by the metainstitutional framework: that means, the idea of convergence can only refer to the metainstitutional framework, whereas divergence of institutions takes place on the level of spatially confined agents and organizations creating and maintaining institutions. Whether such a scenario would be called "convergent" or "divergent", seems to be a matter of taste.

REFERENCES

Amsden, Alice, 'Diffusion of Development: The Late-Industrializing Model and Greater East Asia', in *American Economic Review* 81, AEA Papers and Proceedings, 1991, pp. 2–286.

Aoki, Masahiko, 'An Evolutionary Parable of the Gains from International Organizational Diversity', in Landau et al. 1996, pp. 247–280.

Aoki, Masahiko, 'Information, Incentives, and Bargaining in the Japanese Economy'. Cambridge et al. 1988.

Barney, Jay, 'Firm Resources and Sustained Competitive Advantage', in *Journal of Management,* Vol. 17, No. 1 (1991), pp. 99–120.

Bellet, Michel, Corine L'Harmet (eds.), *Industry, Space and Competition.* Cheltenham 1999.

Bhagwati, Jagdish, 'The Demands to Reduce Domestic Diversity among Trading Nations', in Bhagwati/Hudec, Vol. 1 (1996), pp. 9–40.

Bhagwati, Jagdish, Robert E. Hudec (eds.), *Fair Trade and Harmonization. Prerequisites for Free Trade?.* Cambridge/London 1996.

Binger, Brian R., Elizabeth Hoffman, 'Institutional Persistence and Change: The Question of Efficiency', in *Journal of Institutional and Theoretical Economics,* No. 145 (1989), pp. 67–84.

Casella, Alessandra, 'Free Trade and Evolving Standards', in Bhagwati/Hudec, Vol. 1 (1996), pp. 120–156.

Chandler, Alfred D. jr., Peter Hagström, Örjan Sölvell (eds.), *The Dynamic Firm. The Role of Technology, Strategy, Organization, and Regions.* Oxford 1998.

Cimoli, Mario, Giovanni Dosi, 'Technological Paradigms, Patterns of Learning and Development: An Introductory Roadmap', in *Journal of Evolutionary Economics* 5, (1995), pp. 243–268.

Coriat, Benjamin, Giovanni Dosi, 'Learning How to Govern and Learning how to Solve Problems: On the Co-Evolution of Competences, Conflicts and Organizational Routines', in Chandler et al. 1998, pp. 103–133.

Dasgupta, Partha, Ismail Serageldin (eds.), *Social Capital. A Multifaceted Perspective.* Washington 1999.

Dixit, Avinash K., *The Making of Economic Policy: A Transaction-Cost Politics Perspective.* Cambridge 1996.

Dopfer, Kurt, 'Reconciling Economic Theory and Economic History: The Rise of Japan', in *Journal of Economic Issues* XIX, No. 1 (1985), pp. 21–73.

Dosi, Giovanni, Pavitt, Keith, Soete, Luc, *The Economics of Technical Change and International Trade,* New York 1990.

Dyer, Jeffrey H., 'Does Governance Matter? Keiretsu Alliances and Asset Specifity as Sources of Japanese Competitive Advantage', in *Organization Science,* Vol. 7, No. 6 (1996), pp. 649–666.

Dyer, Jeffrey H., 'Effective Interfirm Collaboration: How Firms Minimize Transaction Costs and Maximize Transaction Value', in *Strategic Management Journal*, Vol. 18 (1997), pp. 535–556.

Ebner, Alexander, 'Understanding Varieties in the Structure and Performance of National Innovation Systems: The Concept of Economic Style', in Groenewegen/Vromen 1999, pp. 141–169.

Eggertsson, Thráinn, *Economic Behavior and Institutions*. Cambridge 1990.

Feenstra, Robert C., Huang Deng-Shing, Gary Hamilton, 'Business Groups and Trade in East Asia, Part I: Networked Equilibria', in *NBER Working Paper* 5886, 1997.

Feenstra, Robert C., Maria Yang, Gary G. Hamilton, *Business Groups and Trade in East Asia, Part II: Product Variety*, 1997.

Feenstra, Robert C., Tzu-Han Yang, Gary G. Hamilton, 'Business Groups and Product Variety in Trade: Evidence From South Korea, Taiwan and Japan', in *Journal of International Economics*, Vol. 48 (1999), pp. 71–100.

Furubotn, Eirik, *Economic Efficiency in a World of Frictions*, MPI Jena Discussion Paper 0998, 1998.

Gerken, Lüder, 'Ursprungslandprinzip, Wettbewerb der Staaten und Freiheit', in *ORDO*, 50 (1999), pp. 405–430.

Greif, Avner, 'Contract Enforceability and Economic Institutions in Early Trade: The Maghribi Traders' Coalition', in *American Economic Review*, Vol. 83, No. 3 (1993), pp. 525–548.

Greif, Avner, 'Cultural Beliefs and the Organization of Society: A Historical and Theoretical Reflection on Collectivist and Individualist Societies', in *Journal of Political Economy* 102, No. 5 (1994), pp. 912–950.

Groenewegen, John, Jack Vromen (eds.), *Institutions and the Evolution of Capitalism: Implications of Evolutionary Economics*, Cheltenham/Northhampton 1999.

Grossman, Gene M., Giovanni Maggi, *Diversity and Trade*, NBER Working Paper 6741, 1998.

Haitani, Kanji, 'The Paradox of Japan's Groupism: Threat to Future Competitiveness?', in *Asian Survey*, Vol. XXX (1990), pp. 237–250.

Hanson, Gordon H., Matthew J. Slaughter, *The Rybczynski Theorem, Factor-Price Equalization, and Immigration: Evidence From U.S. States*, NBER Working Paper 7074, 1999.

Hayami, Yujiro, 'Toward an East Asian Model of Economic Development', in Hayami/Aoki 1998, pp. 3–35.

Hayami, Yujiro, Masahiko Aoki (eds.), *The Institutional Foundations of East Asian Development*, Proceedings of the IEA Conference held in Tokyo, Japan. Houndsmills/London 1998.

Herrmann-Pillath, Carsten, 'Wirtschaftspolitische Steuerung versus institutionelle Selbstorganisation politisch-ökonomischer Systeme: Die Transformation post-sozialistischer Volkswirtschaften', in Schweitzer/Silverberg 1998, pp. 333–360.

Herrmann-Pillath, Carsten, *Evolution von Wirtschaft und Kultur: Bausteine einer transdisziplinären Methode.* Marburg 2000.

Herrmann-Pillath, Carsten, *Institutional Convergence: The Evolutionary Disenchantment*, Diskussionspapier Heft 59 der Fakultät für Wirtschaftswissenschaft der Universität Witten/Herdecke, Mai 2000. (2000b).

Hoekman, Bernhard M., Michel M. Kostecki, *The Political Economy of the World Trading System.* Oxford 1995.

Hunt, Shelby D., Robert M. Morgan, 'The Comparative Advantage Theory of Competition', in *Journal of Marketing,* Vol. 59 (1995), pp. 1–15.

Ikegami, Eiko, *The Taming of the Samurai. Honorific Individualism and the Making of Modern Japan.* Cambridge/London 1995.

Iwata, Ryushi, 'The Japanese Enterprise as a Unified Body of Employees: Origins and Development', in Kumon/Rosovsky 1992, pp. 170–197.

Jones, Eric R., *Growth Recurring.* Oxford 1988.

Kali, Raja, 'Endogenous Business Networks', in *Journal of Law, Economics and Organization* 15, No. 3 (1999), pp. 615–636.

Kerber, Wolfgang, 'Zum Problem einer Wettbewerbsordnung für den Systemwettbewerb', in *Jahrbuch für Neue Politische Ökonomie,* (1998), pp. 199–230.

Kirby, M. W., 'Institutional Rigidities and Economic Decline: Reflections on the British Experience', in *Economic History Review* XLV, No. 4 (1992), pp. 637–660.

Kotabe, Masaaki, Wheiler, Kent W., *Anticompetitive Practices in Japan, Their Impact on the Performance of Foreign Firms.* Westport/London 1996.

Kranton, Rachel E., 'Reciprocal Exchange: A Self-Sustaining System', in *American Economic Review* 86, No. 4 (1996), pp. 830–851.

Kremer, Michael, 'The O-Ring Theory of Economic Development', in *Quarterly Journal of Economics* 108, (1993), pp. 551–575.

Krishna, Anirudh, Elizabeth Shrader, 'Social Capital Assessment Tool', in *mimeo.* Washington 1999.

Krugman, Paul, *Development, Geography, and Economic Theory.* Cambridge, Mass./London 1995.

Kumon, Shumpei, Henry Rosovsky (eds.), *The Political Economy of Japan,* Vol. 3 in *Cultural and Social Dynamics.* Stanford 1992.

Landau, Ralph, Timothy Taylor, Gavin Wright (eds.), *The Mosaic of Economic Growth.* Stanford 1996.

Langlois, Richard N., Nicolai J. Foss, 'Capabilities and Governance: The Rebirth of Production in the Theory of Economic Organization', in *Kyklos,* 52 (1999), pp. 201–218.

Leebron, D. W., 'Lying Down With Procrustes: An Analysis of Harmonization Claims', in Bhagwati/Hudec, Vol. 1 (1996), pp. 41–118.

Leipold, Helmut, 'Informale und formale Institutionen: Typologische und kulturspezifische Relationen', in Helmut Leipold und Ingo Pies, (eds.), *Ordnungstheorie und Ordnungspolitik. Konzeptionen und Entwicklungsperspektiven,* Band 64 (2000), pp. 401–428.

Loasby, Brian, 'Industrial Districts as Knowledge Communities', in Bellet/L'Harmet, 1999.

MacDonald, Glenn M., James R. Markusen, 'A Rehabilitation of Absolute Advantage', in *Journal of Political Economy,* 93, No. 2 (1985), pp. 277–297.

Melo, Martha de, Alan Gelb, 'Transition to Date: A Comparative Overview', in Zecchini, 1997, pp. 59–78.

Melo, Martha de, Gur Ofer, 'The Russian City in Transition: The First Six Years in Ten Volga Capitals', in *mimeo.* Washington 1990.

Milgrom, Paul, John Roberts, 'The Economics of Modern Manufacturing: Technology, Strategy, and Organization', in *American Economic Review,* 80 (1990), pp. 511–528.

Mummert, Uwe, *Informal Institutions and Institutional Policy – Shedding Light on the Myth of Institutional Conflict,* MPI Jena Discussion Paper 02-99, 1999.

North, Douglass C., *Institutions, Institutional Change, and Economic Performance.* Cambridge et al. 1990.

O'Flaherty, Brendan, Jagdish Bhagwati, 'Will Free Trade with Political Science Put Normative Economists Out of Work?', in *Economics and Politics,* Vol. 9, No. 3 (1997), pp. 207–219.

Okazaki, Tetsuji, Masahiro Okuno-Fujiwara, 'Evolution of Economic Systems: The Case of Japan', in Hayami/Aoki 1998, pp. 482–521.

Platteau, Jean-Philippe, 'Behind the Market Stage Where Real Societies Exist – Part I: The Role of Public and Private Order Institutions, and Part II: The Role of Moral Norms', in *Journal of Development Studies* 30/3 + 4, (1994), pp. 533–577, 753–817.

Penz, Reinhard, *Legitimität und Viabilität. Zur Theorie der institutionellen Steuerung der Wirtschaft.* Marburg 1999.

Porter, Michael E., *The Competitive Advantage of Nations.* London 1990.

Radnitzky, Gerard, 'An Economic Theory of the Rise of Civilization and Its Policy Implications: Hayek's Account Generalized', in *ORDO,* 38 (1987), pp. 47–90.

Rauch, James, Alessandra Casella, *Overcoming Informational Barriers to International Resource Allocation: Prices and Group Ties,* NBER Working Paper 6627. (1998).

Rodrik, Dani, 'Understanding Economic Policy Reform', in *Journal of Economic Literature* XXXIV, (1996), pp. 9–41.

Rodrik, Dani, 'TFPG Controversies, Institutions and Economic Performance in East Asia', in Hayami/Aoki 1998, pp. 79–101.

Sala-i-Martin, Xavier, 'The Classical Approach to Convergence Analysis', in *Economic Journal,* Vol. 106 (1996), pp. 1019–1036.

Shleifer, Andrei, 'Government in Transition', in *European Economic Review*, Vol. 41 (1997).

Schweitzer, Frank, Gerald Silverberg (eds.), *Evolution und Selbstorganisation in der Ökonomie, Selbstorganisation: Jahrbuch für Komplexität in den Natur-, Sozial- und Geisteswissenschaften*, Band 9, 1998.

Sutcliffe, Kathleen M., Akbar Zaheer, 'Uncertainty in the Transaction Environment: An Empirical Test', in *Strategic Management Journal* 19, (1998), pp. 1–23.

Thompson, Michael, Richard Ellis, Aaron Wildawsky, *Cultural Theory*, Boulder/Oxford 1990.

Weede, Erich, 'The Impact of Interstate Conflict on Revolutionary Change and Individual Freedom', in *Kyklos*, Vol. 46, No. 3 (1993), pp. 473–496.

White, Colin, *Russia and America, The Roots of Economic Divergence*. London 1987.

Williamson, Oliver, 'Strategy Research: Governance and Competence Perspectives', in *Strategic Management Journal*, Vol. 20 (1999), pp. 1087–1108.

Woolcock, Michael, 'Social Capital and Economic Development: Toward a Theoretical Synthesis and Policy Framework', in *Theory and Society*, 27 (1998), pp. 151–208.

World Trade Organization, *Annual Report 1997*, Volume I, Special Topic: Trade and Competition Policy. Geneva 1997.

Zecchini, Salvatore (ed.), *Lessons From Economic Transition – Central and Eastern Europe in the 1990s*. Dordrecht 1997.

Discussant: Carsten Schreiter

I agree with most points Herrmann-Pillath makes in reviewing different approaches tackling convergence. The idea of convergence is the outcome of equilibrium thinking. There is no possibility of proving this tendency in general, not even for economic performance indicators. If we take von Hayek's message seriously, we know that the outcome of competition is not predictable. This is especially true for predicting details. Therefore, the question of this conference is unanswerable, purely in logical terms. But Hayek left one option open to get a glimpse of future developments, in what he calls pattern predictions. It is possible, therefore, to speculate about convergence on a very abstract level. But in Herrmann-Pillath's opinion this cannot be done very fruitfully. So there is only one option left open: convergence cannot be expected. I am not sure if this outcome is exaggerated, that is, that if we restrict our investigations to the economic subsystem of the society there may be some convergence. At this level we find the market system spreading all over the globe, encompassing very heterogeneous institution bundles, but with some properties in common. Therefore, I would like to challenge the main thesis of Herrmann-Pillath's paper, in so far as there may actually be some convergence of institutional systems in a wider sense, restricting ourselves to the economic sphere. My agenda is as follows: first some affirmative remarks, second some criticism and third some possible outcomes of convergence.

- *Agreement*: One requisite of convergence is a selection mechanism, weeding out inefficiencies and bringing about equi-efficient institutional set-ups, governance structures, etc. This selection force must dominate innovations. Innovations will disrupt selection processes and in this respect heterogeneity indicates an evolution and is a necessary starting point for new developments. In this respect convergence is not to be expected on the market level. This outcome does not preclude the imitation of business techniques, organizational structures, etc. Thus, a general tendency is more than questionable. There is no clear connection between the performance of firms and institutions. If at all, the connection only exists in the form of a lose transmission link from competition on the product level to the organizational level, to the institutions. For a general tendency to develop, there have to be system or country wide problems that cannot be solved on the firm level alone, thus necessitating a reaction of the total system. Herrmann-Pillath maintains that there is no criterion stemming from economics, which can be used to identify a convergence of institutions, because his vantage point is not a general problem.

- *Criticism*: A general problem of social systems is evolution and coping with complexity. Systems must generate and use knowledge. Knowledge creation necessitates resources and spending. There is no guarantee of having successful outcomes, and a lot of resources are wasted in the trial and error process. A system that has to produce knowledge cannot be efficient in an allocative manner. At the same time, there has to be a selection mechanism in force doing its job. Without selection, knowledge creation is both meaningless and useless, just wasting resources. From a system perspective the forces of selection and innovation have to be balanced in that way, in order that selection is not too harsh to jeopardize innovations and, on the other hand, not too weak to produce unused knowledge. To realize this trade-off between selection and innovation there are two extreme possibilities, facing the firm level: The first one is to finance generic and other sorts of more general R&D by government. In this case, there has to be a strong selection machinery forcing private firms to use this knowledge, if inefficiency is excluded. The second case is just the opposite one. Knowledge and research have to be financed completely by private enterprises, but in this case there cannot be strong selection forces at work at the same time. These different patterns can now be identified in reality. Comparing now the United States with Japan, we find in the former system a very strong selection mechanism, the market for corporate control, a strong anti-trust law and more radical innovative activities, while much research is financed by the government. In Japan, on the contrary, we find that there is a rather weak selection mechanism, combined with a high ratio of private R&D to total R&D expenditures, more incremental innovation activity at the firm level. Germany lies in between and the UK has had strong selection forces but not enough public financed R&D efforts. The reason for these different mixtures lies in history, as is well known. Systems are following paths. The argument, so far, shows that, in principle, there is no reason for convergence of the extreme constellations, because both countries, Japan and the USA, are managing the balance between allocative and dynamic efficiency. This was not the case for Germany and the UK.

- *Convergence*: Why should the systems converge or why should one or the other copy the institutional set-up, then? We need to explain the advantage of one mode over the other, if there is any. The advantage cannot lie in the balance of allocative and dynamic efficiency. But it may be the case that one system favours a firm behaviour that is damaging the other system. This brings me to my point. Globalization is speeding up innovations and technical change. The different institutional set-ups have different ways to cope with disturbances and structural change, and the organizational differences between Japan and the USA reflect these differences. When US firms are much more oriented to use external sources of knowledge, they are trained (and forced) to change their knowledge base to foster more radical innovations. They can fire workers and hire new labour. They are using the hierarchy as a means to adapt to very volatile environments. Japanese organizations are very good in adapting to continuously changing circumstances, because they are using horizontal mutual adjustment and inside learning. There is some evidence of this from Marengo, who runs a simulation model, getting these results.

This brings me to my conclusions. First, there may be an escalation to the disadvantage arising from the Japanese way of organizing business, because the method of mutual adjustment inside organizations is too slow, and not useful, when the knowledge base of the firms changes dramatically. Therefore, there should be a tendency to steeper hierarchies in Japan and to more top-down decision making. Second, the innovation system of Japan has a disadvantage insofar as knowledge externalities may have positive effects on the economy as a whole. There is always the presumption that there will be less production of knowledge than optimal, especially when generic or basic research is meant. But there is still another effect. If the assumption is correct that US firms are more efficient in a static sense, increasing competition in world markets will narrow the margins for Japanese firms to finance their R&D efforts. Therefore, I expect that the Japanese system will change the balance between external and internal funding of R&D. Less R&D will be financed by firms and more by government spending. The mechanisms of selection have to adapt to more static pressures. It is still true that both systems have to pay for R&D inevitably. The public financed system has to raise taxes, which will raise costs and narrow the margins, too. But there may be some good reasons to believe that innovating firms are better off, because tax-effects are distributed to the total system. This may be a first, very general suggestion, which requires further research. The result seems therefore to suggest, that a tendency of convergence should be expected. This result is not really in conflict with Herrmann-Pillath's main thesis, because he excludes the search for abstract convergence patterns, stemming from the inner forces of market economies. My idea is to show that it might be useful not to exclude pattern predictions, even if they are very abstract.

REFERENCES

Hayek, Friedrich A. von, 'The Theory of Complex Phenomena', in Hayek, Friedrich A. von, *Studies in Philosophy, Politics and Economics*. London 1967, pp. 22–42.

Marengo, L., 'Coordination and Organizational Learning in the Firm', in *Journal of Evolutionary Economics*, Vol. 2 (1992), pp. 313–326.

4

A COMPARATIVE INSTITUTIONAL ANALYSIS OF JAPANESE COMPUTER NETWORK SYSTEMS

Seiichi Kawasaki

4.1 INTRODUCTION

The main purpose of this paper is to analyze the evolution of Japanese IT industries in comparison with the U.S. developments. We also try to answer the question why Japan's computer and communications industries succeeded in the 80s and then failed in the 90s. Our analytical framework is based on the comparative institutional analysis (CIA) developed by M. Aoki and others. In Section 2 we first outline the technological developments in the IT industries. Section 3 presents information processing models which are the key tools to explain the performances of IT firms, and Section 4 develops the concept of business models which combine the information processing system with other complementary factors. In Section 5, the rise and decline of three major business models in the IT industries are analyzed.

4.2 THE INFORMATION TECHNOLOGY

The modern history of information technology can be represented by three distinctive but closely related sub-streams, namely the mainframe computer technology, the small computer technology, and the Internet technology. All these three streams have relatively long formative years and they overlapped each other. The mainframe computer technology established the basic architecture of the electronic computer. It started from military research during World War II and generated a major industry in the 50s and 60s until its maturing in the 80s. The small computer technology spread computing power all over societiy. The origin can be traced to the ARPA projects in the late 50s and the technology developed into its full form in the early 80s. The Internet technology connects a multitude of computers scattered all over the world and is becoming an indispensable social infrastructure.

Although the technology started from the invention of packet switching in the early 60s, its full industrial development occurred only in the early 90s.

4.2.1 The mainframe computer technology

The first modern electronic computer was developed for ballistic calculation during World War II by J. Mauchly and J. Eckert. Later J. von Neumann joined the project and the team made an important basic invention, the stored-program-controlled computer, which was to become the standard design of the computer for many years to come.[1]

After the war, several companies including Mauchly and Eckert's new company, started developing computers for civilian use. IBM, the successful office machinery maker, entered the new computer market and rapidly expanded its share for office data processing with its skillful marketing methods, a rich array of solid peripheral equipment, and extensive system support. In 1960, IBM introduced its System 360 series computers. The technological level of their hardware and software was solid, but rather conservative. However, the basic architecture of this series was revolutionary. Up to that time, all series of IBM's computers had different software standards, so that the company had to develop all different versions of major software for each series. IBM decided to set up a unified standard for the new series of computers, so that all software would be compatible with the different 360 series and forthcoming models. Although the converting costs were enormous, the series became the main engine of IBM's rapid growth for almost 30 years to come, because this established the de facto standard of mainframe computers. From then on, all other domestic and foreign computer makers had to either make IBM-compatible machines, or find a niche in which IBM was not interested.

In order to keep off IBM-compatible clone makers, IBM had an ambitious plan to produce a path-breaking computer series code named the Future Series in the 70s. The rumor of this series sent shockwaves through the world's IT industries. However, this project was abandoned in 1975 due to various reasons. One of the most important reasons was that so huge an amount of software had already accumulated that switching costs became intolerable. Hardware technology also became commonplace, so that other computer makers could attain better quality at cheaper costs relatively easily. Thus the mainframe computers entered into the stage of maturity.

4.2.2 The small computer technology

In 1957 the Advanced Research Projects Agency (ARPA) was established under the Department of Defense in order to prevent major technological

[1]For the history of the mainframe computer, see, for example, Campbell-Kelly and Aspray (1996: ch. 4–6) and Flamm (1988).

surprises in response to Sputnik. ARPA targeted, in particular, long-term, high-risk research and contracted out all projects to universities and companies, giving them considerable free hand. J.C.R. Licklider took charge of ARPA's Information Processing Techniques Office in 1962 and initiated interactive computing projects. Many important elements of human computer interface emerged from these projects, and they formed the basic concept of the modern small computers.[2]

The most important hardware base of the small computer is the integrated circuit (IC) and microprocessors. The integrated circuit technology was introduced during the period between 1965 and 1975, and reduced the price of computing power drastically. Taking advantage of this technological progress, Digital Equipment Corporation (DEC) successfully developed a series of powerful, low-cost minicomputers (PDP series) and spread scientific and technical computing. Around 1970, Intel developed the first microprocessor (IC including basic computer functions on one chip), and it was to form the core hardware of personal computers later.

In 1964, J.G. Kemeny and T.E. Kurz developed BASIC, a computer language for beginners in order to expand the user circle of time-sharing computing. Due to its simplicity, BASIC was to become the main language and operating system of the first generation of personal computers later. From 1969 to 1974, K. Thompson and D.M. Ritchie developed the Unix operating system and the C language. Due to its compactness, portability, and liberal license policy, Unix spread rapidly among universities and research institutes as the standard OS for minicomputers. The Unix users developed gradually a huge amount of software exchanging ideas freely among themselves, and formed the unique Unix culture and Unix communities.

At first microprocessors were used for constructing small computers by a growing number of enthusiastic hobbyists and the suppliers of computer kits and other peripheral electronic equipment started to grow. In 1977, Apple II and other personal computers were introduced in the market in assembled forms for the first time, and began to spread rapidly. At the same time, Microsoft's Basic and several application softwares (VisiCalc, WordStar, and dBase in particular) made a hit in the market.

Although IBM was rather late in coping with the new trend of computer downsizing, the impact and decision to enter the PC business in 1981 was drastic. IBM abandoned its century-old tradition of making everything inside the company, and outsourced almost all main parts of the personal computer, providing heaven-sent chances for Intel and Microsoft. Although the IBM PC was a success, many clone makers soon started to make more efficient compatible models one after another to make IBM one of the minor

---

[2]For the history of the minicomputer, the work station, and the personal computer, see, for example, Campbell-Kelly and Aspray (1996: ch. 9–11), Freiberger and Swaine (1984), Chopsky and Leonisis (1988), and Langlois (1992).

players in this field. However, the IBM PC architecture established a de facto open standard for the personal computer hardware.

Graphical user interface (GUI) is critically important for the personal computer to appeal to a wide circle of non-specialist users. ARPA's basic research on computer-human interface by D. Englebart and others laid the foundation for personal computers' GUI systems. In 1984 Apple's Macintosh first incorporated GUI commercially inspired by the prototype Alto computer of Xerox, and Microsoft followed Apple by developing the Windows systems.

4.2.3 The Internet technology

The core technology of the Internet is packet switching. In contrast to circuit switching used in the telephone system, packet switching first divides data into small "packets" labeled with their destination and other information, and then forwards them from node to node until they reach their destination. The advantages of the technology include robustness and efficiency in data communications. The basic idea of the technology was invented in the early 60s first by P. Baran at the Rand Corporation and then D. Davies at NPL in the U.K. independently.[3]

The implementation and further technological development were undertaken by L. Roberts of ARPA. ARPA initiated and directed the experimental network project with substantial military research funds, but contracted out the actual development to academic and private sectors. The ARPANET succeeded in networking between four institutions in 1969, and demonstrated for the first time that packet switching worked in practice.

As ARPANET's participants (mainly universities) increased, further technical development was undertaken by many net users and this process expanded the number of networking researchers considerably. ARPA originally intended to use the network mainly for sharing limited computing resources located in different sites, but it turned out that the net was mostly used as a communication tool for member academic communities.

In the early 80s, the ARPANET adopted TCP/IP, new communication protocols developed by ARPA researchers (R. Kahn and V. Cerf). TCP/IP made it possible to interconnect different networks. The ARPANET, a network of computers, became the Internet, a network of networks.

During the 80s and 90s, the Internet was transferred from military to civilian control, and participating networks, computers and users grew enormously. The invention of World Wide Web, Web browsers, and other Web technology popularized the Internet as a key medium for commercial and various social activities.

---

[3]For the history of the Internet, see, for example, Abbate (1999), Norberg and O'Neill (1996), Hafner and Lyon (1996), Randall (1997), and Salus (1995).

4.3 INFORMATION PROCESSING MODES

This section presents the information processing model of the firm[4] developed by M. Aoki and M. Okuno-Fujiwara (1996) in a simplified, nonmathematical way.

4.3.1 A Model of information processing system

While neoclassical economics used to regard the firm as a mechanical agent to maximize profits in response to price signals, the CIA explores resource allocation processes inside the firm as the source of efficiency differences.

For simplicity, a firm is assumed to consist of a management unit and two interrelated business units. There are two different kinds of on-site uncertainties; the system shocks which affect the whole firm and the individual shocks which directly affect individual business units.

The firm's cost is assumed to consist of the following function:

$$C = \overline{C} - (\alpha + \gamma_1)x_1 - (\alpha + \gamma_2)x_2 + \tfrac{1}{2}B(x_1 + x_2)^2 + \tfrac{1}{2}D(x_1 - x_2)^2$$

In this equation x_1 and x_2 denote the activity levels of two business units, α and γ_i system and individual stochastic shocks, B the degree of the units' competing for resources, D the degree of necessity of coordination between the units. In order to minimize the expected cost, the management designs and instructs decision making rules for business units. The following are also assumed:

* The management can only observe the distribution of α and γ_i, but not their realized values;

* Each business unit can observe α and γ_i only with some errors.

Due to organizations' limited capacity of processing information, the management cannot use the on-site information α and γ_i collected by business units. Each business unit also faces trade-off when processing different sources of information.

4.3.2 Types of information systems

Although there are many different modes of utilizing the information on these shocks, the following four types are the most relevant for our study.

Classical Hierarchy

In this system the management directs business units using only the observable information on the shocks, while each business unit does not use any

---

[4]This model was developed by Crémer (1990), Aoki (1987), Aoki (1995), and Aoki and Okuno-Fujiwara (1996).

information on two kinds of shocks. This situation may occur in the early stage of capitalism when workers have little education of utilizing on-site information.

Decentralized Hierarchy

Each business unit uses individual shocks, whereas the system shock is not utilized. The information used by this mode is $\gamma_i + \varepsilon_i$, where ε_i denotes the observation error of the i-th unit. Workers acquire specialist capabilities to deal with each unit's on-site uncertainty, and the differences between the two units are adjusted by inventories. This system corresponds to the coordination mode of traditional large American firms.

Horizontal Hierarchy

In contrast to the decentralized hierarchy focusing on individual shocks, one possible mode could only utilize system shocks, so that member units observe the system shocks together and share the same information. Since it is in reality inconvenient to ignore each unit's individual circumstances altogether, each unit may use individual shocks in addition to the shared system information. Due to bounded rationality, however, this mode cannot use the individual shocks as well as the decentralized hierarchy does. Each unit observes and utilizes $\alpha + \varepsilon_0 + \gamma_i + \varepsilon_i$, where $\alpha + \varepsilon_0$ denotes the observed system shock shared by the two units. This mode corresponds to traditional large Japanese firms with job rotation and small circle activities among workers.

Decentralized Information System

In order to cope with increasing system shocks and the need for coordination among business units, the decentralized hierarchy may utilize the system shock. Still mainly based on the professional ability to deal with individual shocks, this new mode called the decentralized information system observes and utilizes the system shock through the new IT technology. However, this mode does not share the observed system shock as the horizontal hierarchy does, so that the utilized information is $\alpha + \gamma_i + \varepsilon_i$. This mode belongs to the new IT firms typically seen in the USA.

4.3.3 Informational efficiency

Aoki and Okuno-Fujiwara (1996: 58) call an information system informationally efficient if it attains lower expected costs per production unit. Among the four information processing modes discussed above, the classical hierarchy is the least informationally efficient, because it does not utilize any on-site information available at business unit levels. The comparative efficiency among the remaining three modes depends on the relative size of the two shocks and also the relative size of two coordination parameters B and D. When individual shocks are much larger than the system shock, the decentralized hierarchy dominates the other modes, regardless of the relative size of B/D. When the system shock is larger than individual shocks, and when coordination is more important ($D > B$), the horizontal hierarchy is more efficient. On the other hand, when the system shock is relatively large but when coordination among units is less important (B > D), the decentralized information system becomes more efficient.

4.3.4 Information processing in the automobile and IT industries

The mass production and distribution systems which first emerged in the late 1980s, attained historically unprecedented productivity growth and introduced an enormous variety of new products into the markets through economies of scale and scope as well as specialization. However, the resulting discrepancy between production and consumption created serious economic problems such as a great amount of inventories and waste. One of the most important agendas of the post-mass-production economy has been how to match increasing production capability and the needs of consumers, so that consumers may obtain products which satisfy their individual needs at reasonable prices, and producers may save inventories and waste by making exactly what is demanded.[5] Thus, current production and distribution systems demand more extensive coordination among various business units and tend to increase the weight of system shocks. After World War II Japanese manufacturers, particularly in the automobile industries, succeeded in developing a new type of coordination system, investing heavily in specific human capital whose human relationship embodied the network of a firm's knowledge base. The coordination skills are embodied in employees working in the same firm for a long time. The critically important condition for this system to work is the stability of technical progress. Incremental improvement can be attained by the coordination of current employees. In this situation, the horizontal hierarchy of the Japanese firms could dominate the decentralized hierarchy of the large American firms in efficiency.

The coordination between production and consumption is still the main problem for IT industries. However, the difference with the automobile industries is the dynamism of technological progress. The IT industries in their early stage of rapid growth experienced many unexpected turns of technical and business development in a short time, though there have been some relatively stable periods. This technological state has several significant implications for information processing. First, the ability to develop new technology becomes particularly important, so that the types of information processing practiced in the USA, emphasizing the specialist capability, have comparative advantages. Second, the coordination has to

---

[5]Toffler (1980) clearly pointed out the importance of this point in a historical framework. Womack et al. (1990) discussed the same point in the context of the automobile industry.

be flexible and adaptive. The Japanese type coordination was based on intimate human interactions among long-term employees and trade partners. This information system cannot deal with rapidly changing technology, because the accumulated skills become rapidly obsolete and useless and because it prevents hiring and acquiring new abilities. In such a situation, the decentralized information system, based on specialization, but incorporating coordination ability with the help of IT technology, is more efficient than the horizontal hierarchy of the typical Japanese firms.

4.4 BUSINESS MODELS

4.4.1 Institutional complementarity[6]

If informational efficiency is significant and external conditions, such as the nature of shocks, differ from industry to industry, we should observe various modes of information processing in different industries in any country. In reality, however, the same mode tends to be dominant across industries in one country: the horizontal hierarchy dominates Japanese industries, while the decentralized hierarchy or decentralized information system is common among many American industries. This is because the information processing mode is complemented by other institutions, such as the mode of workers' skill types. The mode of skills complementary to the U.S.-type information system is the functional ability to deal with individual shocks. Workers' jobs are clearly classified and evaluated in the external labor market. On the other hand, the ability to communicate with members and solve problems together is required for the Japanese-type information system. A large proportion of such skills is firm-specific and formed by long-term on-the-job-training within the same firm.

4.4.2 Structure of business models

In order to analyze the evolution of firms in IT industries, we shall consider a set of four key dimensions characterizing a firm's structure: the information processing mode, the nature of workers' skills, business range, and product standards. This set will be called a business model. As for the information processing mode, we note that there are actually several different levels in the mode. The business unit, as discussed in Section 3, may represent an individual, a workshop in the factory, or a corporate division of the firm. At the abstract level of this paper, we do not distinguish between them. The business range specifies the product diversification (= the degree of

---

[6]Institutional complementarity is one of the key analytical tools of the CIA. See Aoki and Okuno-Fujiwara (1996).

horizontal integration) and the proportion that a firm occupies for its activities in the whole process of development, production, and distribution of its product (= the degree of vertical integration). In the case of parts procurement, for example, a firm may produce parts itself, or may order parts from suppliers, or may buy parts in the markets. Product standards are particularly important for IT industries. IT products have the characteristic of system products: they are mostly used in combination of other IT products as a system. For example, we need a whole range of software and peripheral products, such as a printer, a monitor, network equipment, and so on, when we use a personal computer. Then it is critically important whether or not these components are mutually compatible.

We assume that the success of a business model basically depends on how the four components can deal with the state of technological development and business environment. Other external factors, such as government policies, are also important determinants. We notice that the role of the government was rather large in the IT industries both in the USA and Japan, as seen in Section 2. U.S. government's defense policies produced the first modern computer, ARPA's generous support and long-term visions laid the foundation of personal computers, and ARPA played the vital role in creating the Internet. Japanese IT industries were also nurtured and heavily protected from the beginning by the government and MITI's industrial policies were particularly instrumental in Japan's catching up with the technological lead of IBM and other U.S. firms.

4.5 EVOLUTION OF IT INDUSTRIES

This section presents the rise and decline of three major business models (the A model, the J model, and the N model) in the evolution process of the IT industries.

4.5.1 Dominance of the A model

IBM continued to dominate the world IT industry throughout the period from the 60s to the 80s. IBM's organizational structure during this period can be characterized as one of multi-divisional forms with various complex modifications reflecting the huge multi-product and multi-national nature of its business. Both at the divisional level and at the workshop level, its information processing mode can be basically regarded as a decentralized hierarchy. As discussed in Section 4.1, the corresponding skills are functional specialists trained in the internal labor market within IBM. Another important feature of IBM was that it continued to maintain the policy to supply the whole system of IT products until its entry into PC business in 1981. The result is a business range with a very high degree of vertical integration. It had been IBM's traditional business strategy to secure profits at every possible point of the product chain since the days when IBM was an office machine maker. IBM's business standards, reflecting this business policy, were proprietary and IBM as a monopolistic industrial leader sought to establish de facto standards. The IBM's business model represented by these four elements will be called the A model.

IBM continued to enjoy its supreme position as the unrivaled world leader in the computer industry until 1993 when it recorded the largest loss ever by a private company. This was mainly because IBM was late to notice the paradigm shift in computer technology, namely the maturing of the mainframe computer and computer downsizing. After drastic restructuring, its business model (the A model) was scrapped, and IBM was reborn as a new IT company.

4.5.2 Rise of the J model

This section discusses the characteristics of major Japanese IT firms, such as Fujitsu, NEC, Hitachi, Toshiba, and Mitsubishi Electric. The set of their main characteristics with respect to the four dimensions will be called the J model.[7]

The information processing mode and the nature of skills of the J model are characterized by the emphasis on inter-unit information sharing of system shocks. At the level of individual workers, they are multi-functional and have less specialized job classification, engaging in team problem solving in workshops. Through job rotation and frequent transfer among different branches and sections, a dense human network is formed within the firm and the group of firms. At the level of workshops, they share on-site system information by operating JIT systems between workshops with the results of inventory reduction and quality improvement.[8]

These firms tend to diversify widely in related areas, such as heavy electrical equipment, home electric appliances, consumer electronics, semi-conductors, telecommunications equipment, and computer products, whereas IBM's product range is more concentrated on computers and does not include telecommunications equipment. On the other hand, the J model is less vertically integrated than the A model, using subcontracting extensively. Many parts suppliers do not have a capital relationship with the IT firms. In this sense, the J model uses the market system more than the A model. On the other hand, these subcontractors tend to have a long-term transaction relationship with the large IT firms and belong to the business group formed by the IT firms (Kawasaki and McMillan 1987). So

---

[7] For the history of Japan's IT industries, see, for example, Information Processing Society of Japan (1998), Fransman (1990), Fransman (1995), and Itami (1996).

[8] A theoretical analysis of the Japanese coordination systems was done by Aoki (1988). For an overview of Japanese employment systems, see, for example, Hart and Kawasaki (1999).

this relationship may be regarded as positioned somewhere between vertical integration and pure market procurement. Japanese firms are observed to form business groups at various transaction levels. This generates a situation called market fragmentation (Fransman 1990: 84–86). Since a group member often uses computer systems made by the same group member, there is a relatively large number of computer makers in Japan. This results, to some extent, in more competition. However, competition will be moderated at the same time because inefficient operations can survive with the assurance of minimum group purchase, and because dynamic scale merit may not be attained due to this market sharing.

Reflecting the state of its business range and the prevalence of long-term employment, the business standards of the J model are highly firm- and group-specific and closed to outsiders. They tend to be often in a tacit form, and embodied in human minds but not in manual, which enhances the efficiency of internal communication but at the same time makes external communication costly and difficult. In contrast, the standards in the A model tend to be clearly specified and manualized although they are proprietary and firm-specific.

From early on, after World War II, Japan tried to catch up with the leading Western countries in computer industries by importing foreign technology, protecting infant computer firms, developing prototypes in national research laboratories, and providing various subsidies to the firms. The catch-up efforts by Japanese IT firms with great help from the government resulted in two major achievements in the 1980s. The first success was with DRAM. The semiconductor was developed and produced mainly for military uses in the USA in the 50s and 60s, but a new MOS type DRAM suitable for mass production was developed in the middle 60s. This breakthrough established a clear direction in semiconductor technological progress to increase the degree of integration further (Yamamura 1999: 110–116). All major Japanese IT firms started to invest heavily in DRAM production and succeeded in continuously improving the degree of integration of DRAM in R&D and reducing the defect rate in production, based on the advantages of intense information sharing mode of the J model. Due to the fierce competition among these firms, the DRAM prices went down drastically, but demand increased more rapidly than the price decrease for calculators, computers and so on. In the middle 80s, Japan occupied a share of more than 90% of 256K DRAM (most advanced at that time) in world production, and U.S. IT firms suffered severely from this Japanese drive. The Japanese government played an important role in this process. For example, MITI started the VLSI project in 1976, in order to increase Japanese capabilities in DRAM production drastically, fearing the rumored IBM's Future Series project.[9] Managing a successful coordination among government research

---

[9] MITI's IT projects were analyzed in detail by Fransman (1990).

laboratories, semiconductor manufacturers, and equipment suppliers, the project was evaluated as a great success in increasing the technological level of DRAM production. The second example of Japan's major success was mainframe hardware. With the development of IBM's 360 series, the world standard in mainframe architecture was firmly established. Although it resulted in the dominance of IBM in the world market, it also gave a chance to Japanese IT industries, in that the technological direction was fixed for clone makers. Japanese manufacturers continuously improved the hardware and finally attained an 80% share in the Japanese market. However, they could never succeed in the world market due to the software standard established by IBM.

One major problem in the computerization of Japan was how to deal with the Japanese language in computers. The technical difficulty certainly caused some delay in the early development of Japanese IT industries. On the demand side, Japanese offices could not use computers for word processing in the early days and these circumstances caused a delay in office computerization and resulted in the weakness in Japanese software development. With the advance in graphical display technology, Japanese IT firms succeeded in dealing with Japanese. Since each firm used a different method, the Japanese processing technology became proprietary standards. For a long time this functioned as a natural entry barrier to foreign computer makers. NEC, utilizing its Japanese processing standard fully, succeeded in acquiring a dominating share in the Japanese PC market until IBM Japan developed a new Japanese processing method as an open standard in 1990.

In 1980, MITI initiated the Fifth Generation Computer Project to produce a new generation of computers capable of reasoning based on artificial intelligence technology. The underlying purpose was to overturn the IBM's mainframe architecture, since this would be indispensable for Japanese success in world computer markets. MITI and Japanese IT firms were confident of the success of this ambitious project based on the success experience of the VLSI project, and the U.S. government and IT firms became very concerned. However, the project failed after more than ten years and a large amount of research expenditure. Embarking on such ambitious, risky projects itself was not a mistake. Consider the case of ARPA's various projects as discussed in Section 2. The basic problem of this project was that the development of a new generation of computer systems in this project belongs to basic research, while the development of higher DRAM capability in the VLSI project is applied research. Basic research requires deeper individual thinking in universities and other research institutes, and many experiments and unexpected detours have to be allowed. Furthermore, the Japanese government and IT firms made a major mistake in fudging the direction of Japanese IT industries. Too eager to pursue IBM, they missed the major technological paradigm shift happening in the world of IT technology, namely computer downsizing and networking. After completing the catch-up stage, Japan reached the stage to build national technological capability for frontier research. Nevertheless, Japanese bureaucracy was not able to change their catch-up policy framework because of their past success and for the maintenance of their power and interests. Another problem with government policies is regulation, a result of catch-up lead by the government. Japan has tried to catch up with Western countries through the heavy use and concentration of government power. One result was that the economic, political, and social systems have been highly regulated by laws and bureaucrats' administrative guidance. These regulations now severely limit the freedom of activities of private business and research. In the field of telecommunications, the telephone network was long monopolized by the nationalized company (NTT). Although NTT was instrumental in expanding the telephone services all over the country efficiently after the war, the communication fees NTT charged were rather high due to their bureaucratic business practices. Furthermore, NTT tried to prevent the spread of alternative communications methods, such as the Internet, in order to maintain its telecommunications monopoly. All these policy stances of the government and NTT severely hindered the development of the Internet in Japan.[10]

The Japanese share in the world semiconductor production reached a peak in 1988, and it has continued to decline since then. The leading positions in the market were taken by other Asian and U.S. firms. The mainframe business became outdated, and Japanese IT industries were not able to recover from the major delay in the fields of small computers and computer networking. The J model seems to have major difficulty in managing the current turbulent technological and business developments.

4.5.3 Emergence of the N model

The new developments in IT technology and worldwide business environment in the 90s have given birth to a new business model, which is called the N model (abbreviation of the Network Model).[11] Some examples of the N model are Dell Computer, Cisco Systems and many other IT firms.

The N model can be characterized as follows (Kokuryo 1995: 14):

The firm identifies its core competence and concentrates all its resources on the core competence.

Other products and services that are complementary to the firm's products are all outsourced to other firms by strategic alliances with them.

Since product compatibility is critical for the operation of this system, the firm tends to promote open standards in its business transactions.

---

[10]Fujiwara (1998) critically discussed various problems of Japan's telecommunications systems and NTT's network policies.

[11]For the discussion of various aspects of the N model, see, for example, Shapiro and Varian (1998), Kokuryo (1995), Kokuryo (1999), Saxenian (1994), Hamel and Prahalad (1994), and Dell (1999).

From our framework of business model, the N model has the following characteristics. First, the business range of the N model is highly specialized with respect to both its product range and the degree of vertical integration. It possesses the A model's emphasis on specialization but drives it to the extreme. Second, the N model as a specialist in its business area utilizes the information on individual shocks. At the same time, the system information will also be extensively used through the transaction systems powered by the Web technology. The N model possesses the J model's advantages of inter-unit coordination, but it enhances the speed and flexibility of coordination by computer network technology. JIT systems used by the J model are refined and expanded as the supply chain management system. In the J model, the relationship with parts suppliers and products vendors sometimes tended to be lenient and inefficient due to their close relationships. The N model keeps a more businesslike relationship, but develops extensive cooperation in its transactions. And the third element is open standards as characterized above. The N model possesses the A model's emphasis on standards, but expands the applicability of standards beyond a firm's boundaries. The nature of the skills, the fourth element of the N model, is determined by the focus on individual shocks, core competence management, and rapidly changing technological developments. Therefore, professional skills, coupled with communication ability by IT, are highly regarded, and the labor turnover rate tends to be rather high. Skills are often improved through information exchange beyond the boundaries of the firm as seen in Silicon Valley (Saxenian 1994).

What does the business world formed by the N model represent? Chandler (1977: 12) characterized the modern business tendency by saying that "the visible hand of management replaced the invisible hand of market forces where and when new technology and expanded market permitted a historically unprecedented high volume and speed of materials through the process of production and distribution." Is the IT revolution reversing this historical tendency? In one sense, this seems to be happening, as we see the market system expanding and penetrating deeper and further into every corner of the world and social life in the IT revolution. Web businesses are causing drastic price competition, instantaneously combining a great number of sellers and buyers from every corner of the earth. There is no denying that the N model is more market-oriented than either the A model or the J model. However, we note that distinctively non-market elements are also playing a key role in the system of the N model at the same time. The supply chain management system, one of the most important components of the N model, is the inter-unit coordination of information and products flow. Mechanical price systems are replaced by the conscious cooperation of business units. On the demand side, these Web firms tend to customize their sales to the specifications of their individual customers (one-to-one marketing), providing community-like interactive facilities to the customers. This customization and interactive consumer participation certainly go beyond the framework of the price system described by the economic textbook.

Why and how has the N model emerged? As outlined in Section 2, the history of Internet technology has the following features:

- The development of this technology took a rather long time, beginning with the invention of packet switching by P. Baran in the early 60s. It was finally revealed to the public by the Web browsers in the early 90s. The development was full of unexpected turns and surprises, so that early developers never fully realized the real significance of their technology.

- The U.S. government played a major role in the development of Internet technology by initiating the research projects and providing substantial research funds. The ARPA projects were not regarded as pure military research, but as long-term risk-taking research, and were all contracted out to civilian companies and universities. This style of research management is in a sharp contrast to Japan's industrial policy that often controlled the projects firmly in the hands of bureaucrats.

- The net users in universities and other research institutions also played an important role in the development. As the ARPANET expanded and got connected to various networks, it gradually formed a huge community of Unix programmers, who developed a multitude of network software for their own use. They included WWW, various browsers, Web-server software, and so on.

- Unlike usual technical developments, such as personal computers, commercial firms were not the direct promoters of the Internet until the 1990s. However, private businesses played an indirect, but still vital role. Apple and many other small venture enterprises started the downsizing technological shift in the computer industries. The rapid growth in the number of small computers created a huge demand for network connection and eventually contributed to the formation of the Internet system.

In addition to the technological base, there are some economic circumstances for the emergence of the N model (Kokuryo 1995: 107–112).

More IT products tend to be system products, so that they are used as a part of a system in combination with other IT products, and the development cycle of IT products tends to be shortening drastically. Therefore it is rather costly and risky to try to supply the whole system by one firm.

In order to compete in the current businesses, parts have to be supplied from the optimal sources located all over the world. It is impossible for one firm to own all such supply bases in the world.

4.6 CONCLUSIONS

This paper analyzes the evolution of Japan's IT industries based on a business-model framework, focusing on the information processing mode in comparison with U.S. developments. We found that Japan's success in the 80s and its failure in computer downsizing and networking afterwards were mainly caused by the interaction of the Japanese-type business system with dynamic technological trends and government policy. In the 80s Japanese IT firms succeeded because their horizontal coordination systems, which have a relative advantage in sharing and improving known technology, just matched the steady technological progress in the semiconductor and mainframe computer systems at that time. Industrial policy also managed national coordination and cooperation successfully in catching up with the targeted U.S. technology. On the other hand, the turbulent technological developments in computer downsizing and networking took Japan's IT firms and government by surprise and posed a major difficulty for Japan's information processing systems. The government and bureaucracy, relying on past successes, lacked flexibility for dealing with a rapidly changing world to decide to reform the outdated catch-up policy framework.

REFERENCES

Abbate, Janet, *Inventing the Internet*. Cambridge 1999.

Aoki, Masahiko, 'Horizontal vs. Vertical Information Structure of the Firm', in *American Economic Review*, Vol. 76 (1987), pp. 971–983.

Aoki, Masahiko, *Information, Incentives, and Bargaining in the Japanese Economy*. Cambridge 1988.

Aoki, Masahiko, *Keizai shisutemu no shinka to tagensei* [Evolution and Diversity of Economic Systems]. Tokyo 1995.

Aoki, Masahiko and M. Okuno-Fujiwara (eds.), *Keizai shisutemu no hikaku seido bunseki* [Comparative Institutional Analysis: A New Approach to Economic Systems]. Tokyo 1996.

Campbell, Kelly Martin and W. Aspray, *Computer: A History of the Information Machine*. New York 1996.

Chandler, Alfred D., *The Visible Hand: The Management Revolution in American Business*. Cambridge 1977.

Chandler, Alfred D., *Scale and Scope: The Dynamics of Industrial Capitalism*. Cambridge 1990.

Chopsky, James and T. Leonsis, *Blue Magic: The People, Power and Politics Behind the IBM Personal Computer*. New York 1988.

Crémer, Jacques, 'Common Knowledge and the Co-ordination of Economic Activities', in Aoki, Masahiko et al. (eds.), *The Firm as a Nexus of Treaties*. London 1990, pp. 53–76.

Dell, Michael, *Direct from Dell*. New York 1999.

Flamm, Kenneth, *Creating the Computer: Government, Industry, and High Technology*. Washington, DC 1988.

Fransman, Martin, *The Market and Beyond: Information Technology in Japan*. Cambridge 1990.

Fransman, Martin, *Japan's Computer and Communications Industry*. Oxford 1995.

Freiberger, Paul and M. Swaine, *Fire in the Valley: The Making of the Personal Computer*. Berkeley, Calif. 1984.

Fujiwara, Hiroshi, *Nettowâku no hasha* [The Winner of Computer Network]. Tokyo 1998.

Hafner, Katie and M. Lyon, *Where Wizards Stay Up Late: The Origins of the Internet*. New York 1996.

Hamel, Gary and C.K. Prahalad, *Competing for the Future*. Boston 1994.

Hart, Robert A. and S. Kawasaki, *Work and Pay in Japan*, Cambridge 1999.

Information Processing Society of Japan (ed.), *Nihon no konpyûta hattatsushi* [Evolution of Japanese Computer Industry]. Tokyo 1998.

Itami, Hiroyuki, *Nihon no konpyûta sangyô* [Japanese Computer Industry]. Tokyo 1996.

Kawasaki, Seiichi and J. McMillan, 'The Design of Contracts: Evidence from Japanese Subcontracting', in *Journal of the Japanese and International Economies*, Vol.1 (1987), pp. 327–349.

Kokuryo, Jiro, *Ôpun nettowâku keiei* [Open Network Management]. Tokyo 1995.

Kokuryo, Jiro, *Ôpun âkitekuchâ senryaku* [Open Architecture Strategy]. Tokyo 1999.

Langlois, Richard N., 'External Economies and Economic Progress: The Case of the Microcomputer Industry'; in *Business History Review*, Vol. 66 (1992), pp. 1–50.

Murayama, Yuzo, *Tekunoshisutemu tenkan no senryaku* [Reforming Techno-systems]. Tokyo 1999.

Norberg, Arthur L. and J.E. O'Neill, *Transforming Computer Technology: Information Processing for the Pentagon, 1962–1986*. Baltimore 1996.

Randall, Neil, *The Soul of the Internet: Net Gods, Netizens and the Wiring of the World*. London 1997.

Salus, Peter H., *Casting the Net: From ARPANET to Internet and Beyond*. Reading, Mass. 1995.

Saxenian, Analee, *Regional Advantage: Culture and Competition in Silicon Valley and Route 128*. Cambridge 1994.

Shapiro, Carl and H.R. Varian, *Information Rules: A Strategic Guide to the Network Economy*. Boston 1998.

Toffler, Alvin, *The Third Wave*. New York 1980.

Williamson, Oliver E., *The Economic Institutions of Capitalism*. New York 1985.

Womack, James P., D.T. Jones and D. Roos, *The Machine That Changed the World*. New York 1990.

Section B:

The Pressure for Institutional Change in Japan and Germany

5

EVOLUTION, SPATIAL SELF–ORGANIZATION AND PATH DEPENDENCE: TOKYO'S ROLE AS AN INTERNATIONAL FINANCIAL CENTER

Beate Reszat

5.1 INTRODUCTION

Among the many challenges Japan is facing in a globalizing economic environment Tokyo's position as a financial center both regionally and internationally has become increasingly threatened in recent years. Japan's markets for money, capital and foreign exchange are among the biggest worldwide. But, recently, other places in Asia such as Singapore and Hong Kong have invested heavily to strengthen their competitiveness, and countries like Malaysia and Thailand – although so far on a modest scale – stand in line to follow their example. Although the turbulences of the Asian crisis have overshadowed and temporarily dampened ambitions,[1] these developments raise two related fundamental issues. On the one hand, the question is how the emergence of financial centers can be explained in general. On the other, it has to be asked how Tokyo as a financial place is affected by the various influences and which are its longer-term prospects. Will it manage to maintain its position without making major concessions to the changing international environment or will convergence and institutional adjustment be the only way to meet the growing competition from outside Japan?

The following paper which represents a very early stage of research emphasises the role of evolutionary forces for the emergence of financial centers in general and Tokyo's future prospects in particular. The starting point is

---

[1]See for a thorough analysis of the various financial markets in the wake of the Asian crisis Menkhoff and Reszat (1998).

an approach from the New Economic Geography as it has been developed by Paul Krugman and other authors. In general, those and other proponents of theories of international trade consider financial services as so-called footloose industries. Since – at least, at first sight[2] – their existence does not depend on natural resources, in principle, they seem not restricted in their choice of location. Nevertheless, as the Asian example shows, they are not evenly spread over the world. On the contrary, regionalism and "clustering" prevail.

Taking an evolutionary view of financial markets means considering them as emergent systems which are characterised by a high degree of complexity. This has two aspects. One is *spatial self-organization*. Under certain circumstances the interactions of many actors taken together – of individuals, firms and financial institutions as well as the administration and political authorities – are able to create a new quality or "culture" of a market place allowing it to become a truly international center. Then, in principle, what needs to be explained is that process as well as the emergent quality. The second aspect is *path dependence*. Broadly stated, path dependence means that a system's current state is a function of past initial conditions and developments. This stands in contrast to traditional equilibrium models in economics which take as given that their results are generally valid, holding independently of past trajectories. The term is closely related to another one which is *lock in*: a system which has once reached a particular state may at times stay there even if this does not appear an optimum to outside observers. Path dependence and lock in are strong arguments for a financial center to maintain a once-reached dominant position even if its competitiveness is in decline, but, on the other hand, might also condemn it to a lagging place, to stay behind forever.

The paper is divided into four parts. The first will give a short overview of financial places in Asia and their main characteristics. The second will describe the basic ideas of the New Economic Geography and discuss the strengths and weaknesses of this concept as well as possible alternatives to capture the idea of a system of evolving financial markets. The third part will study the possibilities to apply concepts of self-organization and evolution to international financial markets in general asking how far the analogy to biological systems can be drawn at all. The fourth will come to a tentative classification of financial places in Asia and, in particular, of Tokyo's future role. One important question in this context is to what extent Japan's program of stepwise financial liberalization, the so-called *Big Bang*, may contribute to meet the place's ongoing hollow out or *kûdôka*.

---

[2]A detailed discussion of this aspect can be found in Reszat (2000).

5.2 COMPETING FINANCIAL PLACES IN ASIA

The Asian crisis has somewhat obscured the view for the region's long-term growth potential and its ongoing attractiveness for banks, security houses and other financial institutions. According to World Bank estimates before the outbreak of the crisis infrastructure spendings in east Asia would have required the remarkable sum of 1.5 trillion US dollars and industry projects another hundreds of billion dollars (Marsh 1998). Even if the most ambitious plans have been abandoned or at least postponed, in the long run, the volume of the remaining projects exceeds all that can be expected from other parts of the world.

In contrast to the impression which, at times, emerged during the Asian crisis, there are ample means to finance these requirements. Even with international capital owners shunning to invest strongly in the region's emerging markets after having come down to earth from the euphoria of recent years – and there are already indications that their cautious attitude will not last – there is sufficient capital due to the high saving rates prevailing in those countries. The problem is to make these savings available for productive investments. The biggest obstacles here are underdeveloped securities markets, an insufficient technical knowledge and sophistication, a lack of experience to handle large investment projects and the absence of institutional investors such as pension funds and insurance companies which would add to the markets' depth and liquidity. In fighting these deficiencies some countries appear better equipped than others clearly demonstrating the need for an international hub for the region's capital.[3]

Table 4 Japan's stock and bond markets in international comparison[1]

Country	1990	1991	1992	1993	1994	1995	1996	1997	1998
Japan									
• Stocks	1303	827	476	782	855	889	938	898	744
• Bonds	365	215	117	184	160	218	181	139	68
United States									
• Stocks	1325	1520	1746	2283	2454	3083	4064	5778	7318
• Bonds	11	13	12	97	72	70	55	50	38
United Kingdom									
• Stocks	587	570	674	859	1014	1134	1389	2013	3004
• Bonds	943	1042	1171	1265	1244	1310	1614	–	1744

1 Exchange turnover in billions of US dollars.
Source: Bank of Japan (1999: Table 23, 24).

---

[3]There are several works in Japanese offering a fundamental comparison of financial systems in the region before the outbreak of the crisis. See, for example, Nihon Shôken Keizai Kenkyûsho (1994), SSKKKS (1996) and Igarashi (1996). See also Emery (1997) and Glick and Hutchison (1994).

So far, Tokyo is the biggest financial center in Asia and therefore, at first sight, the best place to play this role. Its rise to one of the three most important international centers beside London and New York dates back to the second half of the 1980s, when first the Japanese stock market, and later the markets for other assets as well, experienced an unprecedented speculative boom.[4] At its peak in December 1989, the stock market made up 42 per cent of the total capitalization of world markets. In 1990, Japan's total property had an estimated value of ĕ2,000 trillion – more than five times the size of the country's GNP at that time and about four times the value of total property in the United States (Wood 1993: 8).

When the bubble burst, a long-lasting overall decline of asset values set in, accompanied by company failures and bankruptcies on a large scale which severely undermined both corporate and consumer confidence. The Nikkei index which stood at 6,870 yen in 1980 and at 12,556 yen in 1985, which survived the worldwide crash of stockmarkets in October 1987, and on its peak on 19 December 1989 reached 38,915 yen, fell within a few months by 48 per cent to 20,221 yen in October 1990 (Nakao 1995: 99 f.). Suddenly, Japanese banks faced a massive overhang of bad loans and the situation worsened with every new wave of company failures.[5] As a result, the banks became reluctant to lend new money and, at the same time, activities in Japan's securities markets became very low (Table 4). All this triggered a serious debate about whether the Japanese financial system would experience a fundamental hollowing out. In this situation, for Tokyo to play a greater role as the region's international financial center became unthinkable.

Table 5 Average daily foreign exchange market turnover in selected countries[a]

Ctry.	April 1989		89-92[b]	April 1992		92-95[b]	April 1995		April 1998	
	Amt.	%		Amt.	%		Amt.	%	Amt.	%
UK	184.0	26	58	290.5	27	60	464.5	30	637.3	32
USA	115.2	16	45	166.9	16	46	244.4	16	350.9	18
Japan	110.8	15	8	120.2	11	34	161.3	10	148.6	8
Singapore	55.0	8	34	73.6	7	43	105.4	7	139.0	7
Hong Kong	48.8	7	24	60.3	6	50	90.2	6	78.6	4
Switzerland	56.0	8	17	65.5	6	32	86.5	5	81.7	4

a In billions of US dollars. b Percentage change.

Source: Bank for International Settlements.

[4]See for the details Reszat (1998).
[5]See for a detailed chronology and analysis of the crisis Fukao (1999).

Since then, a slight recovery has taken place and long-term prospects do no longer look that bleak. Now it may matter that Tokyo still has the biggest stock market in the region, that its foreign exchange market is the third-largest worldwide (Table 5) and that its market share of cross-border international bank lending is only surpassed by the United Kingdom (Figure 7). The resulting scale economies may well establish first-mover advantages and lock-in effects with strengthen its international position. However, so far, these phenomena reflect less the place's international importance than the size of Japan's economy and the activities of Japanese banks and corporations abroad.

Figure 7 Market share of cross-border lending worldwide

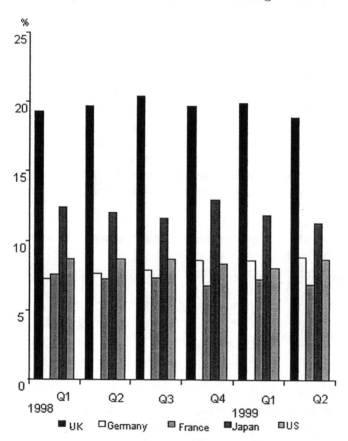

Source: Bank for International Settlements, Bank of England (1999).

In general, Japan's financial system is characterized by several features which make it appear rather unattractive. Traditionally, there is a strict separation and specialization of financial services which has been loosened only recently. The stock market is still rather underdeveloped. Bank lending has an overwhelming importance for the economy and corporate governance is weak (Suto 2000). The so-called main bank system is still working in many respects: companies are linked in a system of long-term interlocking shareholding and borrowing relationships with one or a small number of banks in order to obtain their support in times of crisis (Fukao 1998: 21), making the prospects of both groups hard to judge for investors and observers from outside. These and other factors weaken the place's competitiveness both regional and worldwide.

Nowadays, Tokyo's biggest rivals in the region are Singapore and Hong Kong. In particular, Singapore has taken several steps recently to enhance its international competitiveness. In 1999, the authorities encouraged Singapore's five commercial banking groups to consolidate, lifted a 40 per cent limit on foreign investors' total shareholding in local banks and instituted a five-year liberalization package in order to increase foreign bank access to Singapore's domestic money market and heighten corporate governance. In addition, foreign law firms became permitted to form joint ventures with local firms to provide advisory and drafting services for onshore, cross-border and offshore financial transactions (McNulty 1999). These measures are further improving Singapore's already strong position in Asia which traditionally is explained by the quality of its economy as well as its stability, legal infrastructure and perceived security. Another often mentioned advantage is Singapore's historical role as a trading place going back to its outstanding position in the British colonial system.[6]

Tokyo's other big competitor in the region is Hong Kong. There are many similarities between Singapore and Hong Kong with respect to the underlying strength of the economy, political stability, a well-developed infrastructure of legal, accounting and other services and the British-influenced civil service. Observers generally hint at the complementary rather than competitive relation between the two. This can be explained by the differences between them. Above all, they are located in different time zones. Singapore has the advantage of overlapping business hours with Tokyo and Sidney as well as with European centers such as London and Paris which helped it to develop a more active international money market than Hong Kong. Another difference until 1982 has been the withholding tax in Hong Kong, which was lacking in Singapore. As a result, Singapore attracted offshore funds from Asia as well as from Europe and the Middle East making the place the funding center for international loans to Asian-Pacific borrowers (Park 1983).

Hong Kong is always said to have a deeper and broader market structure than Singapore. In earlier years, the decisive factor here had been its geographic advantage of being located near major international borrowers such as Korea, Japan, the Philippines, Taiwan and, above all, the People's

---

[6] A detailed overview of the place can be found in Teufel (1998).

Republic of China with its enormous demand for capital (Figure 8). Due to this proximity Hong Kong became important for the arrangement, syndication and management of Eurodollar loans to borrowers from those countries. But, the difference is not only geographic but also in government policies: while Singapore is strongly regulated with its financial development depending on government controls and government incentives Hong Kong basically relies on private sector initiatives. In the past, its government had been content to provide the general framework and largely abstained from direct interference. However, to some extent, this was changing with the Asian crisis, when the Hong Kong authorities felt obliged to intervene to stabilise the stock market and intensify monitoring of the banking sector (Schüller 1998).

Figure 8 Financial places in Asia

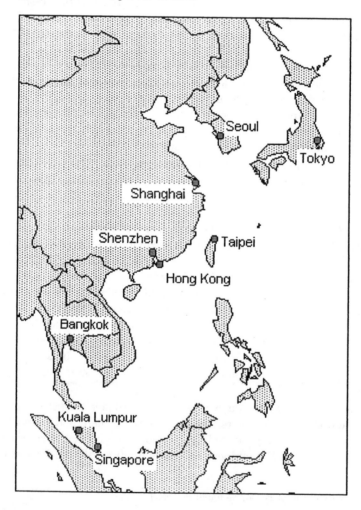

A growing source of uncertainty in recent years has become mainland China's increasing presence in Hong Kong's banking sector raising fears of spillover of financial instability. But, mainland China is still felt in another respect, namely the growing competition from Shanghai and Shenzhen. Since July 1997, Hong Kong belongs to China as a Special Administrative Region. In competing for domestic business its main rival is Shanghai. The Shanghai Stock Exchange, which started operating in December 1990, has several advantages for Chinese investors and corporations, above all, the legal and accounting systems which in Hong Kong differ from those used everywhere else in China. In contrast, Hong Kong's relation to Shenzhen has more cooperative than competitive aspects. Both use the same language, the Guangdong dialect, and the Hong Kong dollar is widely used in Guangdong as well. This opens prospects for an integration of operations by which Hong Kong could position itself as the financial center of the greater Hong Kong/Guangdong region (Fuchita and Osaki 1995).

Beside Singapore and Hong Kong, other financial places in Asia are trying to improve their competitiveness, too. This holds, above all, for Malaysia. The Kuala Lumpur Stock Exchange (KLSE), founded in 1973, is the biggest exchange in Southeast Asia with respect to market capitalisation. For many years it had a system of dual listing with the Stock Exchange of Singapore (SES). Securities listed on one exchange were automatically traded on the other as well. This system was abandoned by Malaysia in 1990. In reaction, Singapore established a new segment within its electronic trading system, the Credit Limit Order Book (CLOB), which had been founded in 1988. Since then, Malaysian and other foreign shares are traded on CLOB International. Competition between Singapore and Malaysia is traditionally fierce. Recently, KLSE's reputation suffered badly when, in the wake of the Asian crisis, it imposed strict capital controls thereby freezing trading in Malaysian shares in the CLOB market.

The Asian crisis temporarily has put an end to the most ambitious plans in some countries to become one of the region's dominant financial centers. However, in some cases, necessary reforms would not have been taken otherwise and the crisis has speeded up progress. In particular, this holds for market access for foreign investors and financial institutions. There is widespread agreement that in the long run, only few financial centers in the region will survive and that the conditions for decline and survival are set now and in the years to come. The question is, to what extent measures taken now by various parties can influence the final outcome. An analysis of the main determinants of this process will have to start with some theoretical considerations.

5.3 CONCEPTS OF SPATIAL SELF-ORGANIZATION AND PATH DEPENDENCE

Lessons from history show that, in general, financial market development and the emergence of financial centers does not take place in a straightforward way but is characterised by high irregularities, self-reinforcing effects and inertia which to overcome often requires an external shock or a "critical mass" of events. One starting point in order to explain the influences behind these processes is location theory which looks at how an economy organizes its use of space and how agglomeration and clustering occur.

Location theory is a strand of economics which has its roots in Germany, in the works of von Thünen, Christaller, Lösch and others.[7] In the 19th century, Johann Heinrich von Thünen first analysed the problem how land around an isolated town supplied by farmers should be allocated for given yields and transportation and production costs taking into account different crops and different intensities of cultivation. More than a hundred years later Walter Christaller and August Lösch developed their theory of central places for a community of farmers who are assumed to be in need of some activities, such as manufacturing or administration, which due to economies of scale cannot be spread evenly among them but have to be provided centrally. Then, there is a tradeoff between scale economies and transportation costs which eventually leads to the emergence of a lattice of central places each surrounded by farmers relying on them.

In principle, the ideas of those early theories can be applied to business districts within a metropolitan area, financial centers in a region or any other phenomenon of spatial agglomeration. Krugman (1996) criticizes them on the grounds that they do not capture the process by which individuals or firms interact, and centralization takes place, and that they do not explicitly deal with complexity and the mechanisms through which macrobehavior emerges from micromotives.[8] In contrast, his edge city model aims at shedding some light on this process. Along the lines of modern urban economic theory the model starts from the assumption of a long narrow city which, in fact, is one-dimensional and located on a circle[9] with

---

[7]Von Thünen (1842), Christaller (1932) and Lösch (1944). The following relies heavily on Krugman (1996), Fujita et al. (1999). See for a description of the early roots of the theory also Kopp 1999.

[8]These terms Krugman refers to are the title of an earlier book by Thomas Schelling. See Schelling (1978).

[9]The assumptions about the nature of the urban area in this context are:
- the city has a single center of fixed size, the central business district (CBD) in which all job opportunities are created;
- there is a dense radial transport system, free of congestion, with travel consisting only of workers commuting between residences and CBD;
- the land is featureless plain, all land parcels are identical and ready for residential use. There are no local public goods and no neighbourhood externalities.

movement only possible along its circumference. To keep the model as sparse as possible there is no land rent and land scarcity is thought of as, in a sense, included only in an implicit reduced form. For the same reason, there is no forward-looking behavior. In addition, although the conceptual weaknesses of the approach are acknowledged, external economies are assumed, that is, agglomeration is, in a sense, explained with the non-specified benefits of agglomeration. These drastic simplifications are considered as necessary to explain the basic idea as clearly as possible.

In the model, locational decisions are determined by two kinds of "forces", a centrifugal and a centripetal one. The decision of each firm where to locate is dependent on all other firms' choices. The two kinds of forces are determined by different interdependencies. On the one hand, firms are assumed to dislike having other businesses nearby because they compete for customers, workers and land. These motives are called centrifugal forces. On the other hand, to have other businesses close also has advantages. For example, they attract customers to the area or add to the variety of local services offered. These considerations are interpreted as centripetal forces that attract businesses and make them locate in "clumps". The interaction of centripetal and centrifugal forces determines the process of businesses migrating from less to more desirable sites over time.

In contrast to what is claimed, the repellent and attracting forces in the Krugman world are not emergent properties of a self-organizing system.[10] They contribute to accumulation and growth of a location. But, at every moment, they are fully attributable to the firms' behavior. There are not really the many interacting units whose interplay adds a new quality to the system which is fundamentally changing its nature in the adaption process. Thus, concepts like this can only serve as a starting point for a further, more elaborate analysis of the emergence of financial centers.

5.4 HOW FINANCIAL MARKETS EVOLVE

In contrast to the approach described here, it is the emergent property, the "organic" change in nature, which is thought crucial for the transition of a financial market place to become an international or regional center. Banks deciding to establish their business in the same location do not constitute a center in this sense. There are many markets and places in the world fulfilling functions and offering kinds of services that can be found in Tokyo,

---

Under these assumptions, the only spatial feature of each location that matters in distance from the CBD which justifies a one-dimensional treatment. See also Fujita (1989): 12.

[10] See in greater detail Reszat (1999). Emergence refers to a quality added to the system which is not inherent in its parts. For example, for Stuart Kauffman "life" is an emergent whole of biological systems which is not located in the property of any single molecule. Compare Kauffman (1995: 24).

London or New York as well. And many of the banks in Tokyo, London and New York have businesses elsewhere, in principle, engaged in the same kinds of activities.

What is thought to make the difference is that with the growth of a market and increasing complexity sometimes – to draw an analogy to the natural sciences – a kind of *self-organized* criticality[11] is reached after which the place is not the same as before. Slowly and perhaps imperceptibly anadaption process to the needs and demands of internationally active participants in the market takes place meeting more and more the criteria of an international financial center, respective facilities grow, and norms, rules of conduct and attitudes and behavior patterns become established. Sometimes, as recent examples in Asia demonstrate, politics try to influence this process from outside. But, if the financial market is a truly emergent system the possibilities are limited. There are certain preconditions which must be met and which can be designed as favorable as possible, but, in the end, whether the odds are in favor of the place or against it is decided by circumstances, or by what evolutionary theorists would call historical accident.

How can the markets' organic nature be explained? In recent years, it has become more and more accepted to regard all kinds of economic processes as the result of evolution and self-organization. In particular, in Japan this strand of research has found a broad resonance.[12] The focus here is not on financial markets but on the real economy. The topic has attracted special attention among authors from the so-called *comparative institutional analysis* (CIA) – hikaku seido bunseki – which is based on the view that an economy is a complex organic system (fukuzatsukei) which is in constant evolution (shinka). This process is path-dependent (keiro ni izon suru) and dependent on initial conditions and historic developments which differ from country to country resulting in the plural nature (tagensei) of the world. Thus, what is best for one country and one economy need not necessarily be so for another one.[13]

---

[11] This term which was coined by Per Bak originally described a type of macroscopic instability in condensed-matter physics. An application to the economics of production and inventory dynamics can be found in Scheinkman and Woodford (1994).

[12] See, for example, Shiozawa (1997) and the literature cited there. Compare also the contributions of Sechiyama (1997), Kuratsu (1997), Hattori (1997), Aruka (1997) and Asari (1997).

[13] CIA served to confirm the view of Japan's uniqueness offering a rationale for peculiarities such as *keiretsu* relations of firms, interlocking shareholdings, the main-bank system, life-long employment and many more. Internationally best-known proponent of this strand of research is Masahiko Aoki from Stanford University (see, for example, Aoki 1996). The results of the comparative institutional analysis have also found their way into politics where one of their most prominent proponents is Eisuke Sakakibara, Japan's former vice-minister of finance and highly influential "Mr Yen". He holds the view that over the years Japan has developed its own model of market economy which in many respects is superior to those of many Western industrial countries. Compare

Nowadays, in economics there is a wide variety of evolutionary theories searching explanations for all kinds of social and economic change. Most of them share several characteristics which constitute a kind of common basis on which the following considerations are founded, too.[14] For example, there is an emphasis on dynamics. None of those concepts is interested in simply explaining something being but is asking how it became what it is. Theories are explicitly microfounded. There is no "macrobehavior" without "micromotives". And, in a very broad sense, rationality is "bounded". Agents are assumed to have at best an imperfect understanding of their environment.

In general, evolutionary theories consider three factors as decisive for evolution. Those are mutation, natural selection and chance. *Mutation* provides the material, i.e. the genetic difference, on which natural selection acts. As one famous geneticist puts it: mutation proposes but selection decides (Cavalli-Sforza and Cavalli-Sforza 1995: 102). *Natural selection* enables a system or an organism to adapt to its environment driving it toward fitness maximisation and reproductive success. *Chance* comes in in several ways. On the one hand, there is a statististical effect known as genetic drift. The carrier of a mutation may die without passing the mutation on to subsequent generations. Or, in contrast, the mutation may be spreading widely due to casual events. On the other hand, mutation itself occurs randomly. Chance makes evolution not just the survival of the fittest but also the survival of the luckiest.

For evolution to take place by natural selection there must be *replicators* and *interactors*. A replicator passes on its structure intact in successive replications. Genes are replicators. Interactors are by their very name entities that "interact as a cohesive whole with their environment in such a way that this interaction causes replication to be differential" (Rosenberg 1994: 403). In biology, this can be organisms, but also cells, genes, tissues, organs and the like. Another useful term in evolutionary theories is *lineage* standing for the entity which actually evolves. In general, lineage is defined as the line of descent which can be traced from a common ancestor. Interactors are composed of lines of descent and some proportion of types of interactors in the cohesive whole is changing from generation to generation. In order to demonstrate the meaning of the different terms, the analogy can be tried on an example from economics. A firm which is switching to more adapted routines is developing, growing in size and increasing its profitability. But, for evolution to take place at the firm level, it must become its own descendant, otherwise the analogy breaks down. According to evolutionary theory, changes within one member of the lineage do not count as evolution. They

---

Sakakibara (1993). One recent application of CIA to the subject of corporate governance in Japan is given in Tsuru (1999).

[14] The following is not by any means an exhaustive list of common characteristics. Compare also Dosi (1997).

are simply a matter of development. The improved adaptation has to be passed on to descendants, successors, subsidiaries or the like.

Thus, each analysis of an evolutionary economic system has to find an answer to the following questions: What is it that is evolving and what is the lineage? What are the generations? Which are the replicators and interactors and how is "fitness" measured? The answer to some of these questions has been suggested earlier. The evolving entity in the analysis intended here is the international financial system consisting of various centers and subcenters of international financial activity as well as other bank places at the periphery. The interactors in this system are individuals and firms but also markets and market segments as well as institutions and other entities developing the "rules of the game" in a market place. Those rules may consist of laws and regulations but may include norms, conventions and behavior patterns passed on from generation to generation of actors as well.

In this framework, the replicators which pass on their structures intact in successive replications may be thought of, not as the banks and financial institutions and other actors themselves, but as the inherited characteristics, laws, rules of conduct and long-term behavior patterns those actors develop over time, and over generations, which eventually make up for the market "culture". What is reproduced again and again, constantly adapting to the environment, are the interacting components of this culture which allows the place to survive.

Each financial center is distinct from another and from any other market place in the world. What determines its market culture's competitiveness or complementarity and its ability to survive? One could think of several measures of "fitness". One might be a place's share, regional or worldwide, in particular market segments such as stocks or derivatives trading. Another could be the range of financial instruments available or the number of foreign institutions present at that place.

As mentioned earlier, there is one phenomenon deserving special attention in this context which is *path dependence* and *lock-in*. For the spatial organization of financial centers this point is of special importance. Although financial services are considered widely as "footloose industries" which are not restricted in their choice of location, once established they shun changing places which then becomes costly and cumbersome. One reason for this inflexibility and the resulting lock-in and concentration of the industry in few places is found in their size and range of activities, which has at least three aspects.

- First, nowadays, financial institutions depend on a vast net of suppliers of so-called producer services. Those include advertising, accounting, management consulting, legal services and many more. Central to the rise of those services was the growing size, complexity and diversification of financial firms. They have a vast diversity of separate functions, and often geographical dispersal, with the result that banks' central headquarters are no longer simply centers for administration and control but function as centers for orientation of the firm within its business environment. They not only have to decide about overall policies concerning clients' business, trading strategies, risk management and the like but also about product development and expansion and mergers and acquisitions in a multiplicity of situations and countries. In this environment, providing certain highly specialised services in-house is costly and often no longer possible (Sassen 1991).

• Reliance on producer services is one argument against the financial industry's being footloose. Another is dependence on the built environment. This is a rather new phenomenon. In former times, developers used to put up offices for financial institutions, which, in principle, were able to move easily in and out, on a speculative basis. Now banks' requirements have become too specialized for this to work and for major houses the trend is to design their own buildings.[15] For example, financial institutions need large trading floors – in the order of 300,000 square feet and even larger – and, depending on a certain technology to handle the huge volume of transactions traded every day, they require adequate space for cables and outlets as well as a pool of technical personnel to operate and repair equipment, including building managers who continuously upgrade the information and telecommunication systems (Fainstein 1994).

• A third argument against the footloose nature of financial industries is the ongoing need for personal, face-to-face contacts in financial markets. Although this does not only mean spatial proximity – other forms such as organizational, cultural, social, technological and institutional proximity may be of equal importance[16] – the spatial aspect is the one which is a crucial argument for "clustering". The core of financial activities can be described as "information, expertise, contacts" (Thrift 1994: 334). In general, all of these require spatial proximity although the advantages vary in their intensity from product to product. For small securities trades, interbank payments or standardized foreign exchange dealing they are probably minuscule. For mergers and acquisitions, the management of investors' portfolios or the lead management of syndicates they are high.

Besides, there is still another argument for financial agglomeration in the big centres which is identification with a place in its broadest sense. In general, people living and working in world cities like New York, London

---

[15] Compare, for London, for example, Eade (1998). One side effect is an increase in the banks' demand for another kind of producer services provided by architects, consulting engineers, planners and project managers.

[16] See for a general discussion of this aspect, for example, Grote et al. (1999).

and Tokyo are aware of their special status. They may complain about the disadvantages such as air pollution and traffic jams, but they also enjoy the advantages. Some of these are in part imaginary by nature, consisting of an experience of a certain way of life, the feel of being part of a special culture, which differs from those elsewhere. This holds in particular for the financial community located in those cities, which has become a wholly distinct class breeding its own rules, norms, rituals and behavior patterns. Their view is largely determined by the way they see themselves and their industry and by the way they interact. Financial places in this sense are not only places of financial intermediation but interactional proving grounds, centers of representation (of "where the stories are") as well as centers of discursive authority (Thrift 1994). They are places where individuals are bound together by a common "market culture", differing from center to center, which is not easily given up in exchange for another environment. The question is, how these influences affect the future financial landscape in Asia.

5.5 TOKYO'S FUTURE PROSPECTS IN ASIA

The answer to the question about Tokyo's future role as a financial center in Asia has many facets and to develop a classification including all the major centripetal and centrifugal forces involved would clearly go beyond the scope of this paper. Instead, in order to give an impression of Tokyo's relative position with respect to some of the factors mentioned earlier the attention will focus on three groups of influences. The first includes those related to the supply of finance, its quality and availability. The second draws attention to the demand for finance and the third concentrates on some influences from the vast range of determinants of the place's general environment which affect its overall attractiveness and "market culture".

On the supply side, there is a wide range of possible indicators of the relative performance of financial places. Among these access of foreign financial institutions to a market seems of crucial importance. Table 6 shows the respective results of a survey among the world's leading executives conducted regularly by the International Institute for Management Development (IMD) in Lausanne.[17] According to their general perception in Asia it

---

[17]In a sense, the views behind the concept of the IMD are very similar to those followed in economic theories of evolution and spatial self-organization. Here as well the picture of two counteracting forces is drawn: of *attractiveness* and *aggression* in response to the economic environment. Attractiveness refers to criteria describing a country's willingness and ability to trade with, and invest in, foreign places. Aggression includes all factors representing a country's international presence and activities in world markets. The institute admits that the distinction between the two is not clear-cut. There are criteria which signal both a country's attractiveness and aggression.

Table 6 Supply determinants in Asian financial markets in comparison

	Japan	Singapore	Hong Kong	Malaysia	Thailand	Taiwan	Korea	UK	USA
Access of foreign financial institutions[a]	6.88	7.37	9.04	6.17	6.65	6.70	6.57	8.35	8.02
Stock market capitalization[b]	2.102,0	104,1	321,0	63,5	23,5	260,5	41,9	2.097,6	8.607,4
No. of banks among the world's top 500[c]	105	4	5	7	7	14	12	18	63
Banking sector assets[d]	143,60	138,81	211,05	201,00	116,58	150,73	80,09	125,24	78,37

a Results of a survey among 4,160 executives in 47 countries, rating on a scale of 0 (worst) to 10 (best).
b In 1998, in billions of US dollars.
c In 1997.
d Percentage of GDP.

Source: IMD (1999).

Table 7 Demand factors in Asian financial markets in comparison

	Japan	Singapore	Hong Kong	Malaysia	Thailand	Taiwan	Korea	UK	USA
Population[a]	125.5	3.9	6.7	22.2	61.2	21.8	46.4	59.2	270.5
Gross domestic savings[b]	31.10	51.80	30.60	43.80	34.90	24.70	34.20	14.60	16.50
No. of firms among the world's top 500[c]	70	4	11	2	–	8	1	51	222
Direct investment stocks inward[d]	33.16	78.06	26.87	45.20	23.10	19.85	14.83	274.37	720.79

a In 1998, estimates in millions.
b In 1997, gross domestic savings (residents and non-residents) as a percentage of GDP.
c In 1997.
d In 1997, in billions of US dollars.

Source: The Financial Times (1998), IMD (1999).

is Hong Kong which is leading the ranks while for Japan the score reflects its notoriously strong formal and informal barriers to foreign influence.[18] Other important factors, in particular with regard to scale economies and lock-in effects, are market size, the share of leading banks in the world and the size of assets in the banking sector. While with respect to the former two Japan has clear advantages, for the last one, the results, with higher values for such different places as Hong Kong and Malaysia, are not clear and need further interpretation.

On the demand side, again, the overall impression of Japan is at least a mixed one (Table 4). The country has by far the highest population among all competitors considered here. However, the figures do not take into account the huge hinterland China represents for Hong Kong and, on a smaller scale, Malaysia for Singapore. A clear advantage in an economy of this size is the high savings rate, although this is somewhat lower than in other countries. Another clear advantage is the number of Japanese firms among the world's top 500. A by far less favorable impression is gained by the volume of foreign direct investments into Japan. It is not only small compared to other Asian countries but in particular to other highly industrialized economies such as the United States and the United Kingdom.

Table 8 summarises a whole range of "environmental" influences just to give an impression of the direction in which further research will have to proceed. Again, for Japan, the picture is not a positive one. This holds for factors directly related to economc activity such as shareholder culture, the question whether new information technology meets business needs or the role of bureaucracy as well as for more indirect influences like the questions of how the political system is adapting to economic challenges or how open national culture is to foreign influence.

At this point, it would lead too far to search for the reasons behind these various responses. With respect to the role of policy in enhancing a financial place's international attractiveness one aspect seems of special interest: the adequateness of legal regulation for ensuring financial stability. As the results in Table 4 indicate, in this respect, the Japanese system is perceived as particularly weak. This may change with the process of financial liberalization and reform, Japan's so-called Big Bang, which has begun in 1998. However, as many critics observe, the prospects so far do not look convincing. Many promising starts have been reversed, many plans delayed or postponed. One example is the Japanese stock market.

Since April 1999, physical trading on the Tokyo Stock Exchange has ended, fixed commissions are abolished, the exchange has begun merging with regional exchanges and, facing a threat of Nasdaq Japan, even started

---

[18]See for respective experiences, even in times when the country economically highly depended on foreign presence, Ogata (1996: 5) and Bailey, Harte and Sugden (1994: 7–45).

Table 8 Asian financial markets' environment[a]

	Japan	Singapore	Hong Kong	Malaysia	Thailand	Taiwan	Korea	UK	USA
Adequateness of legal regulation for financial stability[a]	4.38	8.36	7.14	6.25	4.09	5.89	4.39	6.35	7.53
Insider Trading[a]	6.08	7.88	5.86	4.94	3.74	4.02	4.28	6.34	6.59
Rights and responsibilities of shareholders[a]	3.53	8.00	7.54	6.21	4.81	6.38	2.86	7.27	7.58
New Information Technology[b]	5.87	9.02	6.91	7.46	5.23	7.36	4.39	6.62	7.93
Bureaucracy[c]	2.61	7.45	6.28	4.20	3.14	4.34	1.80	3.80	3.86
Adaption of the political system to economic challenges[a]	2.07	8.24	4.79	5.88	4.16	5.62	2.26	5.70	6.29
Openness of national culture to foreign influence[a]	5.75	8.06	8.24	6.59	7.33	8.49	4.13	6.88	7.58

a Results of a survey among 4,160 executives in 47 countries, rating on a scale of 0 (worst) to 10 (best).
b The implementation of new information technology meets/does not meet business requirements. Results of a survey among 4,160 executives in 47 countries, rating on a scale of 0 (worst) to 10 (best).
c Bureaucracy is hindering/not hindering business development. Results of a survey among 4,160 executives in 47 countries, rating on ascale of 0 (worst) to 10 (best).

Source: IMD (1999).

a new market for growth companies, called Mothers. But, the positive signals of these and other developments are overshadowed by two still unsolved problems. One is lax financial regulation. Although, officially, there is an independent financial-markets regulator, the Securities and Exchange Surveillance Commission (SESC), it is under strong influence of the ministry of finance which is said to explain why the phenomena survey respondents complain about like insider trading and stock manipulation are going on. A second obstacle is the prevailing system of cross-shareholdings which still accounts for about 42 per cent of the stock market (The Economist 2000). Both are incompatible with Tokyo's claim to play a stronger role internationally.

5.6 CONCLUSIONS

As stated in the beginning, this paper represents a very early stage of research. Future efforts must be directed at a more stringent classification and categorization of those centripetal and centrifugal forces affecting the shifting financial landscape in Asia. Nevertheless, with respect to Tokyo's role in the region two general impressions are worth emphasizing even from this first rudimentary analysis. On the one hand, apparently the place can benefit from scale economies resulting from the sheer size of its economy and markets, the strength of Japanese firms both at home and abroad and the role Japanese banks play in international financial markets. On the other hand, there are many disadvantages which, above all, affect market culture such as a still very limited openness to foreign influences on every scale or the slowness of the political system to adapt to changing circumstances. Just as the former present strong competition barriers to other places in the region the latter may easily result for Japan to end up in a kind of negative lock-in with its financial system staying in an eternal state of backwardness.

REFERENCES

Aoki, Masahiko, *Keizai shisutemu no shinka to tagensei.* Tokyo 1996.

Aruka, Yuji, 'Fukuzatsukei to kaosu keizai dôgaku', in *The Keizai Seminar*, 6 (1997), pp. 29–32.

Asari, Ichiro, 'Naiseiteki keiki junkanron to fukuzatsukei', in *The Keizai Seminar*, 6 (1997), pp. 33–39.

Bailey, David, George Harte, Roger Sugden, *Transnationals and Governments: Recent Policies in Japan, France, Germany, the United States and Britain.* London 1994.

Bank of England, *Practical Issues Arising from the Euro*, December 1999.

Bank of Japan, *Comparative Economic and Financial Statistics.* Tokyo 1999.

Cavalli-Sforza, L. L., F. Cavalli-Sforza, *The Great Human Diasporas.* Reading, MA 1995.

Christaller, Walter, *Die zentralen Orte in Süddeutschland*, Reprint 1968. Darmstadt 1933.

Dosi, Giovanni, 'Opportunities, Incentives and the Collective Patterns of Technological Change', in *The Economic Journal*, 1997, pp. 1530–1547.

Eade, Philip, 'A Place of Your Own', in *Euromoney*, February 1998, online edition: http://www.euromoney.com.

Emery, Robert F., *The Bond Markets of Developing Asia.* Boulder 1997.

Fainstein, Susan S., *The City Builders – Property, Politics and Planning in London and New York.* Cambridge MA 1994.

Fuchita, Yasuyuki, Sadakazu Osaki, *Asia's Securities Markets in the 21st Century*, in Internet: http://www.nri.co.jp/nr...iqF/95autumn/gaiyo.html, 1995.

Fujita, Masahisa, *Urban Economic Theory.* Cambridge 1989.

Fukao, Mitsuhiro, 'Japanese Financial Instability and Weaknesses in the Corporate Governance Structure', in *mimeo*, Keio University. Tokyo, 18 October, 1998.

Fukao, Mitsuhiro, *Financial Crisis in Japan*, paper presented at the ERI International Symposium on "Financial Fragility in Transition Economies". Budapest, 22–23 November, 1999.

Glick, Reuven, Michael M. Hutchison (eds.), *Exchange Rate Policy and Interdependence: Perspectives from the Pacific Basin.* Cambridge 1994.

Grote, Michael H., Sofia Harrschar-Ehrnborg, Vivien Lo, *Technologies and Proximities: Frankfurt's New Role in the European Financial System*, Johann Wolfgang Goethe-Universität Working Paper Series on Finance and Accounting, No. 46. Frankfurt December 1999.

Hattori, Shigeyuki, 'Shûkaku teizô no keizai gaku to fukuzatsukei', in *The Keizai Seminar*, 6 (1997), pp. 23–28.

Igarashi, Masao, *Ajia no kin'yû shijô.* Tokyo 1996.

International Institute for Management Development (IMD), *World Competitiveness Yearbook 1997.* Lausanne 1999.

Kauffman, Stuart, *At Home in the Universe*. London 1995.

Kopp, Andreas, *The New Geographical Economics and the German Founders of Regional Economics*, working Paper. Kiel July 1999.

Krugman, Paul, *The Self-Organizing Economy*. Oxford 1996.

Kuratsu, Yasuyuki, 'Kin'yû shijô o fukuzatsukei de yomu', in *The Keizai Seminar*, 6 (1997), pp. 19–22.

Lösch, August, *Die räumliche Ordnung der Wirtschaft*. Jena 1944.

Marsh, Peter, 'Building Machinery Boost', in *The Financial Times*, Internet: http://www.ft.com, 1998.

McNulty, Sheila, 'Singapore Works Hard to Keep its Competitive Edge Sharp', in *The Financial Times*, 8 July, 1999.

Menkhoff, Lukas und Reszat, Beate (eds.), *Asian Financial Markets – Structures, Policy Issues and Prospects*. Baden-Baden 1998.

Nakao, Shigeo, *The Political Economy of Japan Money*. Tokyo 1995.

Nihon Shôken Keizai Kenkyû Sho (ed.), *Ajia-ôsutoraria no shôken shijô*. Tôkyô 1994.

Ogata, Shijuro, *En to nichigin*. Tokyo 1996.

Park, Yoon S., 'Asian Money Markets', in George, Abraham M., Ian H. Giddy (eds), *International Finance Handbook*, Vol. 1, Section 4.10. New York 1983.

Reszat, Beate, *The Japanese Foreign Exchange Market*. London 1998.

Reszat, Beate, 'Emerging Financial Centres, Self-Organisation and Evolution', in *Homo Oeconomicus*, XV, No. 4 (1999), pp. 459–481.

Reszat, Beate, *Centripetal Forces in European Financial Markets – Cultural Identity and Collective Memory as Determinants of Financial Agglomeration*, paper presented at the HWWA-Annual Conference on "Glocalisation in Europe" Hamburg, May 3–5, 2000.

Rosenberg, Alexander, 'Does Evolutionary Theory Give Comfort or Inspiration to Economics?', in Mirowski, Philip (ed.): *Natural Images in Economic Thought*. Cambridge 1994, pp. 384–407.

Sakakibara, Eisuke, *Beyond Capitalism*. Lanham 1993.

Sakura Sôgô Kenkyûsho Kantaiheiyô Kenkyû Sentâ (SSKKKS), *Ajia Shin Kin'yû Chizu*. Tokyo 1996.

Sassen, Saskia, *The Global City – New York, London, Tokyo*. Princeton 1991.

Scheinkman, José A, Michael Woodford, 'Self-Organized Criticality and Economic Fluctuations', in *American Economic Review*, 2 (1994), pp. 417–421.

Schelling, Thomas C., *Micromotives and Macrobehavior*. New York 1978.

Schüller, Margot, 'Hong Kong's Financial Market Development', in Menkhoff, Lukas, Beate Reszat (eds), *Asian Financial Markets – Structures, Policy Issues and Prospects*. Baden-Baden 1998, pp. 103–127.

Sechiyama, Satoshi, 'Fukuzatsukei toshite no keizai', in *The Keizai Seminar*, 6 (1997), pp. 14–18.

Shiozawa, Yoshinori, 'Fukuzatsukei to shisutemu riron', in *The Keizai Seminar*, 12 (1997), pp. 44–49.

Suto, Megumi, *New Development in the Japanese Corporate Governance – A Role of Corporate Pension Funds*, HWWA Discussion Paper, Hamburg, forthcoming.

Tsuru, Kotaru, *Japanese Corporate Governance in Transition*, paper presented on the CEPR Conference of the European Network on the Japanese Economy. Oxford 30/31 July, 1999.

Teufel, Hariolf, 'Singapore', in Menkhoff, Lukas und Reszat, Beate (eds), *Asian Financial Markets – Structures, Policy Issues and Prospects*. Baden-Baden 1998, pp. 129–150.

The Economist, *Slow Financial Starvation*, 1 April 2000.

The Financial Times, *Financial Times 500*, 22 January, 1998.

Thrift, Nigel, 'On the Social and Cultural Determinants of International Financial Centres: the Case of the City of London', in Corbridge, Stuart, Ron Martin, Nigel Thrift (eds), *Money, Power and Space*. Oxford 1994.

Von Thünen, Johann Heinrich, *Der isolierte Staat in Beziehung auf Landwirtschaft und Nationalökonomie*. Stuttgart 1842 [1966].

Wood, Christopher, *The Bubble Economy*. Tokyo 1993.

Discussants: Günter Heiduk and Nicole Pohl

Empirical studies show that one sign of the rise of the global economy in the past decades is the growing importance of the three major centers of international finance: London, New York and Tokyo. There is no difficulty in getting data which give us information on the expansion in international financial transactions and their concentration on the three centers.

Beate Reszat's paper has the aim to analyze the future competitiveness of Tokyo as an international financial center. Particularly, the intention is to analyze this by answering three questions:

- How can the emergence of financial centers be explained?

- How is Tokyo as a financial place affected by growing competition of Singapore, Hong Kong and other locations?

- What are Tokyo's long-term prospects as an international financial center?

Reszat chooses an evolutionary view as her starting point. This implies that she assumes that the international financial system can be characterized by those features that are emphasized in evolutionary theories, such as emergent, self-organizing properties of a system whose dynamics are the result of the interaction of heterogeneous agents. Certainly, this is a good starting point as a number of authors have nowadays realized that the economic system in its whole has to be understood as an evolving system. Research in the sources of change, its diffusion as well as in the stability of economic "equilibria" has risen strongly during the last decade (Marengo/Willinger 1997; Fujita 1997). However, the theoretical basis for this kind of dynamic explanation is still weak. Moreover, interest for the way economic activities are embedded into the spatial system of the economy has been growing. Quite a lot of research has been done on the phenomenon of agglomeration in the industrial sector and on the way central and peripheral regions emerge. The theoretical arguments used to explain the growth and dominance of some cities are scale economies and agglomeration economies. It remains to be explained why these arguments are not restricted to manufacturing industries, but also relevant for producer services, especially financial services which are often characterized as footloose industries. Therefore, we can without doubt conclude that answering these questions is a daunting challenge as "the empirical literature lacks an analytical framework and therefore intellectual coherence" (Drennan 1996: 360).

In any case, the combination of empirical observation and theoretical thinking only makes sense if it leads us to new insights about the appropriateness of theoretical models to describe reality or about ways to build new models. However, Reszat's paper leaves a gap between the theoretical intention and the empirical picture that is drawn. Theoretical approaches and empirical description do not fit together. Thus, the emergent features of the financial system in the past and also in the future are not illustrated, nor do we get a clear picture of the interaction of the relevant agents of the system. Most certainly, this is a difficult task as it requires a broad range of empirical data and it may well go beyond the scope of Reszat's paper. Moreover, Reszat does not really introduce a concrete model that might be applied to the problem of international financial centers. Most of the time she remains at the level of conceptional work. She states that Krugman's model of the "edge city" might be a good starting-point, explains however her doubts on whether this model really expresses the emergent properties of the economic system (Krugman 1996). Further doubts about the possibility to apply this model to the problem of international financial centers may be reasonable. Paul Krugman aims at explaining the locational behavior of the industrial sector. This is determined by the existence of transport costs that are related to geographical distance. Moreover, the spatial patterns to be derived from this model are due to price interaction. Whether these are also the laws that govern the spatial system of international financial centers may be doubted.

Which are the questions that will have to be answered in order to elaborate the idea of the international financial system as an emergent system from a theoretical point of view (Figure 9)?

Figure 9 A guide to modelling the evolution of the international financial system

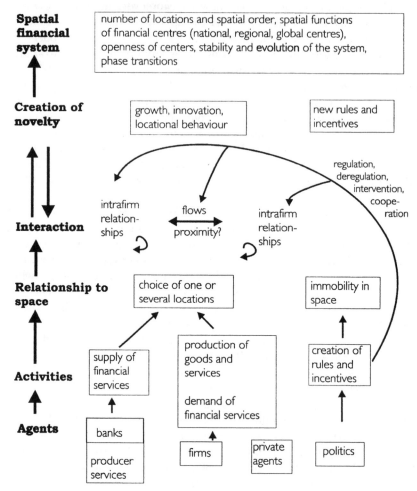

Source: Authors.

Which are the *agents* interacting in the system considered? Which are their relevant characteristics and scopes of action?

- Banks having the possibility to offer financial services and innovation and to use competitive advantages; most of the time the banks that are engaged in financial centers will be multinational firms active at various locations of the world.
- Suppliers of producer services in a broad sense.
- Firms which choose locations for their production, develop innovations, determine the growth of locations and decide about the sources and use of their capital.

- Private agents and their saving behavior.

- National political decision-makers deciding about the openness of locations and the rules of operation.

- How is *novelty* created? How does agents' *interaction* lead to evolution in the international financial system?

- If deeper empirical studies are able to show that New York is the leader in financial innovations, the forces behind the heterogeneity of IFCs have to be analyzed (Sassen 1999: 84).

- Which are the forces that preserve or break up an existing status quo (*lock-in effects*)?

We may suppose that processes of learning at established centers and the creation of routines might be relevant. Thus, there are dynamic lock-in effects that are different from static economies of scale.

It seems that nowadays besides the still dominating "big three" the spatial structure of the international financial network is emerging towards a hierarchical system with financial second-tier centers like Frankfurt, Hong Kong, Singapore. Sassen expects that "... by its (the global financial system) very design – based on connectivity, mobility, and speed – it will continue to be enormously volatile" (Sassen 1999: 87).

Which conclusions can we derive about the resulting spatial structure of the international financial system?

The interaction on the micro-level has to be transferred into macro-developments. The spatial structure of the financial system will be characterized by the number of dominant financial centers, their location and the spatial horizon of the flows reaching and leaving them. Thus, the spatial preferences of suppliers and demanders of capital will have to be taken into account.

It is an open question in which ways the "cyberspace" will influence the geographic structure of the international financial markets. The digital space might strengthen the position of the dominant IFCs or not (Sassen 2000).

Empirically, it can be observed that financial centers have developed in regions of industrial growth. This might lead us to conclude that industrial enterprises, their innovation and expansion, are the dominant driving forces also for the international financial system. Historically, waves of growth have swept from Europe to the USA and to Japan and South East Asia (Figure 10). On the other hand, innovations in the financial sector that are localized in certain markets may influence locational decisions of the industrial sector. In any case, we will have to analyze in how far spatial proximity matters for the interdependent locational decisions of the financial and industrial sector or whether financial centers can be considered hubs where flows of capital meet independently from their sources and destinations. Thus, the analysis of the relationship between financial and industrial sectors will have to be at the heart of any theoretical analysis. In this respect, the influence of multinational firms may deserve special interest. Where do multinational firms look for sources of finance: at the location of their headquarters or those of their subsidiaries? Are their regional or cultural differences in their behavior? Are there region-specific relationships between firms and banks? What about the intrafirm relationships within multinational banks ? Can they help us to understand whether financial centers at different locations are competitive or complementary? Finally, the question of the initial growth of financial locations will be prevalent. Can our theories go beyond the idea of "historical hazard" to explain the selection among different locations? What role can politics take in this respect? It might be interesting to analyze the influence of monetary policy respecting monetary integration on the evolution of IFCs (Frankel 1993; Frieden 1993).

Figure 10 Long-term world economic development and international financial centers

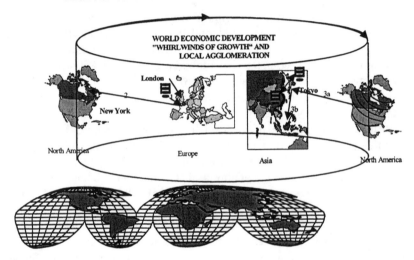

Source: Authors.

The following hypotheses seem to be reasonable:

- Financial centers differ in their degree of openness. Thus, some of them have global or regional functions, others are limited to a national level. Openness is a result of the regulation valid at a location and the possibility of penetration by foreign firms in the industrial sector (multinationals). Financial centers can be considered point economies in a more or less spatially extended system of regional growth.

- The future changes in the spatial structure of international financial centers will depend on historical developments and the strength of lock-in effects, but also on the reaction of agents on new stimuli and their behavior within a global economic system. For example, it has been argued that the growth of Singapore's financial sector is due to the investment of Japanese multinationals. Thus a region-specific structure of financial locations may be derived that has different functions and may be competitive as well as complementary. This structure and its evolution may be due to more or less dynamic patterns of openness and aggressiveness of different regions and agents. Evolution can be related to the change of important locations and to shifting relative importance of existing locations.

These very preliminary ideas already indicate that a very broad view of the economic system will have to be taken in order to fully understand the driving forces of change. The different sectors of the economy are interlinked. Stimuli for changes can have various sources so that we will have to deal with models that are much more open in their outcomes than in the past. Explaining the rising complexity in the globalized world economy will make it necessary to accept declining determination of the results.

To get deeper insights into the microeconomic foundations of change and evolution we may have to complement the knowledge that can be derived from economic theories by ideas from other disciplines like (economic) sociology. Researchers in this field have for a long time realized that culture and organization matter. Biggart and Guillén (Biggart/Guillén 1999) show that developed logics of organization may even result in different export structures. How far these aspects matter for the international financial system has up to now received littel interest. Further interdisciplinary research might help us to understand cultural and organizational influences on the spatial economic system. Obviously, the basis for new insights will be improvements of our methodological tools.

To summarize: The questions raised in Reszat's paper show that we are still at the very beginning of empirical and theoretical research that sheds light onto space- and time-related aspects of the international economy.

REFERENCES

Drennan, Matthew P., 'The Dominance of International Finance by London, New York and Tokyo', in Daniels, P.W: and Lever, W.F. (eds.), *The Global Economy in Transition.* Longman 1996, pp. 352–371.

Biggart, Nicole, Guillén, Mauro, 'Developing Difference: Social Organization and the Rise of the Auto Industries of South Korea, Taiwan, Spain and Argentina', in *American Sociological Review*, Vol. 64 (1999), pp. 722–747.

Frankel, Jeffrey A., 'Is Japan Creating a Yen Bloc in East Asia and the Pacific?', in Frankel, J.A., Kahler, M. (eds.), *Regionalism and Rivalry – Japan and the United States in Pacific Asia.* Chicago 1993, pp. 53–87.

Frieden, Jeffry A., 'Domestic Politics and Regional Cooperation: The United States, Japan, and Pacific Money and Finance', in Frankel, J.A., Kahler, M. (eds.), *Regionalism and Rivalry – Japan and the United States in Pacific Asia.* Chicago 1993, pp. 423–447.

Fujita, Masahisa, *Urban Economic Theory*, Cambridge 1989.

Fujita, Masahisa, Mori, Tomoya, 'Structural Stability and Evolution of Urban Systems', in *Regional Science and Urban Economics*, Vol. 27 (1997), pp. 399–442.

Fujita, Masahisa et al., *The Spatial Economy: Cities, Regions, and International Trade*, Cambridge, Mass. 1999.

Krugman, Paul R., *The self-organizing economy.* Cambridge Mass. 1996.

Marengo, Luigi, Willinger, Marc, 'Alternative Methodologies for Modelling Evolutionary Dynamics: Introduction', in *Journal of Evolutionary Economics* Vol. 7 (1997), pp. 331–338.

Sassen, Saskia, 'Global Financial Centers', in *Foreign Affairs*, Vol. 78 (1999), pp. 75–87.

Sassen, Saskia, *Cities in a World Economy*, Thousand Oaks, 2000.

Suto, Megumi, *New Developments in the Japanese Corporate Governance in the 1990s – The Role of Corporate Pension Funds*, HWWA Discussion Paper 100, Hamburg 2000.

6

TECHNOLOGY AND INNOVATION MANAGEMENT IN GERMAN AND JAPANESE MANUFACTURING FIRMS: STRATEGIC REORIENTATION AND IMPLICATIONS FOR TECHNOLOGICAL COMPETITIVENESS

Martin Hemmert

6.1 INTRODUCTION

Throughout recent decades, the innovation systems of Germany and Japan have been regarded as strongholds of the economic systems of the two countries. They played a crucial role in the upgrading of the German and the Japanese economies after post-war recovery to give them a competitive edge on the world markets in medium and high-tech manufacturing industries like automobiles and machinery (in both countries), electronics and semiconductors (particularly in Japan), and chemicals and pharmaceuticals (particularly in Germany).

Within the innovation systems of both countries, industrial R&D (research and development) has been playing a predominant role. As in other advanced countries, the clear majority of the national R&D activities has been performed in the manufacturing business sector. Moreover, in contrast to other industrialized countries like the United States, the United Kingdom, and France, where governmental R&D spending (particularly in the military sector) provided a major financial source of business R&D, industrial firms in Germany and Japan have been financing the overwhelming part of their R&D activities themselves.

Notably, German and Japanese manufacturing firms have not built up a reputation on the whole as world leaders in breakthrough innovations. Rather, they have succeeded very often in leapfrogging new technologies and innovations that were developed first somewhere else, particularly in the United States. In many cases, they succeeded in implementing such technologies and innovations rapidly into marketable products, thereby often leaving the initial innovators behind on the market. A prerequisite for this ability was a strong absorptive capacity for external technological knowledge within German and Japanese firms.

Since the 1990s, however, there are rising concerns in both countries that German and Japanese firms may be left behind in terms of future technological competitiveness by Anglo-Saxon firms. These concerns are based on the observation that technological competition between manufacturing firms is not simply intensifying, but that the rules of high-tech competition may be fundamentally changing. In particular, it appears that due to the proliferation of new IT technologies, the relative importance of speed and of flexibility for high-tech competition has increased significantly. This may imply an unfavorable competitive shift for large German and Japanese manufacturing firms which have been the backbone of industrial R&D in these two countries. It raises the question whether German and Japanese firms possess the flexibility to adapt themselves to the altering competitive rules or are left behind as the dinosaurs symbolizing a former industrial era.

In order to address these issues, a profile of German and Japanese manufacturing firms concerning technology and innovation management is given first. Thereafter, the upcoming developments in the field of international technological competition are discussed. In particular, the requirements for structural change in the R&D management of German and Japanese firms that are implied by these changes will be looked at. Subsequently, the strategic reactions of German and Japanese firms to the environmental changes are scrutinized. Thereafter, some empirical evidence concerning their recent technological competitiveness is given, and the influence of external institutional factors and of path dependency are also discussed. The paper closes with a brief reflection on the issues of international diversity and convergence in technology and innovation management and some implications for firms' managers and for policymakers.

6.2 TECHNOLOGY AND INNOVATION MANAGEMENT IN GERMAN AND JAPANESE MANUFACTURING FIRMS: MANAGERIAL PROFILES

Subsequently, based on results from empirical research, a description of the managerial characteristics of technology and innovation management in German and Japanese manufacturing firms will be conducted. The results of this analysis are summarized in Table 9. It has to be stressed, however, that this description of managerial characteristics is based on limited empirical evidence and therefore does not necessarily apply to all firms in all manufacturing industries. Rather, the findings may be interpreted as very rough classifications of managerial characteristics of German and Japanese firms in an international context.

Table 9 Features of technology and innovation management in German and Japanese manufacturing firms

Field of technology and innovation management	Features of...	
	German firms	Japanese firms
Technology strategy	conservative	conservative
Human resource management	low internal mobility moderate external mobility	moderate internal mobility low external mobility
Internal organization	primarily field oriented	strongly project oriented
External linkages	primarily horizontal	primarily vertical
Internationalization	high	low
Industrial organization	concentration on large firms	concentration on large firms
	significant role of independent medium-sized firms	technological dependency of medium-sized firms on final producers
	few innovative venture firms	few innovative venture firms

Source: Author's composition.

When turning to the **technology strategies** of the German and Japanese manufacturing firms, technological conservatism appears to be a common attitude among the firms' management in both countries. Casework in high-technology industries like semiconductors has shown that in contrast to US firms, which changed their process technologies and main product lines in order to seize new technological opportunities, Japanese business firms tended to stick with technologies already familiar to them (Okimoto and Nishi 1994: 200–202). Likewise, the management of German manufacturing firms has a reputation for being risk averse concerning technology strategies, i.e. concentrating on familiar technologies rather than tapping into new technological fields (Schröder 1997: 121–122). This tendency might have been reinforced by the managerial paradigm to focus on core competencies (Pralahad and Hamel 1990) which supposedly has become very influential among business managers during the 1990s.

Another crucial area in technology and innovation management is **human resource management** concerning R&D personnel. In contrast to technology strategy, wide differences between German and Japanese firms can be observed in this field. In large Japanese manufacturing firms, long term employment of highly qualified personnel in fields like R&D is the normal case, whereas in Germany the mobility of such personnel between firms appears to be somewhat higher. In an international survey of R&D workers conducted around 1990, only 6% of the Japanese respondents reported a change of their employer during their hitherto careers. The proportion of the German respondents was 35%, respectively (Ernst and Wiesner 1994: 104).

At the same time, there is a widespread belief that the mobility of personnel *inside* Japanese firms is comparatively high. This perception, however, does not necessarily match with the results of empirical surveys on this issue. In the international study of R&D workers cited above, the length of stay of the Japanese respondents with their present working assignment was not shorter when compared with respondents from Germany and the United States. When asked about probable future assignments, however, a clear majority of the German respondents perceived their future area of work restricted to other R&D departments. The percentage of responses quoting construction and design, production technology, and other firms within the same group as possible future working areas was much higher in Japan than in Germany (Ernst and Wiesner 1994: 124).

Additional evidence from a survey of the career paths of more than 200 engineers in a large Japanese manufacturing firm suggests that particularly in the early stages of the career, transfers of engineers between different functions and departments are relatively frequent in Japan (Kusunoki and Numagami 1997: 197). This finding is consistent with the results of earlier work by Aoki on this issue (Aoki 1988: 240–242).

Altogether the mobility of R&D personnel between firms appears to be relatively low in Japan, with the intra-firm mobility somewhat higher. In the case of German firms, the mobility of technical personnel seems to be mainly restricted to transfers between different R&D units, with few assignments to other business functions. At the same time, the mobility of such personnel between firms appears to be significantly higher than in Japan.

Concerning the **internal organization** of technology and innovation related activities, the views about German and Japanese manufacturing firms are quite different. Concerning R&D activities in Japanese firms, the early involvement of managers and technical personnel from a variety of departments inside and outside R&D has been emphasized (Wakasugi 1994: 165–166). An earlier empirical survey showed that when compared with US firms, a much higher proportion of R&D projects has been suggested by other departments than R&D in Japanese firms (Mansfield 1988: 172). These findings are consistent with the perception that R&D activities are strongly project-oriented in Japanese manufacturing firms (Clark and Fujimoto 1991: 247–285), with overlaps between different project stages to enhance a speedy development of new products and processes (Nonaka 1994: 211–219).

In German firms, in contrast, a lack of communication between R&D and other departments has been perceived as a major problem that often results in delays of R&D activities (Brockhoff 1990: 111). This suggests that such activities are organized in a more functional way in German firms than in Japanese firms.

These differences in internal organization of R&D activities between German and Japanese firms interfere with the earlier findings on human resource management. It can be argued that the relatively high mobility of personnel between R&D and other departments and the relatively strong project orientation of R&D activities in Japanese firms reinforce each other.

Another aspect often emphasized in the context of technology and innovation management is the issue of **external linkages**, particularly of R&D cooperation. The historical cases of a few successful horizontal research consortia in Japan like the VLSI project (Sakakibara 1995: 79–100) have resulted in the widespread view that the horizontal R&D ties between large Japanese manufacturing firms are extraordinarily strong. Surveys with a broader empirical base, however, have led to findings contrary to this view. Empirical evidence from a survey covering a wide range of manufacturing industries suggests that in Japan, vertical R&D collaborations between firms are much more common than horizontal ones (Gotô 1993: 88). Aldrich and Sasaki (1995: 308), who compared a large number of (primarily horizontal) R&D consortia in Japan and the USA, have come to the conclusion that the management of such consortia is more decentralized in Japan than in the US, indicating a weaker flow of technological information between the Japanese firms.

R&D collaborations between German firms have gained much less attention on the international level than in the Japanese case. However, an empirical survey of most leading German manufacturing firms has shown that horizontal cooperation is more common there than vertical cooperation (Rotering 1990: 101). This suggests substantial differences to the external linkages of Japanese firms which appear to be focused much more on vertical ties between suppliers and customers.

Another issue raised in the discussion on the features of technology and innovation management in German and Japanese firms is the **internationalization** of the firms in this field. Here the common perception is that while German firms have a relatively strong track record of internationalization of their R&D activities since the 1980s (Brockhoff 1990: 16–17), Japanese firms are still relatively little internationalized in technological terms. These assessments are confirmed by statistical findings. Whereas the

German manufacturing firms spent almost 20% of their total R&D budget abroad in 1997 (BMBF 2000: 51), the corresponding figure for the Japanese firms was only 3% (Tsûshô Sangyôshô 2000: 48). Although the quoted statistical result for the Japanese firms might be significantly underestimated,[1] the findings altogether suggest a wide difference concerning the technological internationalization of German and Japanese manufacturing firms.

Finally, the **industrial organization** of manufacturing firms in the field of R&D is taken into consideration. It is an outcome of the overall structure of R&D activities in an industrial system, rather than of technology and innovation management inside each firm. Industrial organization strongly affects, however, the competitive position and the competitive behavior of the firms and is therefore treated here as well. Aggregated statistics indicate that both in Germany and in Japan a large proportion of industrial R&D activities is concentrated in large firms. In Japan, the large manufacturing firms with an equity of 10 billion Yen or more accounted for 25.2% of the total manufacturing employment and 44.9% of the total manufacturing sales in 1998, but for no less than 75.9% of the total R&D spending in the manufacturing sector (Sômuchô Tôkeikyoku 2000: 72–75). The twenty manufacturing firms with the largest R&D budgets in Japan alone spent 36.9% of the total R&D expenditures in manufacturing (Sômuchô Tôkeikyoku 2000: 74, 140). In Germany, the manufacturing firms with 1,000 or more employees spent 82.0% of the total R&D of the manufacturing sector in 1997 (Grenzmann, Marquardt and Wudtke 2000: A7). A firm-specific calculation revealed that in the beginning of the 1990s, the top seven R&D performing firms in Germany accounted for 31% of total industrial R&D employment (Keck 1993: 138).

It has to be added, however, that the phenomenon of concentration of R&D activities on large firms in the manufacturing sector is not limited to Germany and Japan. In the United States, for instance, firms with 1,000 or more employees spent no less than 90.8% of the total R&D in manufacturing in 1997 – a much higher proportion than in Germany. The 10 firms with the largest R&D budgets accounted for 29.8% of the whole R&D expenditures in manufacturing (National Science Board 2000: 2–24, 2–26).

Also, the degree of the overall concentration of R&D on large firms does not shed light on the vertical division of labor between the firms and on their competitive position. Empirical evidence suggests the existence of significant differences between Germany and Japan concerning these aspects. In the German manufacturing sector, in some industries strong independent medium-sized firms play an important role in the development of new

---

[1] Belderbos (1997: 337–338) raises the point that the data on international R&D expenditures of business firms in Japan are collected as a part of the survey on foreign direct investment. A majority of responding firms in this survey supplies no data on R&D in foreign countries. In many cases, however, this does not necessarily mean that no such overseas R&D activities are conducted.

products and processes. Sectoral statistics show that in the German machinery industry, firms with less than 1,000 employees in 1997 spent some 45.3% of the total R&D expenditures of the industry (Grenzmann, Marquadt, and Wudtke 2000: A15). In Japan, medium-sized firms conduct as well a substantial part of the overall industrial R&D. But in contrast to Germany, many of these firms do not manufacture final products under their own brands. Rather, they are highly dependent or sometimes even quasi-integrated suppliers of large producers of final products (Hemmert 1999: 499–501). Therefore, it can be assumed that their technological independence may be much lower than in case of many medium-sized German manufacturing firms. Altogether, while on the surface the concentration of industrial R&D on large firms in Germany appears to be as high or even higher than in Japan, the amount of R&D activities performed by independent medium-sized firms seems to be higher in Germany than in Japan.

One aspect that appears to be common in both countries, however, is the relative scarcity of small, innovative venture business firms. The role of such firms in the R&D of the manufacturing sectors is significantly larger in the United States than both in Germany and in Japan (Schröder 1997: 122–123; Kutsuna, Yamada and Akashi 1999: 53–57).

The above discussion has shown that on one hand, some similarities of German and Japanese firms seem to exist in certain fields of technology and innovation management. This applies to the important role of large firms in industrial R&D as well as to a seemingly common conservative attitude in technological strategies. On the other hand, however, in many important issues like human resource management, internal organization, external linkages, and internationalization, empirical and statistical evidence suggests significant differences between German and Japanese firms.

Subsequently, the discussion turns to recent international developments in technology and innovation management, and the implications of these developments for German and Japanese manufacturing firms. In particular, it will be scrutinized to what extent the international developments create a pressure on German and Japanese firms to change their style of technology and innovation management pointed out above.

6.3 CHANGES IN INTERNATIONAL COMPETITION ON TECHNOLOGY AND INNOVATION

Due to a number of interrelated technological and institutional trends, the rules of international competition among business firms in the field of technology and innovation have been changing significantly during the last two decades. In particular, the following developments appear to be important for this field:

(1) Due to a spread of technological knowledge among an increasing number of firms and countries, the breadth of technological competitiveness has globally increased (Porter, Roessner, Newman, and Jin 2000). Therefore, the intensity of technological competition among firms has intensified.

(2) Although it is an open question whether this intensifying of competition has resulted in a shortening of product life cycles (Gerpott 1999: 216–220), an increase in the importance of speed vis-à-vis the importance of cost in technological competition is generally acknowledged (Perillieux 1995: 279–280; Specht and Beckmann 1996: 3).

(3) A vast increase of available technological knowledge and the intensified technological competition among business firms imply that even large firms now lack the resources to conduct all the necessary R&D activities in a wide range of technological fields in-house. This development has exerted pressure on firms to focus their R&D activities on a narrower range of fields and/or to increase the outside sourcing of technological knowledge (Corey 1997: 147–148; Mowery 1998: 646).

(4) The efforts particularly of large firms to make use of particular technological competencies in different countries has resulted in a globalization of firms' R&D activities and therefore of technological competition (OECD 1999: 11–13).

(5) Finally, the recent progress in information and communication technologies, particularly the proliferation of the internet, has induced firms to intensify the use of these technologies when communicating between different business units and locations on the national as well as on the international level. Moreover, it has led the way for the buildup of virtual bases of technological knowledge (Goodman and Olivera 1998; Wirtz 2000: 98–99).

From these changes in the competitive environment a number of pressures for managerial change can be expected to evolve from the perspective of German and Japanese manufacturing firms. When considering the managerial profiles discussed in the previous section, technology and innovation management of the firms particularly may have to be redirected concerning the following issues:

- As a consequence of the increased importance of speed in technological competition, the technological strategies of German and Japanese firms may have to become more progressive to prevent a situation of being left behind on the markets by technological leaders.

- The management of human resources may have to be redirected towards a higher internal and external mobility of R&D personnel in order to make better use of external knowledge (embodied in new personnel coming from outside) and to increase the speed and efficiency of R&D processes.

- The internal organization of R&D in German firms may have to become more project oriented to attain a more timely development of new products and processes.

- There is a need to strengthen external technological linkages to focus internal resources to fields of relative competitive strength and at the same time make increased use of external technological knowledge.

- Particularly the Japanese firms may have to increase the internationalization of their R&D and thereby enhance their competitiveness by intensified use of technological knowledge in different countries.

- Firms may have to make more extensive use of new information and communication technologies and to build up virtual knowledge bases.

- Finally, as a result of the firms' individual efforts for managerial change, the concentration of industrial R&D on large firms may decrease, and the role of innovative small firms may become more important for technological progress and innovation.

Subsequently, based on recent empirical data, changes in German and Japanese manufacturing firms concerning technology and innovation management will be discussed. In particular, it will be scrutinized whether and to what extent the changes in the competitive environment of the firms listed above are addressed by the observed managerial reorientation of the firms.

6.4 REORIENTATION OF TECHNOLOGY AND INNOVATION MANAGEMENT IN GERMAN AND JAPANESE MANUFACTURING FIRMS

The discussion of the strategic reorientation of German and Japanese firms will be conducted in the order of issues listed in the previous section and therefore starts with the technology strategies of the firms. Concerning technological strategies of business firms, no quantitative empirical data covering a large number of firms are available. The analysis therefore has to rely here on the qualitative discussion of case-based observations.

Concerning German manufacturing firms, a few prominent cases of strategic reorientation have become widely known. Mannesmann was, up to the mid-1990s, a rather traditional conglomerate engaged mainly in the production of steel tubes and automotive parts as well as in the engineering sector. Thereafter, Mannesmann went through a metamorphosis to become a leading telecommunications firm in Germany within a few years. A less radical but still significant case is that of Daimler-Benz. Having been a renowned producer of luxury cars for many decades, the entry into the compact car market was attained through the launch of the Mercedes A-class and the Smartcar. In both cases, entirely new product platforms have been developed internally.

Despite these prominent cases, however, it cannot be overlooked that the majority of large German manufacturing firms has not significantly changed its strategic technological conservatism in recent years, i.e. its tendency to concentrate on familiar technologies rather than to tap into new technological fields. Concerning large Japanese firms, the overall situation is still clearer. The technological conservatism appears to have remained the predominant attitude of the firms' managers in Japan. In contrast to Germany, no significant cases of strategic reorientation of firms have become known in this field.

Concerning the human resource management of the firms in the field of R&D, particularly the issue of internal and external mobility of R&D personnel, there is – similar to the field of technology strategies – no direct quantitative evidence available on recent developments. Subsequently, some results of an empirical survey conducted by the author in 1999 are discussed to gain an indirect assessment of the tendencies in this and some other managerial fields. In this study, questionnaires from 165 R&D managers working for 16 leading pharmaceutical and semiconductor firms in Germany and Japan were collected. In the questionnaire survey, the respondents gave assessments on a wide range of issues concerning technology acquisition in their working areas. Additionally, 44 R&D managers from the same firms were interviewed about their views concerning technology acquisition.[2]

In Figure 11, the assessments of the German and the Japanese respondents on the effect of a number of factors related to R&D personnel on technology acquisition are compared. A majority of the items is evaluated more favorably by the German respondents than by the Japanese ones, but in most cases the differences of the average assessments are not statistically significant. However, the two factors related to the availability of R&D personnel are rated much better by the Germans than by the Japanese, indicating an important difference between the two countries concerning this aspect.

In the interviews, Japanese R&D managers specified their assessments on this issue. They stressed the lack of availability of qualified R&D personnel with former professional experience. Thus the external mobility of R&D personnel appears to be still very low in Japan, although the firms are now more interested in experienced personnel than before. In contrast, in the surveyed German firms the hiring of scientists and engineers working formerly for research institutions and other business firms, including competitors, has become more common than before.

---

[2]For the methodological details of this survey, refer to Hemmert (2000: 116–132).

Figure 11 Effects of factors to human resources on technology acquisition in the working areas of German and Japanese R&D managers (average values)

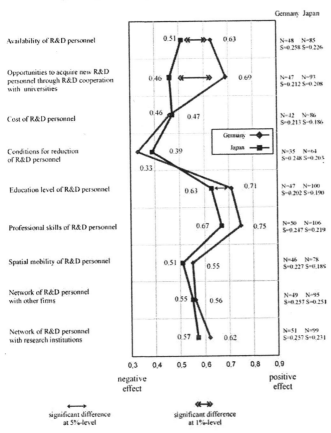

Source: Author's composition.

Concerning the aspect of internal mobility of human resources, fewer hints can be derived from the results of the survey. Notably however, the spatial mobility of R&D personnel was rated slightly higher by the German than by the Japanese questionnaire respondents. During the interviews, the spatial as well as the working assignment flexibility of scientists and engineers was raised neither by the German nor by the Japanese managers as a major problem. These findings indicate that at least in perception of the firms themselves, the internal mobility of R&D personnel is not now regarded as a major problem to be addressed in technology and innovation management.

Concerning the issue of internal organization of R&D activities, there is, again, no broad empirical evidence on recent tendencies, particularly in

German firms. Apparently, however, there has been a broad reception of project-based R&D organization practices by Japanese firms in Western countries. This discussion is centered around buzzwords like 'lean development' (Åhlström and Karlsson 1996; Bürgel 1995) and appears to have led the ground for wide-spread efforts in German and other Western firms to speed up R&D activities by adapting a more project-based organization. This seems to have resulted in major improvements in the cases of many German firms (Sommerlatte 1995: 324), thereby diminishing the relative advantage of Japanese competitors in this field.

How about the development of external linkages of German and Japanese manufacturing firms in the field of technology and innovation management? An aggregated indicator for the importance of external R&D is the part of the R&D budget spent outside the firms. Figure 12 shows the importance of such external R&D spending and its recent development in Germany, Japan and the United States. The statistical data reveal that external R&D is generally gaining importance, a finding which is consistent with the general trend of the externalization of industrial R&D outlined above. The data further indicate that the relative importance of external R&D spending appears to be higher in Germany than in both Japan and in the United States. Interestingly, US firms are spending the relatively smallest part of their R&D funds externally among the firms in the three countries. This casts doubt on the conventional view that US firms play a leading role in all recent developments in technology and innovation management.

Figure 12 External R&D expenditures as a part of the total R&D expenditures of manufacturing firms in Germany, Japan and the United States

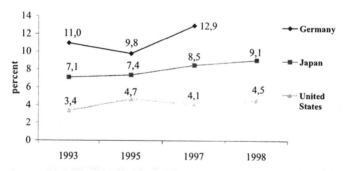

Source: Grenzmann, Marquardt and Wudtke 2000 (and earlier editions); Sômuchô Tôkeikyoku 2000 (and earlier editions); National Science Foundation 2000.

The issue of external linkages in the field of technology and innovation management was also investigated in the author's survey of German and Japanese R&D managers mentioned above. In Figure 13, the assessments of the respondents on different items related to the acquisition of external

Figure 13 Effects of factors related to external sources of technological knowledge on technology acquisition in the working areas of German and Japanese R&D managers (average values)

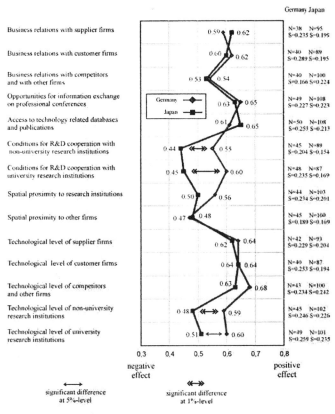

	Germany	Japan
Business relations with supplier firms	N=38	N=95
	S=0.235	S=0.195
Business relations with customer firms	N=40	N=89
	S=0.289	S=0.195
Business relations with competitors and with other firms	N=40	N=100
	S=0.166	S=0.224
Opportunities for information exchange on professional conferences	N=49	N=108
	S=0.227	S=0.223
Access to technology related databases and publications	N=50	N=108
	S=0.253	S=0.213
Conditions for R&D cooperation with non-university research institutions	N=45	N=89
	S=0.204	S=0.154
Conditions for R&D cooperation with university research institutions	N=48	N=87
	S=0.235	S=0.169
Spatial proximity to research institutions	N=44	N=103
	S=0.234	S=0.201
Spatial proximity to other firms	N=45	N=100
	S=0.189	S=0.169
Technological level of supplier firms	N=42	N=93
	S=0.229	S=0.204
Technological level of customer firms	N=40	N=87
	S=0.253	S=0.194
Technological level of competitors and other firms	N=43	N=100
	S=0.234	S=0.242
Technological level of non-university research institutions	N=45	N=102
	S=0.246	S=0.226
Technological level of university research institutions	N=49	N=101
	S=0.259	S=0.235

N: number of observed cases; S: standard deviation

Source: Author's composition.

knowledge are depicted. Concerning the items which address external linkages to and the technological level of other firms as external sources of technology, no significant differences were found between German and Japanese respondents. These result are suggesting that the differences concerning horizontal and vertical linkages between German and Japanese firms which have been raised in section 2 may not be very strong any more. However, the technological links to and the technological level of research institutions have been rated significantly better by the German than by the Japanese respondents. This finding is consistent with statements of R&D managers in the interview survey. The German managers expressed some criticism on certain features of German research institutions like a high geographical and institutional dispersion which probably is inefficient in capital-intensive fields like wafer technologies. But on the whole, they were satisfied with the level of research institutions and the conditions for technological collaboration with them. In contrast, the Japanese managers viewed the technological level of research institutions in general as insufficient. Moreover, they pointed to significant bureaucratic barriers concerning collaborative R&D between industry and governmental research institutions which further reduce the potential value of the latter as external sources of technological knowledge for business firms.

The findings concerning the evaluation of research institutions as external sources of technology are by and large consistent with the results of other empirical work. In Germany, due to a gradual opening up of research institutions for collaboration with industry, business firms have overwhelmingly expressed full or at least partial satisfaction with the current role of research institutions in a recent survey (Nicolay and Wimmers 2000: 13). In Japan, criticism about the low public investment in the research infrastructure and a therefore weak technological performance of governmental research institutions is widespread (Sakakibara 1995: 178–181; Barker 1998: 75–78). This discussion also sheds light on the growing role of public research institutions (including universities) for technology and innovation management of business firms. An increasing interrelatedness between public research and industrial R&D has been observed in recent years (Gambardella 1995: 42–61; Mansfield 1998).

Concerning internationalization of R&D activities, in the discussion of the previous subsection a particular need for Japanese manufacturing firms to increase their overseas R&D activities to make better use of technological capabilities in foreign locations has been identified. How about the recent development regarding this aspect?

In Figure 14, the percentage of respondents to the author's questionnaire survey who have attained technological knowledge exclusively from domestic sources is reported by country. This percentage is higher among the Japanese respondents than among the German ones for all sources of technology. In the cases of firm-internal sources, the country-specific differences are particularly stark. These findings suggest that while most R&D managers of Japanese firms are accustomed to use external technology from international sources, the internal R&D activities are still very much centered in their home country. The results also demonstrate that whereas the internationalization of Japanese firms' R&D undoubtedly has increased in the last two decades, there is still a large gap concerning this aspect when comparing with German firms.

A remaining issue is the proliferation of the use of new information and communication technologies in German and Japanese business firms. In general terms, both countries are considered to be latecomers concerning the use of such technologies when compared with the United States or many other industrialized countries. For instance, in 1997 the number of internet hosts per one million inhabitants was 13,772 in Germany and 9,265 in Japan, very few when compared with 76,984 in the United States (World Economic

Forum 1999: 292). Such statistics, however, reveal little about the actual use of information and communication technologies in the specific field of technology and innovation management of manufacturing firms.

Figure 14 Percentage of questionnaire respondents who have acquired technology exclusively from domestic sources by country

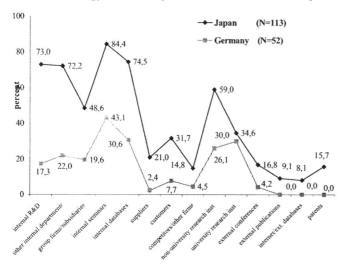

Source: Author's composition.

Figure 15 Effects of factors related to the exchange of technological information on technology acquisition in the working areas of German and Japanese R&D managers (average values)

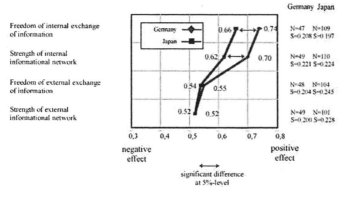

Source: Author's composition.

In the author's questionnaire and interview survey among German and Japanese pharmaceutical and semiconductor firms, some results were obtained on this issue. In Figure 15 the assessments of questionnaire respondents on items related to internal and external information exchange are shown. While on average there is almost no difference between the German and the Japanese respondents concerning the conditions for external exchange of technological information, the circumstances for internal information exchange have been evaluated significantly better by the Germans than by the Japanese.

Additional information on this issue was obtained during the interviews. Most German R&D managers emphasized the widespread use of the Internet and other new tools of information and communication technologies when exchanging technological information inside and outside the firm. Moreover, at least in some German firms surveyed by the author, company-wide virtual knowledge bases have been established. In contrast, while the use of the Internet and other kinds of information networks has proliferated as well in the Japanese firms, the establishment of virtual bases of technological knowledge was not progressed beyond the stage of planning in most cases.

Given the fact that Nonaka's and Takeuchi's path-breaking work on knowledge management is predominantly based on casework about Japanese manufacturing firms, these findings are surprising at a first glance. When thoroughly studying their book however, it becomes clear that (1) their empirical findings are centered on a very limited number of excellent Japanese firms, but not on a broad, representative sample, and that (2) their discussion of knowledge management emphasizes informal management tools like the conscious creation of organizational redundancy or the use of socialization among R&D personnel to enhance knowledge transfer (Nonaka and Takeuchi 1995: 80–82, 114–116). In contrast, recent treatments on knowledge management in Western countries focus much more on the use of information and communication technologies rather than on the implementation of such 'soft' management tools (Davenport and Prusak 1998: 123–143; O'Dell and Grayson 1998: 85–106). Thus the actual meaning of knowledge management emphasized by Japanese and Western authors appears to be rather different. The findings of the author's survey address the use of information and communication technologies and not the tools of knowledge management emphasized by Nonaka and Takeuchi. Concerning the use of such technologies, German firms appear to have made stronger progress than Japanese firms so far.

Finally, the trends in industrial organization concerning activities related to technology and innovation remain to be discussed. A comparison of the most recent statistics on the concentration of R&D expenditures among manufacturing firms with earlier results reveals that both in Germany and in Japan the share of R&D expenditures spent by large firms remained almost unchanged throughout the 1990s. Thus, on the aggregated level there is no evidence of structural change of the R&D activities in the manufacturing sector.

On the micro-level however, the picture in Germany is quite different. During the second half of the 1990s, the number of innovative venture businesses has been soaring. A very prominent case is the biotechnology sector: The number of biotechnology firms increased from 75 to 440 between 1995 and 1998 (Lehrer 2000: 100). But also the total start-up venture capital has rapidly increased since around 1997, resulting in a total venture capital investment of more than 1 billion Euro in 1998, which has been more than the combined venture capital investment in France and the UK (Lehrer 2000: 90). The judgements of R&D managers in large German firms concerning the technological level of high-tech venture firms have also been mostly positive in the interview survey of the author.

In Japan, serious efforts to enhance the activity of small and medium venture firms have taken place as well. As a part of the implementation of the Science and Technology Basic Plan that was launched by the Japanese government in 1996, substantial budgets have been set up to support the growth of innovative venture businesses. But due to a lack of applications by firms, only small fractions of those budgets have been actually spent (Hemmert and Oberländer 1998: 15). The views of most of the Japanese R&D managers interviewed by the author concerning high-tech venture firms were also mostly reserved, particularly stressing the fact that still only few such firms are existing in Japan. In contrast to Germany, a significant increase of the role of innovative small and medium firms in industrial R&D could not be witnessed yet in Japan.

6.5 MANAGERIAL EVALUATION, INSTITUTIONAL FACTORS AND PATH DEPENDENCY

The discussion in the previous section has revealed that the extent to which German and Japanese manufacturing firms have reacted to changes in their competitive environment by a reorientation of their technology and innovation management is quite different. Because of the very limited empirical evidence concerning some issues, the results should be regarded as tentative findings. In this meaning, however, the following observations were made:

(1) Strategic conservatism among German and Japanese manufacturing firms concerning technology and innovation is, with some exceptions in Germany, prevailing.

(2) The external mobility of human resources in R&D has been increasing among German manufacturing firms and appears to be much higher now than among Japanese firms.

(3) The internal organization of R&D activities has become more project oriented in German firms, thereby diminishing the initial advantage of Japanese firms in this field.

(4) Both German and Japanese manufacturing firms have been strengthening their external linkages in technology and innovation management. However, external sources of technology presently play a greater role for German firms than for Japanese firms.

(5) Whereas the internationalization of industrial R&D is increasing both in German and in Japanese firms, its level is currently much higher in the case of the German firms than of the Japanese firms.

(6) The overall concentration of industrial R&D on large firms remains unchanged in both countries. Germany has recently witnessed a large increase of innovative small venture firms however, whereas in Japan no such development could be observed yet.

Altogether, the results strongly suggest that the strategic reorientation of German manufacturing firms concerning most of the issues raised in this paper has been much more dynamic than in the case of the Japanese firms. If the assumption that such reorientation measures are necessary to address the changes in the competitive environment of the firms holds true, a better performance of German firms than of Japanese firms in technology and innovation management should be expected.

In fact, in the questionnaire and interview survey by the author, the German R&D managers evaluated their technology acquisition performance much better than the Japanese. As shown in Figure 16, the average rating of all yardsticks with the exception of transferability of new technologies differed significantly between the German and the Japanese questionnaire respondents. The different perceptions concerning technology acquisition performance between German and Japanese managers were confirmed during the interview survey. Additionally, an analysis of the number of US patents granted to the surveyed firms revealed that the development concerning this measurable output of R&D activities was much more positive during the second half of the 1990s among the German firms than among the Japanese firms (Hemmert 2000: 337).

These empirical results have to be viewed carefully not only due to the general difficulties of measuring the managerial performance of firms in areas not directly connected to the market, but also because of the fact that the topic of the author's study was technology acquisition, which is a very important, but not the only part of technology and innovation management. Nevertheless, the findings together with the data collected from other sources suggest a stark difference between German and Japanese manufacturing firms concerning the amount of strategic reorientation during the 1990s as well as concerning their performance in the field of technology and innovation management.

When evaluating the managerial performance of the firms however, the institutional surroundings have to be taken into consideration. An issue where these surroundings are apparently important is industrial organization, which is beyond the scope of the management of individual firms.

Figure 16 Assessment of technology acquisition performance by German and Japanese R&D managers (average values)

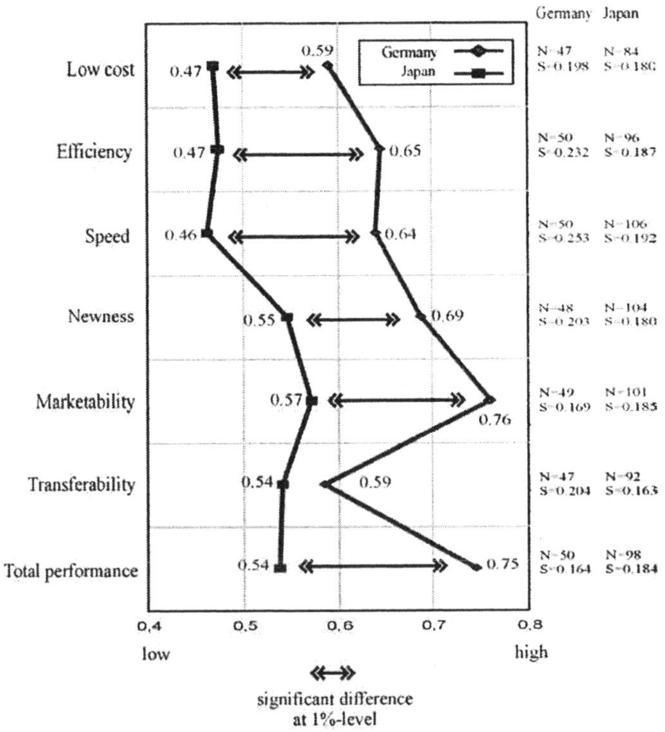

N: number of observed cases; S: standard deviation

Source: Author's composition.

The differences between Germany and Japan concerning the emergence of innovative venture businesses are mainly the result of different conditions on the two countries capital markets and probably of country-specific differences in technology policy.

However, managerial aspects also must not be seen alone. For instance, the observed conservatism of German and Japanese firms concerning technology strategies has to be seen in the context of corporate governance. In both the German and the Japanese corporate governance system the stances of managers, employees and loan providers (banks) are perceived to be relatively strong. All these groups are regarded to be relatively risk averse concerning the strategic orientation of firms.[3] It therefore does not come as a surprise that German and Japanese firms tend to be more cautious concerning technology strategies when compared with US firms where

---

[3]Concerning this aspect, refer to the contribution by Franz Waldenberger in this volume.

stockholders, who may be less cautious about entering new technological fields as long as profitability is secured, are said to have a stronger position.

External institutional settings also play a significant role for other facets of technology and innovation management. As has been discussed above, German manufacturing firms are holding stronger external linkages with research institutions than Japanese ones due to the fact that the technological level of research institutions is higher and the conditions for cooperating with them are more favorable in Germany when compared with Japan.

Concerning other managerial fields, the matter of path dependency has to be taken into consideration. This applies to human resource management as well as to internationalization. In the Japanese employment system, high investment of large firms into the vocational training of their employees and therefore the formation of firm-specific skills as well as high income penalties for employees who change their employer in the latter part of their professional careers have been long-term characteristics (Demes 1998: 145–147). Recently, firms appear to be more positive about hiring technical personnel with former working experience. Due to the overall structure of the Japanese employment system, however, there are still very few such scientists and engineers available.

When analyzing the low degree of internationalization of Japanese firms, the relative lateness of Japan's industrial development has also to be taken into consideration. Up to the 1970s and the 1980s, Japanese manufacturing firms have still been in a process of catching up to their Western competitors – particularly concerning technology and innovation. The internationalization of the R&D activities of most large Japanese manufacturing firms only started seriously during the second half of the 1980s (Asakawa 1996: 26), at a time when many North American and European firms already had built up considerable overseas R&D units. Given the fact that the Westerns firms were, like the Japanese firms, still forging ahead with the internationalization of their R&D since then, it is not surprising that the Japanese firms are still lagging behind their Western competitors concerning this aspect.

When considering the institutional context, it therefore becomes clear that the technology and innovation management of Japanese manufacturing firms cannot be blamed alone for their slowness concerning strategic reorientation and their seemingly weak performance in this managerial field during recent years. The institutional environment in Japan, which in many fields like industrial organization for a long time has been regarded as a competitive advantage for Japanese firms, looks very unfavorable now concerning technology and innovation management, particularly under the recent tendencies in international competition.

6.6 CONCLUSIONS AND IMPLICATIONS: MUTUAL BENCHMARKING AND PREVAILING INTERANTIONAL DIVERSITY IN TECHNOLOGY AND INNOVATION MANAGEMENT

The above discussion has shown that the increasing globalization of economic activities in general and the recent changes in international competition on technology and innovation in particular may to a certain degree result in an international convergence of management practices. For manufacturing firms, mutual benchmarking of best management practices seems to have become organizational routine. Firms that are not willing or not able to follow the changing rules of international competition, like many Japanese firms in recent years, have to pay an increasing penalty in terms of their technological competitiveness.

However, in the debate about globalization and economic convergence it should not be overlooked that the institutional diversity between countries is a strong driver for the internationalization of manufacturing firms R&D activities. Multinational firms are seeking maximum advantage by making use of specific technological competencies in different locations and countries. In other words, a vanishing of national and regional differences in technological competencies by a foregoing international convergence may paradoxically decrease the incentives for firms to spread their R&D activities to different countries and locations. Also, the path dependency of the development of firms and the inertia of economic systems and institutions pose further brakes on global convergence of firms and economic activities. Despite the widespread mutual benchmarking that is forcing firms from different countries to follow certain global trends in certain periods of time, these aspects altogether should assure a prevailing international diversity of institutional structures in the foreseeable future. Rather, it appears likely that in the field of technology and innovation, multinational firms become truly global in the long run, resulting in a decreasing importance of their country of origin. In other words, while the dissimilarities between North America, Europe and Japan are likely to persist, the dissimilarities between large North American, European and Japanese *firms* may gradually vanish as these firms evolve into global technological networks.

The discussion in this paper has also shown that at least in the field of technology and innovation management it makes little sense to think in terms of evolving 'global standards'. Rather, business firms are trying to learn about best practices from their competitors (in their home country as well as in other countries) in a process of mutual benchmarking. While during the 1980s, Japanese firms have drawn very much interest by their competitors, US firms have moved into the center of attention during the 1990s. However, a closer look reveals that US firms do not necessarily play a leading role concerning all developments that have been identified above as international trends in technology and innovation management.

For instance, firms from Germany and also from some other European countries may have progressed further concerning the use of external sources of technology and also regarding the internationalization of their R&D activities than US firms.

However, the supposed persistence of institutional diversity on the international level does not free firms and governments from the need to learn about 'best practices' in the course of international competition. In the actual field of technology and innovation management, need for further strategic adjustment presently appears to be more urgent in Japan than in Germany. The technological performance of Japanese manufacturing firms is suffering from a low degree of internationalization of their R&D activities and also from weaknesses in the institutional environment in their home country, namely from the low technological level of research institutions and the scarcity of innovative venture firms. Therefore, firms should forge ahead with the internationalization of their R&D which should help them to compensate a least partially for institutional weaknesses in their home country. At the same time, the Japanese government should support the technological competitiveness of manufacturing firms by improving their environment in Japan, particularly by upgrading the technological strength of research institutions and by further supporting innovative venture firms.

Concerning other issues however, it is an open question whether Japanese or German firms should strictly adhere to the perceived international trends in technology and innovation management. For instance, conservative attitudes concerning technology strategies may have prevented Japanese and German firms in some cases to become global technological forerunners. But firms from these two countries have often been successful in leapfrogging important technologies with a certain time lag and thereafter taking their share on the international markets for related products. While the technological progress in certain information and communication technologies is certainly very rapid now, there is no clear evidence that the 'follower' strategies that Japanese and Germans have often successfully adapted will not work any more in the future. Therefore, it remains doubtful whether a general turn to more risky strategies will eventually improve the technological competitiveness of large Japanese and German manufacturing firms.

REFERENCES

Åhlström, Pär and Christer Karlsson, 'The Difficult Path to Lean Product Development', in *Journal of Product Innovation Management*, Vol. 13 (1996), pp. 283–295.

Aldrich, Howard E. and Toshihiro Sasaki, 'R&D consortia in the United States and Japan', in *Research Policy*, Vol. 14 (1995), pp. 301–316

Aoki, Masahiko, *Information, Incentives, and Bargaining in the Japanese Economy*. Cambridge 1988.

Asakawa, Kazuhiro, 'External-Internal Linkages and Overseas Autonomy-Control Tension: The Management Dilemma of the Japanese R&D in Europe', in *IEEE Transactions on Engineering Management*, Vol. 43 (1996), pp. 24–32.

Barker, Brendan, 'Internationalizing Japanese Science', in Hemmert, Martin and Christian Oberländer (eds.), *Technology and Innovation in Japan. Policy and Management for the Twenty-first Century*, London and New York 1998, pp. 70–86.

Belderbos, René A., *Japanese Electronics Multinationals and Strategic Trade Policies*. Oxford 1997.

BMBF – Bundesministerium für Bildung und Forschung (ed.), *Zur technologischen Leistungsfähigkeit Deutschlands. Zusammenfassender Endbericht 1999*. Bonn 2000.

Brockhoff, Klaus, *Stärken und Schwächen industrieller Forschung und Entwicklung: Umfrageergebnisse aus der Bundesrepublik Deutschland*, Stuttgart 1990.

Bürgel, Hans-Dietmar, 'Lean R&D', in Zahn, Erich (ed.), *Handbuch Technologiemanagement*. Stuttgart 1995, pp. 335–349.

Clark, Kim B. and Takahiro Fujimoto, *Product Development Performance, Strategy, Organization, and Management in the World Auto Industry*. Boston 1991.

Corey, E. Raymond, *Technology Fountainheads. The Management Challenge of R&D Consortia*. Boston 1997.

Davenport, Thomas H. and Laurence Prusak, *Working Knowledge. How Organizations Manage What They Know*. Boston 1998.

Demes, Helmut, 'Arbeitsmarkt und Beschäftigung', in Deutsches Institut für Japanstudien (ed.), *Die Wirtschaft Japans. Strukturen zwischen Kontinuität und Wandel*. Berlin 1998, pp. 135–164.

Ernst, Angelika and Gerhard Wiesner, *Japans technische Intelligenz. Personalstrukturen und Personalmanagement in Forschung und Entwicklung*. Munich 1994.

Gambardella, Alfonso, *Science and innovation. The US Pharmaceutical Industry during the 1980s*. Cambridge 1995.

Gerpott, Torsten J., *Strategisches Technologie- und Innovationsmanagement. Eine konzentrierte Einführung*. Stuttgart 1999.

Goodman, Paul S. and Fernando Olivera, *Knowledge Sharing via Computer-Assisted Systems in International Corporations*, Carnegie Bosch Institute for Applied Studies in International Management, Working Paper 98-17, 1998.

Gotô, Akira, *Nihon no gijutsu kakushin to sangyô soshiki* [Innovation and industrial organization in Japan]. Tokyo 1993.

Grenzmann, Christoph, Rüdiger Marquardt and Joachim Wudtke, *Forschung und Entwicklung in der Wirtschaft 1997–1999*. Essen 2000.

Hemmert, Martin, "'Intermediate Organization" Revisited: A Framework for the Vertical Division of Labor in Manufacturing and the Case of the Japanese Assembly Industries', in: *Industrial and Corporate Change*, Vol. 8 (1999), pp. 487–517.

Hemmert, Martin, *Erfolgsfaktoren der Technologiegewinnung von Hochtechnologieunternehmen. Eine empirische Untersuchung von Pharma- und Halbleiterunternehmen in Deutschland und Japan*, Professorial Thesis submitted to the Faculty of Economic Studies, University of Essen, 2000.

Hemmert, Martin and Christian Oberländer, 'The Japanese system of technology and innovation: Preparing for the twenty-first century', in Hemmert, Martin and Christian Oberländer (eds.), *Technology and Innovation in Japan. Policy and Management for the Twenty-first Century*. London and New York 1998, pp. 5–19.

Keck, Otto, 'The National System for Technological Innovation in Germany', in Nelson, Richard R. (ed.), *National Innovation Systems*. New York and Oxford 1993, pp. 115–157.

Kusunoki, Ken and Tsuyoshi Numagami, 'Intrafirm Transfers of Engineers in Japan', in Gotô, Akira and Hiroyuki Odagiri (eds.), *Innovation in Japan*. New York and Oxford 1997, pp. 173–203.

Kutsuna, Kenji, Kôzô Yamada and Yoshihiko Akashi, *Nihon no benchâ kigyô. Âlîsutçji no kadai to shien* [Venture firms in Japan. Tasks and support in the early stage]. Tokyo 1999.

Lehrer, Mark, 'Has Germany Finally Fixed Its High-Tech Problem? The Recent Boom in German Technology-based Entrepreneurship', in *California Management Review*, Vol. 42 (2000), No. 4, pp. 89–107.

Mansfield, Edwin, 'Industrial R&D in Japan and the United States: A Comparative Study', in *American Economic Review*, Vol. 78 (1988), pp. 223–228.

Mansfield, Edwin, 'Academic Research and industrial innovation: An update of empirical findings', in *Research Policy*, Vol. 26 (1998), pp. 773–776.

Mowery, David C., 'The changing structure of the US national innovation system: Implications for international conflict and cooperation in R&D policy', in *Research Policy*, Vol. 27 (1998), pp. 639–654.

National Science Board (ed.), *Science & Engineering Indicators 2000, Volume 1*. Arlington 2000.

National Science Foundation (ed.), *Research and Development in Industry: 1998, Early Release Tables*. Arlington 2000.

Nicolay, Rainer and Stephan Wimmers, *Kundenzufriedenheit der Unternehmen mit Forschungseinrichtungen. Ergebnisse einer Unternehmensbefragung zur Zusammenarbeit zwischen Unternehmen und Forschungseinrichtungen*. Bonn and Berlin 2000.

Nonaka, Ikujirô, 'Product Development and Innovation', in Imai, Ken-ichi und Ryûtarô Komiya (eds.), *Business Enterprise in Japan: Views of Leading Japanese Economists*. Cambridge and London 1994, pp. 209–221.

Nonaka, Ikujirô and Hirotaka Takeuchi, *The Knowledge-Creating Company. How Japanese Companies Create the Dynamics of Innovation*. New York and Oxford 1995.

O'Dell, Carla and C. Jackson Grayson, Jr., *If Only We Knew What We Know. The Transfer of Internal Knowledge and Best Practice*. New York 1998.

OECD – Organisation for Economic Co-operation and Development, *Globalisation of Industrial R&D: Policy Issues*. Paris 1999.

Okimoto, Daniel I. and Yoshio Nishi, 'R&D Organization in Japanese and American Semiconductor Firms', in Aoki, Masahiko and Ronald Dore (eds.), *The Japanese Firm. Sources of Competitive Strength*. Oxford 1994, pp. 178–208.

Perillieux, René, 'Technologietiming', in Zahn, Erich (ed.), *Handbuch Technologie-management*. Stuttgart 1995, pp. 267–284.

Porter, Alan L., J. David Roessner, Nils Newman, and Xiao-Yin Jin, *1999 Indicators of Technology-based Competitiveness of 33 Nations*, Report to the Science Indicators Unit, Science Resources Studies Division, National Science Foundation, Atlanta: Technology Policy and Assessment Center, Georgia Institute of Technology, 2000.

Pralahad, C. K. and Gary Hamel, 'The Core Competence of the Corporation', in *Harvard Business Review*, Vol. 68 (1990), May-June, pp. 79–91.

Rotering, Christian, *Forschungs- und Entwicklungskooperationen zwischen Unternehmen. Eine empirische Analyse*. Stuttgart 1990.

Sakakibara, Kiyonori: *Nihon kigyô no kenkyû kaihatsu manejimento. Soshikinai dôkeika to sono chôfuku* [R&D management in Japanese firms. The creation and the overcoming of organizational isomorphism]. Tokyo 1995.

Schröder, Hans-Horst, 'Innovationsstrategien und Technologiepolitik in Deutschland', in Lichtblau, Karl and Franz Waldenberger (eds.), *Planung, Wettbewerb und wirtschaftlicher Wandel. Ein japanisch-deutscher Vergleich*. Cologne 1997, pp. 107–152.

Sômuchô Tôkeikyoku (ed.), *Heisei 11-nen kagaku gijutsu kenkyû chôsa hôkoku* [Report on the Survey of Research and Development 1999]. Tokyo 2000.

Specht, Günter and Christoph Beckmann, *F&E-Management*. Stuttgart 1996.

Sommerlatte, Tom, 'Management von Forschung und Entwicklung', in Zahn, Erich (ed.), *Handbuch Technologiemanagement*. Stuttgart 1995, pp. 323–334.

Tsûshô Sangyôshô (ed.), *Dai 29-kai 1999-nen kaigai jigyô katsudô kihon chôsa gaiyô* [Overview on the 29th basic survey of overseas business activities]. Tokyo 2000.

Wakasugi, Ryûhei, 'Organizational Structure and Behavior in Research and Development', in Imai, Ken-ichi und Ryûtarô Komiya (eds.), *Business Enterprise in Japan: Views of Leading Japanese Economists*. Cambridge 1994, pp. 159–177.

Wirtz, Bernd W., 'Wissensmanagement und kooperativer Transfer immaterieller Ressourcen in virtuellen Unternehmensnetzwerken', in *ZfB-Ergänzungsheft 2*, 2000, pp. 97–114.

World Economic Forum (ed.), *The Global Competitiveness Report 1999*. New York and Oxford 1999.

Discussant: Ivan Botskor

Knowledge is in the head
Innovation management = transfer of technological knowledge

Where does the first transfer of this type take place in a company?

Put very bluntly: It takes place in the hiring of new employees, in whose heads there is already accumulated knowledge.

This is the point I would like to elaborate regarding the paper of Mr. Hemmert. He mentions it in his Table 3, dealing with intra and inter fluctuations. But the problem is somewhat deeper, not unlike the famous question of 'what came first: the chicken or the egg?'

Assuming that the universities are the primary chickens, how do the German and Japanese eggs, which the firms employ, compare? There are many trends under reform in both countries, but their main educational patterns can be summarized as follows:

Japan: The education of engineers and natural science graduates is more general and shorter. Most graduates are 4-year bachelors of science. Essentially they should know the general scientific laws (or at least know where to look them up), independent research and work capability are not taught or expected.

Germany: The education of engineers and natural science graduates is more general and takes longer. A German Diploma is comparable to a Master's Degree – many students do an additional Ph.D., especially in Physics and Chemistry. The graduates have a solid scientific background and a higher capacity for original thinking.

These differences are rooted in the concrete expectations which the 'market' for these graduates has presented in the past:

Japan: A good general knowledge was welcome, but more important was the adaptability of the student to the company, group workstyle and its goals. The (big) companies were prepared to train the newly graduated engineer or science major whom they hired for many years. This was a substantial investment that would only pay as long as the 'lifetime employment model' kept the trainee in the company. Small companies could not afford the expense of this training and received the information through the keiretsu grapevine.

Germany: The companies expected that their new employees from the universities received a good training in their special subjects, that they were also trained in specifics and not only in basic background knowledge. There is some mobility in the German job market as far as the R&D area is concerned, which increases the intercompany information flow.

Disadvantages

Japan: The cost of training is very high. The new workers will eventually be useful after 5 to 10 years.

Germany: A good worker only stays with sufficient incentive. The longer period of study makes the new R&D employees too old: for a fresh graduate 28 is about the average age. The German graduates specialize in particular fields. An electronics engineer will insist on solving his problems by a different method than a mechanical engineer – building up new interdisciplinary fields like Mechatronics is more difficult in Germany.

Advantages

Japan: The Japanese graduates are young and unprejudiced. They can be readily employed in interdisciplinary activities, where there is a lot of innovative potential.

Germany: Small companies can employ qualified R&D workers without having to train them.

Changes in education

The economic paradigm is now changing. Globalization and shareholders introduce new rules and values in the economies. Who has presently the advantage in innovation management?

Japan: It could be that the Japanese companies will be clamoring for masters in physics, chemistry, engineers, etc. in the next years. But that will not be easy. The whole university educational system has to be changed. Students are not used to working hard in the universities and most universities do not have good training facilities. This is changing, but maybe not fast enough. The introduction of merit pay and the abolition of the seniority system, which the big Japanese companies aim for, will also affect the R&D workers' morale and security. Many will leave, taking with them the expensive training, not only to other Japanese companies, but also to other countries.

Germany: The German disadvantage lies in the lower interdisciplinary interaction between the different special subjects. The time spent on higher education should be shortened. But most of the teaching system and employment rules do not have to be changed as much as in Japan.

Conclusion

Both educational systems have to be reformed, but the Japanese reform has to be more drastic, both at university as well as company level.

7

JAPANESE AND GERMAN CORPORATE GOVERNANCE IN TRANSITION: FORCES OF CHANGE AND PERSISTENCE

Franz Waldenberger

7.1 INTRODUCTION

Does the victory of Vodafone in the battle for control over the assets of Mannesmann's mobile phone service signal the beginning of the end of German corporatist capitalism? Do the similar cases of hostile takeovers by foreign companies in Japan imply the end of the Japanese postwar industrial system? Both in Germany and Japan, restructuring had been the task of corporate insiders. Stable ownership combined with bank control kept unfriendly outsiders from gaining control over company assets. The recent cases clearly indicate that these structural obstacles are no longer insurmountable. However, what does this imply for the German and Japanese systems of corporate governance? The answer is not at all clear. There is room for at least three interpretations.

Endogenous change: The appearance of hostile takeovers could be the result of changes within the corporate system whereby traditional obstacles to this mode of corporate restructuring were lowered.

Exogenous shock: Rather than being the result of changes occurring within national systems of corporate governance, the appearance of hostile takeovers could be related to the severeness of the environment German and Japanese companies are presently confronting. It is interesting to note, that the first hostile takeovers both in Japan and Germany occurred in telecommunications services. Due to fast technological progress, markets in these industries are changing rapidly and the uncertainty about the future course of business is high. In such an environment, speed and size become a decisive factor for survival. Strategic alliances and external growth through mergers and acquisitions are a must. Given the high degree of uncertainty, consensus among prospective partners might be impossible or too time consuming to achieve. Even insider systems might under such conditions be urged to resort to unfriendly means of restructuring.

Evolutionary change: The exogenous and the endogenous change interpretations can both be true and they might not be unrelated to each other, but mutually re-enforcing. Changes in the market environment might require adaptations in the pattern of ownership, or they might create the need to redefine traditional stakeholder relationships.

In what follows I will opt for the evolutionary interpretation, but with a caveat. The title of my paper mentions not only forces of change, but also forces of persistence. The evolutionary argument stated above, while being more comprehensive than the first two interpretations, still represents a very simplistic model of change. It does not allow for obstacles in the process of transformation, nor does it allow for variety in the outcome. To make the evolutionary argument a bit more realistic, we will have to consider problems of system complementarities. In the age of computers, everyone is familiar with the term "system requirements" when installing new software. You cannot run a Windows application on a Macintosh. Similar arguments apply to systems of corporate governance. The introduction of market based instruments of control in the relationship between management and shareholders require adjustments in the relationship with other stakeholders of the firm. Incompatibilities will result in a malfunctioning of the system as a whole.

The compatibility issue is developed in more detail in the next section by sketching a general model of corporate governance. The model allows a simple characterization and interpretation of the Japanese and German systems of governance. It will also provide the framework for section 7.3, where the forces of change and persistence will be analysed and evaluated. The paper concludes by stressing that the direction of change will not be from one particular system to another, but from a low number of alternative models to a larger variety of choices of corporate governance systems.

7.2 CORPORATE GOVERNANCE AS A SYSTEM

Modern economic theory views the firm as a nexus of contracts (Milgrom and Roberts 1992: 20). The term contract is to be understood in a very broad sense, as it includes not only written, but mostly implicit obligations by the respective parties. A firm entertains contractual relations with employees, managers, equity owners, creditors, suppliers, dealers and customers. These are groups with conflicting interests. Owners want to earn a high return on their equity. Employees prefer high wages. Customers demand cheap products of high quality. Suppliers want a good price for their own products. Managers pursue interests of their own. At the same time, they have to manage the various contractual relations of the firm. In doing so, they have to reconcile and trade off the conflicting interests of owners, employees and other contractual parties. How can this be done?

The "stakeholder- versus shareholder-value" discussion (see for example OECD 1998) gives a naive answer to this question. Managers with a shareholder-value orientation are said to put shareholder interests first. So when asked whether they would lay off employees in order to increase dividends for shareholders, such managers would say "yes". Stakeholder oriented firms would answer to this question with "no". They will try to balance out conflicting interests. Decisions tend to be more consensus-based. Contractual relations are regarded as long-term commitments and as important assets for future business.

According to this classification, Japanese and German firms are regarded as stakeholder oriented, whereas companies in the US or the UK are classified as shareholder oriented. In a survey conducted by Masaru Yoshimori in the mid 1990s, managers of large companies from these countries where asked how they would decide when given the choice between (A) increasing profits through laying off employees or (B) keeping both the level of profits and the level of employment (Yoshimori 1995: 28). Of the US and of the UK managers 98% opted for the "more profit" alternative. In Germany, the preference for this alternative was down to 41%. In Japan, the "more profit" alternative would have been chosen by just 3% of the respondents.

I have called the "shareholder- versus stakeholder-value" discussion naive. Although it captures differences of managerial behaviour in various countries, it does not explain at all where these differences come from. Therefore, it is of little help in the analysis of change. The discussion suggests, that companies can more or less freely choose between being shareholder- or stakeholder-oriented. Whether managers give shareholder interests more emphasis or whether they follow a consensus-based approach is seen as the outcome of modifiable regulations and incentive structures. For example, stakeholder-oriented managers are seen to lack control from the shareholder side. So simply strengthening the legal position of shareholders would turn a stakeholder-oriented management into shareholder-value maximisers.[1]

This viewpoint is naive, because it neglects the constraints managers have to consider when they trade off opposing owner, lender, employee, customer and supplier interests. Also, these constraints are defined by the economic environment and not by legal stipulations. For the purpose of analysis, it is helpful to assume, that managers in all countries pursue first of all their own personal interests. As Adam Smith noted, in the context

---

[1] Automative industry which product is quite complex, is also the industry that has the more formalised and representative purchasing system.

of division of labour, pursuing ones own income interests requires that one serves the income and consumption interests of others. This holds true for managers in all countries. Differences in managerial behaviour are thus not due to the fact that managers in different countries have a different goal function, different patterns of behaviour are rather the result of differences in the way the interests of owners, employees and other contractual parties are to be served.

There are basically two ways to protect economic interests. One is managerial commitment. For example, in Japan management is highly committed to employment stability. This is not only apparent in the responses to questionnaires; it is also evident in the actual behaviour of companies. The reluctance to lay off employees is again shown in the present recession (OECD 1999: 47–50, Keizai Kikaku Chô 1999: 160). The alternative way of protecting contractual interests is through competition. Competition is certainly the cheaper way of protecting income and consumption interests, but it is not always available. To put it more clearly, the explicit commitment of management to the protection of specific stakeholder interests is directly related to the fact that these interests are insufficiently protected by competition. This is a central proposition; so let me explain it in more detail with regard to the employment relation, which is after all the most important contractual relation in this context.

Under ideal market conditions, the additional income that one employee contributes to the value added of the firm is just equal to the income she can earn somewhere else. In that case the market not only prices the marginal product of the employee correctly, it also assures that the income interest of the employee is perfectly protected. If she does not get what she can earn elsewhere, she will quit. The short-term exit option provided by the market is a perfect safeguard for the employee. However, the protection provided by the exit option only works to the extent that the market prices the marginal product correctly. Prices measure opportunity costs. They measure the income to be earned at other companies. Opportunity costs will only be close to the employees' present marginal product if labour qualifications and work place specifications are sufficiently standardized, so that labour services can, without productivity loss, be transferred to other companies. The less the standardization requirement is fulfilled, the more firm-specific labour services are and the wider will be the gap between actual marginal product and opportunity costs, i.e. market price. Asset specificity, here the specificity of the human capital employed in labour services, implies that income interests are only insufficiently protected by the exit option of the market. Consequently, these interests must be protected by other means, namely by commitments on the part of the firm. Insufficient commitment will lead to underinvestment in firm-specific assets and will forfeit the associated productivity gains.

How about the capital side? Here, management will have to serve the interests of equity owners and long-term lenders. These interests are also not protected by short-term exit options. Equity capital is completely locked-in. Long-term debt cannot be withdrawn before the maturity of the underlying contract. How can management commit to both employees and to providers of capital? As long as the company is profitable enough to serve its long-term debt and to generate enough return for equity owners, there is no problem. However, in rough economic conditions that require the restructuring of assets the situation is different. Here, the task is to find a compromise that will ensure that the various groups of stakeholders continue to believe in the commitment of management to protect their interests. Under restructuring, protection can of course only be interpreted in relative terms. Every stakeholder group will have to be convinced that the burden they share in the total cost of restructuring is fair.

The requirement to negotiate the terms of restructuring among employees, equity owners and long-term lenders has far-reaching implications for the organization of capital markets. Capital finance relationships will have to be stable. This means that secondary markets for trading equity and debt-contracts cannot be developed to the full extent. Equity ownership and lending relationships have to be stable in order to built up trust. Without trust from the side of capital providers, management will not be able to make a commitment to protect the interests of other stakeholders, namely employees. Without trust, there would be the fear that in situations of restructuring the capital side will not extend funds. This uncertainty would in turn prevent other contractual parties from investing in company specific assets.

So here we have a first system complementarity. The underdevelopment of markets for qualified labour requires the underdevelopment of secondary markets for equity and long-term capital. The complementarity requirement is well demonstrated by the traditional German and Japanese corporate systems. Stable ownership of stock and stable main bank or Hausbank-relationships, the pillars of the German and the Japanese corporate finance (OECD 1995, 1996), has supported the commitment of management vis-à-vis employees.

It should be noted that this complementarity has long been acknowledged in the corporate governance literature (Blair 1995, Porter 1997). But to my knowledge, it has not been related to the characteristics of the market environment. According to the argument developed here, asset specificity is not a variable that can be controlled by management. It is dictated by the development of markets for the respective productive resources.

A third element of the German and Japanese system completes the picture of an insider system. Insider systems are typically characterized by a strong information asymmetry between insiders and outsiders. This asymmetry arises from two sources. Firstly, the existence of asset specificity implies that the market does not correctly price essential resources of the firm. This creates a basic problem for the evaluation of company assets. Secondly, the underdevelopment of secondary stock markets impedes the pricing function of these markets. With little stock turnover, analysts will find it not profitable to specialize in the evaluation of stock. Also, because of stable relationships with the capital side, management has little incentive to provide the markets with company information.

7.3 SCENARIOS OF CHANGE

The market environment in which the contractual relations of companies are embedded as described above determines systems of corporate governance. Instead of making the distinction between stakeholder- and shareholder-oriented systems, it is more adequate to talk about market-based versus relational systems of governance. Shareholder-orientation arises in an environment where contractual relations are embedded in well-developed markets. Stakeholder-orientation is the typical approach of companies that operate in a less developed market environment.

The above characterization of governance systems has two direct implications for the analysis of change. Firstly, change can only result from changes in the market environment. Secondly, attention has to be paid to system complementarity. Speaking of the German and the Japanese system, structural change as such and the development of secondary markets for stock and external debt alone will not shift these systems away from their stakeholder-orientation and insider quality. For this to happen, the functioning of other markets, especially labour markets, will have to improve. If this condition is not met, strategies that, under the pressure of structural adjustment, one-sidedly defer to the interests of capital markets will be bound to fail. In what follows, I will elaborate on this proposition.

7.3.1 Structural change

Structural adjustment can be dealt with in relational systems of corporate governance. The success of Japanese companies in overcoming the two oil crises in the 1970s showed that stakeholder systems could be quite good in coping with structural change. However, this episode also demonstrates that success hinges on one very important precondition. There must be new fields of business and technology into which companies can diversify. Only if companies can find new fields of growth, will they be able to overcome the conflict between employee and capital interests. This situation was met in the 1970s, when Japanese companies entered the semi-conductor industry and could use the micro-electronic revolution as an engine for growth.

The condition was not met in the 1990s. Instead, the specific problems of the relational system of corporate governance became apparent. Structural adjustment requires the reallocation of resources, especially labour and capital, from old to new industries. In the relational governance system, both skilled labour and risk capital are stuck with the companies in old industries. If these companies cannot manage to diversify into new industries, the reallocation of resources will fail or it will at least consume much more time. Here, market-based systems are in an advantage, because labour and capital can move out of the old industries leaving the old companies behind. The ongoing sluggishness of the Japanese economy tells us that companies in old industries have indeed much more difficulty in coping with the structural challenges of the 1990s. At the same time, the slow process of restructuring confirms that the relational system of governance is still in place.

In Germany, the growth potential of companies seemed to have been already exhausted in the 1970s. Since then, unemployment has been rising steadily and this certainly undermined the trust relationship between labour and management. The reluctance of management to lay off workers was further reduced in the restructuring phase following German unification. The separation rate (number of lay-offs and quits in per cent of total employment) was 4.3% in the 1990s compared to 1.6% in the 1980s (OECD 1997: 148). According to the complementarity argument, markets for skilled labour should thus be more developed in Germany than in Japan. Employment and wage data for 1992 indeed suggest that, in comparison with Japan, asset specificity of human capital plays a minor role in Germany (Waldenberger 1999: chapter 6). This can be related to differences in German and Japanese skill formation systems, which tend to be more professional-oriented and less company-based in Germany.

7.3.2 Corporate governance and stages of economic development

Whether consensus based governance systems can cope with structural change seems to depend very much on the overall stage of economic development. Both Japan and Germany are successful latecomers among the industrialized nations. The latecomer position provided Japanese and German corporate systems with the incentives to create company based skill formation and employment systems. In order to close the technology gap, companies in latecomer nations had to train employees. They could not wait for the market to provide them with the skills required by new industrial technologies. At the same time, the catch-up position created the growth environment in which relational commitments could be fulfilled.

Sectoral employment and income per head data indicate that Germany was about 30 to 50 years ahead of Japan (Waldenberger 1998: 403–404). This means that the German corporate system lost the growth potential and with it its ability to sustain company based training and employment systems earlier than Japan. Seen under the longer historical perspective, Japan might by now have reached the position the German corporate system confronted in the 1970s. The crucial point would then not be how to preserve the stakeholder approach of management, but how to move to a more market based system of corporate governance.

7.3.3 Capital markets in Germany: The age of shareholders?

Will pressure from globalised capital markets force management in Japan and Germany to further defer to shareholder interests? Empirically, the following developments are of relevance: (1) the spread of shareholder-value concepts of management, (2) the decline of banking and the growth of secondary markets for stock and debt, (3) growing efforts of companies in the field of investor relations, (4) the rise of a shareholder-culture among small private investors, (5) the use of market-based management incentive systems such as stock-options for managers and high-level employees. Let us first look at the German case.

The concept of "shareholder value" has become quite popular in Germany (Hilpert et al. 1999: 16). Restructuring strategies of large traditional German companies, for example Siemens or Hoechst, suggest that this is more than just part of a new rhetoric. Also, large companies have become less and less dependent on bank credit. Instead they rely on in-house funds and capital markets. As a consequence, investor relations activities by large German companies started to be systematically pursued since the mid 1980s (Günther and Otterbein 1996). In the 1990s, this trend became further supported by a rising interest of private households to invest their savings in securities (Monopolkommission 1998). Recently, companies are experimenting with stock-option schemes for top managers (Bernhardt and Witt 1997).

However, despite these changes and despite the well developed infrastructure of German stock exchanges, the number of listed companies in Germany is comparatively low, ownership of listed stock is still highly concentrated and stable, and high volume turn-over of stock is limited to a few publicly held companies (Schmidt et al. 1997). I am not aware that the new listings at the Neue Markt, the German version of Nasdaq, have US like patterns of diversified ownership. How is this reluctance of German companies, to move away from "old" structures of ownership control to be interpreted?

First of all, it should be noted that concentrated and stable ownership is a necessary, but not a sufficient condition for relationship based systems of corporate governance. If a large portion of stock is traded in the market, stable and influential owners can use the advantage of market evaluation without giving up effective control. Of course, they forgo the benefits of diversification. So there must also be an advantage for sticking to the old pattern of ownership. Three reasons are probably relevant.

Firstly, many shareholdings are kept within the corporate sector. They have a market value, which is far above the book value. Selling them would result in extra-ordinary profits. These would be highly taxed. Therefore, not selling preserves value. This argument will, however, become irrelevant if the presently planned tax reform of the German government should take effect. One point of the reform is to free income gains from the sales of shares from taxation.

Secondly, influential owners might be necessary to balance out the influence of the employment side, which is guaranteed by the German co-determination law. German co-determination law gives employees a representation in the supervisory board. Without a strong board representation of owner-interests, the employee side might one-sidedly control management.

Thirdly, dispersed ownership of stock, which is the rule in the US, requires that managers of large companies built-up a reputation in the investment community for serving ownership interests. This reputation substitutes the personal trust relationship managers can entertain with stable and influential groups of owners. To build up a reputation requires that manager careers are visible to the investor community. The prevalence of in-house recruiting of management positions (Sato 1998) obstructs the market visibility of management careers. Germany will need to develop its market for top managers in order for the market reputation mechanism to function.

7.3.4 The Japanese task: Developing external markets for skilled labour

Japanese companies, while experiencing the same changes in the capital market environment, still confront a different labour market situation. Top management in Japan, as well as representatives of the Japanese industrial community – apart maybe from the international division of Keidanren and Nikkeiren – proclaim that concepts of shareholder-value maximization are not applicable and not preferable in the Japanese context. However, the present crisis forces Japan in many industries to move to a market-based system of corporate governance. The reason is simply that the mid-term growth potential of the Japanese economy is too low for reconciling both employee and capital interests. Japanese employees, present and prospective, have already lost confidence in the ability of firms to keep up their commitment to employment stability. The crucial question is: how swiftly can Japan develop an external market for skilled labour to allow for the necessary structural adjustment of labour and capital?

Economists know little about how markets develop. Most of economics is based on the assumption that markets already exist. It is therefore hard to speculate how fast markets for qualified labour services can develop. All one can do is to point out various channels of influence that support their development.

Undoing artificial mobility barriers: Seniority-based pay- and promotion-schemes as well as company centred pensions have long obstructed the mobility of labour. As they represent artificial barriers, they could most easily be undone. There are attempts undertaken in this direction. For example, the age factor in wage payments has steadily been reduced (Waldenberger

1997: 12–15). Especially larger firms are experimenting with new performance based wage schemes and try to introduce more flexible employment schemes (Dirks 1997). Further incentives for mobility result from new labour market policies. Employment policies tended to subsidise existing employment within companies in recessions. The focus here is shifting to instruments that support labour mobility (OECD 1999: 205).

Developing a market infrastructure: Deregulation has widened the scope for agencies offering services in the field of recruitment and job search (OECD 1999: 207). With rising unemployment, their business will further grow and contribute to the development of external labour markets.

Developing standardized skill-formation systems: The underdevelopment of external labour markets is directly related to the fact that human capital is firm specific. One way to lower the importance of asset specificity is to offer more outside facilities and programmes of skill formation. This requires a redefinition of the role educational institutions, especially universities, play with regard to skill formation. Japanese universities are presently under pressure to develop new fields of business, as the number of students will, for demographic reasons, predictably decline. They will thus be ready to respond to new demands. However, respective strategies will need to be coordinated with the business community, and such coordination will take time.

It is to be expected that the development of external labour markets will proceed, but that it will take time. Changes in professions, where the requirements of standardization can more easily be met are already observable (Demes 1998: 156–159). The transformations will certainly not occur at once. As companies reduce the number of core employees and show less willingness to bear the costs of human capital investment, the proportion of more flexible employment patterns will grow, also among the more qualified groups of employees.

7.4 CONCLUSION

The German and Japanese relational systems of corporate governance are products of a successful catch-up era both economies enjoyed as late-developers. The overall economic growth potential made investment in relational contracts both necessary and sustainable. Thus, this mode of governance became characteristic for the national economy as a whole. Given the present stage of economic development, the necessity of restructuring in many old industries and the reduced growth expectations for the economy as a whole, relational governance will no longer be supportable on a great scale. As a national characteristic it will lose its importance. But this does not mean that in prosperous new industries where the application of new technologies requires investment in firm specific skills, the option of relational governance will be precluded. It can easily be introduced. It is only on the *national* scale that it has lost its importance in Germany and that it will lose its predominance in Japan. As can be seen by the variety of legal forms of businesses and by the variety of financial instruments, companies can choose among a whole set of governance types. In Germany and Japan the traditional national bias of this set will shift from relational to market-based forms of governance. But this will widen and not narrow the choice of German and Japanese companies.

REFERENCES

Bernhardt, Wolfgang and Peter Witt, 'Stock Options und Shareholder Value', in *Zeitschrift für Betriebswirtschaft*, No. 67 (1997), pp. 85–101.

Blair, Magret, *Ownership and Control. Rethinking Corporate Governance for the Twenty-First Century.* Washington 1995.

Demes, Helmut, 'Arbeitsmarkt und Beschäftigung', in Deutsches Institut für Japanstudien (ed.), *Die Wirtschaft Japans. Strukturen zwischen Kontinuität und Wandel.* Berlin 1998, pp. 135–164.

Dirks, Daniel, 'Employment Trends in Japanese Firms', in Economic Section German Institute of Japanese Studies (ed.), *The Japanese Employment System in Transition. Five Perspectives.* Tokyo 1997, pp. 35–53.

Günther, Thomas and Simone Otterbein, 'Die Gestaltung der Investor Relations am Beispiel führender deutscher Aktiengesellschaften', in *Zeitschrift für Betriebwirtschaft*, No. 66 (1996), pp. 389–417.

Hilpert, Hanns Günther, Helmut Laumer, Silvia Martsch and Franz Waldenberger, 'Wandel der Unternehmenskultur in Deutschland und Japan im Zeitalter der Globalisierung', in *Japan Analysen Prognosen*, No. 152/153, 1999, pp. 1–50.

Keizai Kikaku Chô, *Keizai hakusho* [White paper on the economy]. Tokyo 1999.

Milgrom, Paul and John Roberts, *Economics, Organization and Management.* Englewood Cliffs. Prentice Hall 1992.

Miller, Merton H., 'Is American Corporate Governance Fatally Flawed?', in Donald H. Chew (ed.), *Studies in International Corporate Finance and Governance Systems. A Comparison of the U.S., Japan, and Europe.* New York 1997, pp. 38–45.

Monopolkommission, *Ordnungspolitische Leitlinien für ein funktionsfähiges Finanzsystem. Sondergutachten 26.* Baden-Baden 1998.

Nihon Rôdô Kenkyû Kikô, *Rôdô hakusho* [White paper on labour]. Tokyo 1999.

OECD, *OECD Economic Surveys*, Germany 1995. Paris 1995.

OECD, *OECD Economic Surveys*, Japan 1996. Paris 1996.

OECD, 'Special Feature: Shareholder Value and the Market in Corporate Control in OECD Countries', in *Financial Market Trends*, No. 69 (1998), pp. 15–37.

OECD, *OECD Employment Outlook 1997.* Paris 1997.

OECD: OECD *Economic Surveys* Japan 1999. Paris 1999.

Porter, Michael E., 'Capital Choices: Changing the Way America Invests in Industry', in Donald H. Chew (ed.), *Studies in International Corporate Finance and Governance Systems. A Comparison of the U.S., Japan, and Europe.* New York 1997, pp. 5–17.

Roe, Mark J., *Strong Managers, Weak Owners. The Political Roots of American Corporate Finance.* Princeton 1994.

Sato, Hiroki, 'Career Formation and Development of White-Collar Workers' Individual Capabilities: An International Comparison of Japan, Germany, and the United States', in The Japan Institute of Labour (ed.), *Human Resource Development of Professional and Managerial Workers in Industry: An International Comparison* (= JIL Report Series No. 7). Tokyo 1998, pp. 14–30.

Schmidt, Harmut, Jochen Drukarczyk, Dirk Honold, Stefan Prigge, Andreas Schüler and Gönke Tetens, *Corporate Governance in Germany*. Baden-Baden 1997.

Waldenberger, Franz, 'The Aging Society. A Structural Challenge for the Japanese Employment System', in Economic Section German Institute of Japanese Studies (ed.), *The Japanese Employment System in Transition. Five Perspectives*. Tokyo 1997, pp. 5–17.

Waldenberger, Franz, 'Japan. Das Erfolgssyndrom als Krisenursache', in *Internationale Politik und Gesellschaft* (1998), pp. 403–412.

Waldenberger, Franz, *Organisation und Evolution arbeitsteiliger Systeme. Erkenntnisse aus der japanischen Wirtschaftsentwicklung*. München 1999.

Yoshimori, Masaru, 'Whose Company Is It? The Concept of the Corporation in Japan and the West', in Long Range Planning, No. 28 (1995), pp. 33–44.

Section C:

The Impact on the Economy: What Must Change, What Can Stay?

8

THE JAPANESE FIRMS' PURCHASING SYSTEM: STRATEGIC AND STRUCTURAL CHANGES OF THE 80s AND 90s

Yveline Lecler

8.1 INTRODUCTION

Today, globalisation of firms appears to be the main factor of change in the purchasing strategies. The liberalisation of Asian countries enhancing regulations to attract Foreign Direct Investment, the reinforcement of local content policies and the pace of growth in this area until the financial crisis of 1997, are elements which contributed to the increase in relocation of firms and thus to the globalisation of the purchasing networks.

But, observing the evolution during the 80s, leads us to think that globalisation cannot be held responsible for all the changes that occurred in the relationships between the Japanese large customers firms and their suppliers/subcontractors. The labour force shortage of the 80s, the commercial frictions with the US and Europe, the rise of the yen after 1985, and the recession in Japan in the 1990s are other elements, which challenged some foundations of the organisation inherited from a more or less remote past. As a matter of fact, those elements were not without any relation with the globalisation process, the necessity of which they tend to reinforce.

Facing new constraints in Japan and abroad, Japanese firms began to reconsider their purchasing strategies in the 80s and 90s tending to adapt to the necessity of cutting costs and to the globalised production. The changes are not easy to summarise from a general point of view, however. A new paradigm is sought through experiments that differ from firm to firm, from industry to industry. Some changes were already initiated in the 80s, some others began more recently. Taken separately, these changes may appear as having few effects in terms of structural transformations. But, whatever they are, firms' new experiments are cumulative and the observation leads us to think that much broader changes will finally occur. The present period appears as a transition one. The following points will try to explain what is at stake as far as the purchasing system and the buyers/suppliers relations are concerned through statistical surveys and branch or case studies.

The most interesting survey for our purpose is an exhaustive survey on subcontracting and division of labour in Japan. This survey occurs only every 5 years and is broadly referred to in the White Paper on SMEs. The last one was conducted in November/December 1995. Some of the data used are not up to date and do not take the Asian crisis impact into account. This is however not very important as the main stream of structural evolution took place in the late 80s in the electric/electronic appliances industry and in the mid-90s in the car industry that we are taking as sample branches. The Asian crisis does not seem to constitute a strategic turning point in this regard. The new strategies were already implemented before and the crisis direct impact behaves more as an accelerator of previous trends than as a new factor of transformation.

Of course, the repercussions of the Asian crisis in Japan, and the measures taken by firms and by the government, could play a part for further restructuring. For example the present situation in Japan leading to an increase in mergers and acquisition, not only between Japanese firms but also between Japanese and foreign firms could generate new converging behaviours.

Extrapolation of the present trends mainly in the car industry which is the more investigated by the author,[1] will give an image of what could happen in the coming years, and on the converging process of the purchasing system of Japanese and Western firms.

8.2 THE INVESTMENTS ABROAD AND THE CHANGES IN THE DIVISION OF LABOUR

In the 80s and 90s, production by Japanese firms abroad drastically increased along with the growth of Foreign Direct Investments (FDI) both to advanced economies and to Asian countries.

8.2.1 The FDI in advanced economies: an adjustment strategy

In the 80s, Japan had to cope with pressures linked to commercial frictions, notably from the US, and with the re-appreciation of the yen at

---

[1] The automotive industry, whose product is quite complex, is also the industry that has the more formalised and representative purchasing system.

177

the Plaza G5 meeting. As a consequence, reflecting the Japanese big firms' adjustment strategies, the dynamics of investments abroad, especially in advanced economies was strengthened, including investments from suppliers, both large and smaller firms.

In the manufacturing industry, the amount invested in North America rose from 398 millions US$ in 1980 to 9.586 millions US$ in 1989. In number of cases too, North America received 590 new Japanese establishments in 1988 compared to only 197 in 1980 (Maruyama 1997: 39). The USA, followed by some European countries, are indeed taking more and more measures to compel the big Japanese manufacturers established abroad (the transplants) to increase their supply in parts and components from the local suppliers. In a context of expensive yen, such measures drove the numerous suppliers/subcontractors to invest abroad, whether it be further to a request from their customer unsatisfied by the quality, the delivery times, etc. of the American/European suppliers, or further to a decision of the Japanese suppliers themselves for whom the decrease in the orders (to be exported from Japan) would endanger their survival.

8.2.2 The FDI in Asian countries: cost-cutting and market strategies

If North America is the main direction of Japanese FDI in the 80s, cases of investments in Asian countries (mainly in the Asian NIEs), also increased drastically: 936 in 1988 compared to 321 in 1980. This reflects the necessity to cope with the rising cost of production in Japan due to the increasing yen in a context where the labour shortage is pushing wages up and makes it difficult especially for SMEs to find workers.

But in the first half of the 90s, the situation appears to be quite different. Japanese firms are redirecting their FDI to Asian countries, mainly ASEAN and Continental China. This is true whatever the size of the firms. But the predominance of Asia appears particularly strong for SMEs: 64.7% of investment cases in 1989, 91.6% in 1995 and still 64.9% in 1997. The shift is clearly favouring China from 1993 to 1995.

The main reasons for redirecting FDI are manifold:

- The fast growing markets offering significant potential prospects for the future;
- The further increase in the yen currency, and especially the low level reached by the dollar at that time (under 100 yens for a dollar) making it too expensive to produce in Japan;
- The loss in competitiveness, making in the 90s price becoming more important than quality again, with 39.4% of customers giving such an answer when asked about their priority for purchasing parts (chushokigyo hakusho 1996: 224);

178

* The regulations by Asian countries pushing firms to implement a strategy of exports substitution by purchasing as many parts as possible locally.

These reasons are often acting together because shifting production to ASEAN market for example is a means to catch the new market potentiality, to cope with local regulations in terms of local content, while cutting production costs thanks to cheap labour forces.

In the survey on firms' globalisation conducted in December 1995, suppliers and subcontractors were asked about what they intended to do depending on the yen fluctuation. It appears that the value of the yen in the middle of the 90s was the main factor for SMEs especially to deepen the relocation of activities even though few firms were thinking to withdraw with a decreasing yen (Table 10).

Table 10 Relocation strategies for subcontracting SMEs depending on the yen value

If 1 US dollar =	80 yens	100 yens	120 yens
Increase of production abroad	70.2	4.3	20.9
No change in present volume of production abroad	28.8	54.5	61.9
Increase the production in Japan	0.9	1.2	17.2

Sources: Chushokigyo hakusho 1996:221.

For small as well as for big suppliers/subcontractors, with a dollar at 100 yen, increasing production abroad is first of all a means to cut cost through cheap labour (74% of both firms category). Secondly it is the occasion to benefit from market potentiality (50% and 64% respectively). The loss in competitiveness if exporting from Japan is more important for big suppliers (44%) than for SMEs (37.7%) while cutting cost through purchasing raw material locally is a more frequent reason for SMEs (43.2%) than for big suppliers (35%). The request of the customer to relocate activities comes far behind with only 19% of big suppliers and 15.1% of smaller ones giving it (chushokigyo hakusho 1996: 221).

Looking at the markets where products are sold is another indicator of the investment motivation. It appears that Japanese big firms are re-importing less (21.4%) of their Asian production on Japanese market than SMEs do (32%) but are exporting more outside Japan: 39% and 21.9% respectively (chûshôkigyô hakusho 1999: 401).

This strongly depends on industries though. While the car industry sells the major part of its production on local markets, electric/electronic appliances industries focus much more on exports.

Whatever the motivation is, investing abroad implies for firms to adapt to national labour standards, to local industrial institutions, etc. It provides firms with an opportunity to test outside Japan the adaptability of some

Japanese principles of management of the customers/suppliers relations, and to learn how to work in a different social context.

8.2.3 The international division of labour revisited: The case of electric/electronic appliances industry

In the case of electric/electronic appliances industry, relocation of activities began rather early if compared with car industry. Already in the 70s, after the Nixon shock ending the fixed currency system of 360 yen for a dollar, some companies decided to relocate labour intensive production to cheap labour countries to cut production cost and stay competitive. For example, Sharp opened its first foreign plants in Korea in 1973 and the second one in Malaysia in 1974. These plants only aimed at exporting products to the US and Europe.

At the end of the 70s and during the 80s, Japan had to cope with commercial frictions with advanced economies and firms starting to invest in the US and Europe. The strategy was of course to secure market by substituting local production for exports. In the case of Sharp for example, half of the products sold in Europe were produced in Europe and the other half was exported from Asian countries in the early 80s. Japanese firms of this sector implemented two different FDI strategies which coexisted at least until the mid-80s: plants in advanced economies were dedicated to local markets while plants in Asian countries, whether NIEs or ASEAN, were dedicated to exports.

After the mid-80s, these two strategies became less differentiated. The economic growth in Asian countries, NIEs first then ASEAN, making it possible to sell product on these markets too (Audio, TV, white goods), production volume increased and new plants were opened both for exports and for local demand. The re-appreciation of the yen after the Plaza agreement and its further increase contributed to the relocation of ever more activities in cheap labour countries (ASEAN but also China). Production of some products were completely transferred to these countries and production stopped in Japan.

Firms structured their networks within the host country to achieve this goal. The idea was to purchase as much as possible in the country of location because of import taxes. When it was impossible components were procured from neighbour countries or from Japan. Raw material was for the biggest part coming from Japan because of quality problems.

For example, Sharp opened in 1993 a plant in China for the manufacturing of copying machines. The choice of China is related to incentives of the Chinese government, the possibility to procure components locally and the cheap labour force. The plant is selling 80% of its production to the US, 10% is exported to other foreign markets and the 10% remaining are sold on the Chinese market. Final assembly is made in China but parts are coming from Japan, Taiwan, Hong Kong and ASEAN countries, depending on their sophistication level. The organisation of the network is a 'process sharing type'.

Thus, local procurement is the common rule but the suppliers are mainly Japanese relocated firms, or local/Japanese joint venture. For example, on the 80% of local procurement that Sharp achieves in Malaysia for TV production, Japanese affiliated firms deliver around 60%. Sharp never gave any guarantee of orders to its suppliers, but they decided to follow. In the case of electric/electronic appliances industry, the production units being also dedicated to exports the production volume is high enough to make investment by suppliers profitable. For this reason firms of this sector suffered less of the Asian crisis than firms engaged in the car industry. Local procurement ratios are high, exports became cheaper because of fall in currencies. Even if local markets shrunk, the reduction of sales was compensated by exports' better competitiveness.

But suffering less than car industry does not mean that no changes are needed. In electric/electronic industry too, competition increased, and in the mid-90s lowering cost by further economy of scale is also at stake. Matsushita is an interesting example of change in the international division of labour. The firm originally developed a strategy to supply each market through local production creating 'mini-Matsushitas' in each country that offered a sufficient market in sales volume. This mini-Matsushita philosophy aimed at avoiding imports of components from other countries. It can be considered as a reproduction of the Japanese purchasing organisation in each country of location. In the mid-90s, Matsushita decided to change this organisation[2] and began to implement an organisation where each country is specialised in the production of one product to be exported to the other countries of the region. The mini-Matsushita constitutes an embarrassment to develop the new strategy and the evolution is therefore slow. But the firm has decided to act in this direction not only in Asian region but also in the US and Europe. In each region, a network co-ordinator unit or regional headquarter is charged with importing and exporting components and products for the whole network.

Sharp also thinks of such an organisation for the coming years. For the moment, in the ASEAN countries, the firm is producing in each country. For example, TVs are produced in Malaysia, in Thailand and in Indonesia. The firm recognises that it could achieve better economies of scale if producing the TV in one country only and exporting to the others tending to a 'product discrimination' type of organisation. The same can be said for video and so on.

But taxes are still high even between ASEAN countries and complementation scheme like AICO[3] is not suitable. First, only firms having 30% of

---

[2] Case studied by the author in September 1995.

[3] AICO scheme = Asian Industrial Co-operation Scheme. For detailed presentation see Guiheux/Lecler 2000, Legewie 1998.

local capital may use the AICO scheme. It is not the case in most of the Sharp plants. Second, the exchange reciprocity is a condition that Sharp cannot satisfy. But with the AFTA, the possibility is coming, so the firm is studying a reorganisation tending to a 'product discrimination' type of structuring (studied by the author in June 1999).

Whatever the structure of the networks, the international division of labour is rather advanced in the electric/electronic industry where relocation of firms in the Asian Region was drastic and concerned a whole range of products of which production completely disappeared in Japan, leading to a permanent restructuring of purchasing networks to cope with production shift abroad. Thus, in the electric/electronic appliances industries, it seems that the Japanese purchasing system has already achieved its transformation towards a globalised transactional system.

8.2.4 From a national to a regional/international oriented division of labour: The case of the car industry

In the car industry too, relocations of activities in advanced economies were mainly dedicated to secure markets because of commercial frictions. It also aimed to counter the high yen currency after the Plaza agreement, making it more profitable to produce in the US or in Europe than to export from Japan. On these markets, the strategy is quite similar to the electric/electronic appliance industry described above.

However if considering the ASEAN countries' case, the situation is quite different in both industries.

The Japanese carmakers invested the region quite early to supply local market. The first Toyota plant was opened in 1965. The investment aimed at conquering new market in Japan's neighbourhood. Japanese carmakers were for a long time the only ones to have established operation in the region for CKD[4] vehicles. During the 1970s, as the ASEAN countries began to adopt policies that favoured localisation, Japanese parts makers also began to set up operations in the region.

Because they were protected as "national" carmakers, and because the only customers in the local market came from the richest socio-economic classes, carmakers were able to charge high prices for the vehicles they offered. Parts makers also could deliver components at higher price than in Japan. Thus, despite the small size of markets, and the high production costs, the ASEAN located plants were profitable.

This strategy came to an end in the 90s, for several reasons acting simultaneously:

---

[4]CKD = Completely Knock Down.

- The growth potential of the market attracted new competitors, who challenged the Japanese domination;

- The economic growth and the progressive constitution of a middle class in these countries led to a demand for less expensive vehicles and especially Korean carmakers who entered the region seemed to be able to challenge the Japanese market share;

- Purchasing of parts and components from Japan which were still very important in volume became much more expensive due to the high yen, leading to an increase in production cost.

Carmakers had to implement a new strategy aiming at cutting cost by increasing local procurements[5] and achieving economies of scale by concentrating orders. Parts makers had to follow in the same direction.

Increasing local procurements and reducing imports from Japan are not so easy because the technological level of ASEAN countries is still low and capability building is a long lasting process. A new wave of penetration by Japanese suppliers, on the request of their buyers or because of new opportunities of markets, took place in the mid-90s.

Achieving economy of scale is not easy too. ASEAN markets for vehicles were fast growing in the 90s and cumulative annual sales volumes would have justified mass production. However, strongly fragmented, they still remain limited in size. Because of consumer attitudes or because of governmental policies aimed at the development of a local industry, each country market differs from the others. Economies of scale are quite difficult to achieve in such a context. For parts makers, the situation is the same, production volume being quite limited (for more details see Guiheux, Lecler 2000).

Therefore, Japanese firms that oriented production to local markets could no longer reproduce an organisation of purchasing like in Japan. It was quite impossible for suppliers to follow the affiliated carmaker in Thailand or Indonesia just to supply him. Opening a production unit could not be profitable without supplying several carmakers in the region. The borders of industrial keiretsu had to be crossed to make local production possible at a reasonable cost.

Carmakers experienced joint production and joint procurement from parts makers belonging to different keiretsu. Even Toyota and Nissan, never purchasing parts from the same suppliers in Japan, started to experiment joint supply in the ASEAN region. Parts makers had the opportunity to experiment new relations with customers they were not supplying in Japan and also concluded agreements for joint production with out-keiretsu parts makers. This, tending to networks restructuring, also constituted learning to change relations in Japan as will be discussed later.

---

[5]Local content ratios policies also acted in that direction.

This trend is reinforced by the Asian crisis that had a much bigger impact on firms of car industry than it had for the electric/electronic appliance one. Production was exclusively dedicated to local markets and sales shrinkage could not be easily compensated by exports. Believing in market recovery after the crisis though, carmakers and big suppliers did not withdraw. To survive they tend to concentrate production in ASEAN units as much as possible to keep them in activity. They shifted more production from Japan and started exports from ASEAN production bases, mainly re-importation of parts to Japan. This means that orders reduction to suppliers in Japan could be reinforced further. It also means that concentration of orders or production in one plant or in one country to achieve economy of scale in a context of even smaller markets is still more urgent than before.

The ASEAN complementation scheme, BBC,[6] implemented in 1988 and AICO which is also opened to suppliers, implemented in 1996 are addressing the problem of market fragmentation, favouring exchanges of parts within ASEAN countries with reduced taxes. This scheme however does not seem to be the main factor why an Asian division of labour finally progressed in the region. From the moment where cost became the core element to secure market domination in the region, firms tending to achieve economy of scale by purchasing parts locally started to implement an Asian division of labour, leading to a specialisation of each country in one or several type of components.[7] For example, Denso has production units in each of ASEAN 4 countries. Until now, each unit is assembling the whole range of products (starter, alternators, condensers) for the local market needs. This is related to the local regulations, but after applying to AICO and with the perspective of trade liberalisation under WTO, Denso is now changing its organisation towards a specialisation by country and by products. So starters and alternators would only be produced in Thailand while condensers would only be made in Indonesia and so on. In such a dynamics, parts procurements will also be concentrated to a further extend in the country having the best advantage to produce it, leading to a 'product discrimination' type of structuring. Carmakers too are acting in the same direction. For the moment they are producing each model in all the countries where a local demand exists. Without withdrawing from any country, they are aiming at reorganising their assembling units to produce in each country the model which market is the larger (Toyota Kijiang in Indonesia, Hilux in Thailand, etc.). Other markets are supplied through exports from this centralised production unit. So the 'process sharing type' of organisation, that was relevant to the car industry, is being mixed with a 'product discrimination' type of structuring the new division of labour.

[6]Brand to Brand Complementation Scheme, on this point, see Guiheux G./Lecler Y. 2000 or Legewie 1998.
[7]For more details on this matter, see Lecler 1999 and Guiheux/Lecler 2000.

8.3 THE SITUATION OF SUPPLIERS/SUBCONTRACTORS IN JAPAN

Between 85 and 95, all this evolution led most of the suppliers/sub-contractors in Japan to receive orders for more sophisticated products in terms of quality and precision degree (66.5% of firms), with a request for shorter delivery time (59.8%) and lower prices (64.1%) (chushokigyo hakusho 1996: 193). But changes also affected the volume of orders, which in turn implied further changes in the buyer/suppliers relation, as we shall try to illustrate through branch surveys.

8.3.1 Changes in the volume of orders received by suppliers in Japan

Until the late 70s, around half of Japanese parent firms of the manufacturing industries were used to order one component reference to a single firm (mono-sourcing), while the other half preferred reducing risk by ordering to several firms (multi-sourcing). The need for reducing cost by economies of scale led to a concentration of orders to a single firm, making mono-sourcing become the rule for around 70% of firms in the 90s.

Table 11 Buyers' reasons for orders decrease and measures to adapt to sales reduction (in % of firms, November 1995)

Reasons for reduction of orders	manuf. ind.	electronic	transport
sales reduction	69.1	53.5	70.3
production reintegration by buyer	31.3	32.6	37.8
components standardisation/ commonalisation	22.2	41.9	40.5
buyer relocation abroad	21.9	58.1	35.1
re-importation's from abroad	16.3	37.2	16.2
Measures to be taken in coming years (after 95)			
economy of labour cost	61.1	66.1	51.3
reduction in investments	42.2	33.9	53.8
relocation of activity abroad	28.7	51.2	30.8
further components standardisation	17.1	20.7	35.9

Sources: Chushokigyo hakusho, 1996:184.

Between 1985 and 1995, 70% of buyers are admitting they reduced their orders to suppliers/subcontractors in Japan. The reduction of their own sales is the main reasons in the case of transportation industry while relocation abroad is the main reason for electronic industries. Standardisation or communalisation of components[8] is also an important factor for both industries making orders more concentrated to a small number of supplying firms (Table 11). Looking at the measures buyers intend to implement (in 1995) to better cope with sales reduction, suggests that the cut of orders to suppliers/subcontractors in Japan will deepen further. A survey of the MITI shows that compared with 1995, the 1998 turnover of manufacturing Japanese firms is negative whatever the firms' size or categories, but the extent of decrease is broader for subcontracting firms than it is for both subsidiaries of big firms or independent firms (table 12).

Table 12 Evolution of firms' turnover between 1995 and 1998

	SMEs	Big firms
Independent firms	- 3.0	- 2.1
Subcontracting firms	- 4.1	- 3.5
Subsidiaries	- 2.2	- 1.0

Source: Chushokigyo hakusho 1999:157.

N.B.: Evolution of turnover = 1998 turnover - 1995 turnover / 1995 turnover x 100 (%).
Independent firms are firms that are neither subsidiaries nor subcontracting. Subsidiaries are firms whose capital is controlled at more than 50% by outsider. Number of subcontracting firms also includes subsidiaries, which are mainly subcontracting their products while subsidiaries also include subcontracting firms.

But this data does not give a comprehensive picture of what is really at stake as far as the purchasing system is concerned. Case studies show that both reduction and concentration of orders are still in progress. This contrasted move is expected to continue further along with the evolution of criteria for selecting suppliers.

8.3.2 The need for higher capabilities

Maintaining or even increasing one's markets share meant in the 1980s being able to supply new and varied products before the competitors. Consequently the design lead-time of those products had to be shortened as much as could be while their prices had to be kept down to remain affordable to the consumers. Design hence became the basic element of the firms' competitiveness and it was in that field that productivity gains were sought after by revising the former practices and introducing the concurrent engineering way of designing (Lecler/ Perrin/Villeval 1999). To achieve these goals and especially to reduce the launching delay of the new products

[8]Using the same component in several product models to achieve economy of scale and to cut the designing cost.

186

on the market, buyers tended to rely more and more heavily on their suppliers for the design of the parts and components the latter had to produce previously according to given plans or specifications.

The whole set of those changes tended on the one hand to alter the nature of the relations between the customer and the suppliers and on the other hand to increase the gap between suppliers themselves. To enter this new way, not only did the suppliers have to win a higher technological control but they also had to gain organisational and managerial skills of a new kind. As Table 13 suggests, the measures taken often simultaneously by suppliers aimed at securing their orders through increasing the product value-added and so on, but they also aimed at finding new buyers, new markets and new sales channels, finally at developing products outside any subcontracting relation. In fact the share of SMEs engaged in subcontracting activities for the major part of their turnover which permanently increased in the 70s and 80s, is declining since the late 80s.

All of the suppliers/subcontractors do not have the strength or the means to embark on such a dynamics; consequently numerous shifts occurred within the hierarchy of the division of labour.

Table 13 Adaptation measures taken by suppliers/subcontractors
(in firms %, 1995)

	SMEs	Big firms
Increase value-added of products	50.3	51.4
Develop new products	46.1	65.5
Search new markets or new sales channels	36.8	40.5
Increase precision of technologies	35.2	25.9
Increase production rationalisation and economy of labour	27.4	35.0
Diversify production to enter new sector	26.5	25.0
Specialising in small lot production	25.2	13.2
Amelioration of labour force training	18.7	14.1
Reduction of delivery time	11.0	10.0
Increase the qualified technological level	9.7	12.7
Change of buyer	7.7	3.6

Sources: Chushokigyo hakusho 1996:234.

The percentage of buyers considering that the long-term relationship they entertained with their suppliers is a reason for continuing to put orders to them got smaller since the late 70s; it still reaches 21.6% in 1985. In 1995 however, this number dropped to 7.1% with a trend to further drop (3.5% for the future) (*chushokigyo hakusho* 1996: 195).

The criteria that are taking importance in terms of supplier selection may be grouped in two categories taken simultaneously into account by buyers: cost-cutting and capabilities increase. As far as capabilities are concerned, the product quality is still important but capabilities in specialised technologies and R and D or design are becoming the main factors for receiving orders, confirming the shift towards more design activities delegated to suppliers that we mentioned above. These selection criteria already took more importance in the 80s, but the difference in the 90s is that they absolutely have to be achieved with a reduction in production cost.

The evolution of the selection criteria tends to confirm that dependence in terms of turnover with the main buyer should be declining. The numbers of Table 14 effectively show that it is diminishing a little bit, but also that it is remaining still high if compared with Western standards. More recent data would of course be interesting, as they would probably show that the trend is deepening. The survey on structure and management of firms, conducted by the SMEs agency in 1998, shows that 37% of sample firms think their dependence towards their main customers is going to decline in the coming years (*chushokigyo hakusho* 1999: 157).

At a more empirical level it appears that some suppliers are getting more autonomous from their main buyer, while some others are on the contrary getting more dependent because of orders concentration. Some indicators are going in the direction of an extinction (or at least a diminution) of the notion of main customer while others are suggesting there is no clear evidence. This contrasted situation is hidden at average statistics level. The impact of changes in the division of labour in the electric/electronic appliances industry and in the car industry will provide a more comprehensive picture of what is going on in this regard.

Table 14 Evolution of dependence towards main buyer (manufacturing industry average)

Turnover share with the main customer	1985	1990	1995
Less than 30%	9.6	8.6	11.9
30 to 60%	10.1	12.5	17.2
60 to 90%	20.2	24.3	23.0
more than 90%	60.0	54.7	47.9

Sources: Chushokigyo hakusho 1996, p.190.

8.3.3 The changes in the electric/electronic appliances industry in Japan

The relocation of activities abroad had of course repercussions on suppliers in Japan. For example, in the case of the television and video industry, the near totality of the production has gone abroad, especially to the ASEAN countries. The suppliers/subcontractors that once participated in the production process of those goods have consequently lost the corresponding orders. However their main customers have generally been able to give them other goods to produce. For instance, the firms that we visited in 1994 did not register a decrease in orders from their main parent-firm. But they had radically altered their production activities over the past 5 years whatever their size and position within the hierarchy. They had evolved from the production of parts and components for TV sets and videos, to the production of parts and components or the assembly for computers and word processors. In general, although not systematically,[9] the main customer had remained the same as in the past (but the dependence in terms of turnover ration was lower): the latter having altered its production, the supplier had merely followed the change. This shift from one product range to another more sophisticated one gave the opportunity to many suppliers/subcontractors to adapt the new situation. It means however they had to cope with new technologies progressively. Considering the present main items produced in Japan to the 60s ones, give a good idea of the technological gap that firms had to cope with over time. In the 60s, production focused on black and white TV, refrigerators, and washing machine. In the 70s, it was colour TV, stereo sets, and electronic lenses. In the 80s, firms had to turn to air conditioning, VTR, CD players. In the 90s they are concerned with computers and Internet, mobile phone and video games. The 2000-decade should be focusing on DVD, mobile phone of new generation (PDA) and STB computers. Some suppliers, even small ones, introduced very sophisticated automated insertion machines for example and could achieve such an evolution, but suppliers/subcontractors that could not and were left behind are not scarce too. With the acceleration of production transfer to ASEAN countries and China and with the crisis in Japan, making consumption stagnant, firms registering a reduction in order are increasing. In fact, the situation is strongly depending on customers' firms. Some who engaged more and early enough in new products are rather wealthy and so are the suppliers. Others that did not, have difficulties and suppliers had to find new buyers.

Supplying networks in the electric/electronic appliance industry never were as formalised and hierarchical (with several suppliers' ranks) as it is in the car industry, where product complexity is much higher. Big suppliers that could achieve a large increase in capabilities are now supplying Japanese and Western firms and are through this learning of cross-cultural management becoming rather autonomous from any customer. The notion of main customer does not seem to be relevant anymore, at least as far as first rank suppliers are considered.

---

[9] In one of the cases studied, given the decrease in his main principal's orders, the supplier had tried to diversify and turn toward technologically close but more sophisticated products, such as computers hard disk assembly. His attempt to diversify his buyers then drove him to new buyers and little by little this led the main principal to change.

8.3.4 The changing relation between car and parts makers in Japan

In the car industry too relocating production abroad instead of exporting from Japan means reduction of production in Japan. As long as demand was growing in Japan, the impact was not too strong on suppliers units in Japan, but in the 90s when the demand and exports fell, over capacities appeared and the decrease in orders became more patent. Unlike in the electric/electronic appliance case, carmakers could not put orders for a new product range to their suppliers to compensate for the loss in orders of car components. Suppliers had to adapt by themselves. For the first rank suppliers, generally very large firms, designing their products (components, systems or functions), the 90s crisis and the carmakers globalisation acted more as a kind of incentive to go abroad and seek product innovations, rather than as a redistributing factor of the customers. At the other extreme in the pyramid, the small third- and fourth-rank subcontractors that do the undifferentiated tasks in small batches had the opportunity to reorient, as there will always be simple tasks to be done in the near vicinity of the customers (Takeishi/Fujimoto/Sei 1993). This is confirmed by the percentage of firms that withdraw onto small batch productions with express delivery. In other respects, as they are much less specialised, they can ensure their survival by getting out of the car industry. It is true that the subcontractors at the lower end of the pyramid are much more flexible; however there are also many small firms with old executives and no successors, who preferred stopping all production given the bad economic situation. The firms that disappeared – one might say by natural extinction – were not special cases.

The second-rank suppliers seem to be the more threatened by the crisis. Highly specialised, they cannot shift out of the car industry. They are the ones that suffer the most from the competition of the relocated or local firms directly supplying the foreign establishments of their Japanese customers. Most of them tended to move towards more value-added components or functions. They also tried to cut production costs to keep competitive on foreign markets. For them survival means to find new customers to compensate for losses of orders from their affiliated principal. But diversifying customers is not easy. Success stories exist but failure too, leading to changes in the positioning of firms and to a reshaping of the whole chain of purchasing (for more details see Guiheux/Lecler 2000).

But the decrease in orders is not the only consequence of the relocation of activities abroad. Even if no direct link can be established between the learning of new relations that we have quoted in the ASEAN, and the changes presently occurring in Japan, the reshaping of the purchasing chain is now taking place not only within the industrial keiretsu, but also on an inter-keiretsu basis.

Indeed, whereas the suppliers (whatever their size, etc.) belonging to the Toyota keiretsu could hardly supply Nissan and the reverse, those historic principles got more and more questioned. Obviously it was still not really easy in 1994, as the following case of a first-rank Nissan supplier shows.[10] Owing to its production cost superiority in comparison with the traditional Toyota suppliers, the firm had obtained orders from Toyota. As a consequence it had to build a production plant a few kilometres from its original site where the Toyota parts and components would be produced. It was still inconceivable for the executive managers to produce goods for both Nissan and Toyota in the same plant, although this did not prevent them from accepting the job, which they would not have been able to do a few years ago. This trend enlarged further and what was impossible before and still quite difficult in the first half of the 90s became slowly possible in Japan too.

The necessity to cut cost finally led carmakers to put orders to better performing suppliers whatever their original keiretsu was. Cases of production for both Toyota and Nissan became more frequent. Since mid-90s, the examples of parts-makers starting to deliver parts or components to carmakers at the top of another keiretsu are increasing in number (Table 15). The process is just beginning and the dependence towards the affiliated carmaker remains quite high. But the trend is engaged and seems to be irreversible. This is also confirmed by the evolution of a supplier's association membership of each Japanese carmaker. In the past, membership to the supplier's association of a carmaker was rather exclusive. Few parts makers only were members of two-car makers association. Today, 67 suppliers of Toyota are for example also members of the association of Nissan (Table 16).

The trend is now to multi-membership, attesting that customer diversification became a reality and that the notion of main customer is blurring through the network re-composition in Japan and outside Japan. A supplier's capabilities, innovation, competitiveness are emphasised more than long-term relations and so on like in the past. The Japanese purchasing system is not only facing strategic changes, but is now also experiencing a structural transformation.

8.4 THE INDUCED STRUCTURAL TRANSFORMATIONS OF THE JAPANESE PURCHASING SYSTEM

In both industries studied, the purchasing networks are being revised on a globalised basis. Even if conditions are different from one industry to the other, as we have seen, present situation leads to some converging structural changes. Wherever the need is coming from, the necessity to cut costs in both industries pushed firms to turn from a national division of labour to

---

[10]Case studied during the summer 1994 by the author.

Table 15 Example of customer's diversification by some major Japanese suppliers

Suppliers	Belonging Keiretsu	New customer	Nature of the relation
Futaba Corp & Co.	Toyota	Honda	Orders of presses by Honda since 1994. Then delivery of parts
Aisan Industries Co., Ltd	Toyota	Mitsubishi, Nissan	Delivery of regulators to Mitsubishi. In 1997, Asian was intending to reinforce its relations with Nissan to reduce its dependency to Toyota from 75% to 60%
Aisin Seiki Co., Ltd	Toyota	Nissan	Delivers braking components to Nissan since the Spring of 1996
Nippon Denso	Toyota	Nissan	Since 1996, delivers components (lock systems) to Nissan through Kansei, first rank supplier of Nissan
Koito Mfg Co.,Ltd	Toyota	Nissan	Delivers lights to the Nissan Primera
Tokai Rika Co.,Ltd	Toyota	Nissan	Delivers Nissan USA in gear handles for the AT and small parts
Nissan Koki	Nissan	Isuzu	Since 1995 delivers crankshafts for diesel engines
Kansei	Nissan	Honda, Isuzu Daewoo	Since 1994 delivers components to Daewoo, Honda, Isuzu plants in the US
Kansei	Nissan	Honda	Delivers meters for two wheels vehicles. Kansei intends to reduce the share of its sales to Nissan from 80 to 70%
Ichikoh Industries, Ltd	Nissan	Toyota	Delivers lights for the RAV4; Ichikoh has got the market by proposing prices 25% less than Koito, usual supplier of Toyota
Tsuchia Mfg Co., Ltd	Nissan	Toyota	Since 1996 delivering oil and gasoline filters to Toyota plants in GB
Daiichi Forging Co., Ltd	Fuji Heavy Industries	Other makers	Since 1995 delivers forged parts to all carmakers
Shigeru Industries Co., Ltd	Fuji Heavy Industries	Daihatsu	Delivers parts for mini-cars to Daihatsu since 1994
Sakamoto Industries Co., Ltd	Fuji Heavy Industries	Mitsubishi	Started to supply Mitsubishi in Japan in 1995 then also supplied US plants
Nishikawa Chemical Co., Ltd	Mazda	Mitsubishi	Supply parts to Mitsubishi since 1994. Intends to reduce the share of its turnover with Mazda from 95 to 80%

Sources: " Nihon no jidosha buhin sangyo ", (Fourin, 1997).

Table 16 Multi-membership to suppliers association

	Toyota	Nissan	Mitsubishi	Honda	Mazda	Isuzu	Daihatsu	Fuji Heavy Ind.	Total of firms
Toyota		67 27.3%	90 36.7%	82 33.5%	69 28.2%	84 34.3%	106 43.3%	56 22.9%	245
Nissan	67 34.7%		88 45.6%	94 48.7%	71 36.8%	89 46.1%	50 25.9%	84 43.5%	193
Mitsubishi	90 23.8%	88 23.3%		97 25.7%	93 24.6%	106 28%	89 23.5%	77 20.4%	378
Honda	82 24.6%	94 28.1%	97 29%		74 22.2%	87 26%	77 23.1%	78 23.4%	334
Mazda	69 36.1%	71 37.2%	93 48.7%	74 38.7%		76 39.8%	67 35.1%	66 34.6%	191
Isuzu	84 27.7%	89 29.4%	106 35%	87 28.7%	79 25.1%		66 21.8%	82 27.1%	303
Daihatsu	106 58.2%	50 27.5%	89 48.9%	77 42.3%	67 36.8%	66 36.3%		51 28%	182
Fuji Heavy Ind.	56 30.8%	84 46.2%	77 42.3%	78 42.9%	66 36.3%	82 45.1%	51 28%		182

Notes to the table: 1st number: number of suppliers of A (line) also belonging to the association of B (column); 2nd number: percentage that this numbers represents in the total of A association member firms.

Sources: Fourin, 1997, pp. 64-65.

an international division of labour centred on Asia. For several reasons, Japanese firms could not reproduce their purchasing system in the relocation countries. Even if they first tried to do it, regional conditions (increase of local content ratios, necessity to achieve economy of scale, etc.) forced them to progressively adapt their practices. Doing so they progressively turn away from the former relational principles that made the Japanese system consistent and efficient (Lecler 1993).

8.4.1 The Japanese purchasing system's former characteristics: The traditional principles

The Japanese purchasing system efficiency was rooted in the strong dependence towards one main customer. It is because the dependence was strong that the customer could transfer technology and information to its suppliers without fearing to lose the control of the whole production chain, without fearing that innovation could benefit competitors. It is thanks to this dependence that he could concentrate on the most strategic part of the production process, delegating all the intermediate process to suppliers. It is because of this large technology and information transfer implying a lot of human relations that the system could be considered as relational (Lecler 1993). The technology and information transfer constituted an investment that could not have been profitable for the customer without long-term relations. But the strong dependence was a guarantee that the suppliers will respect the rule of the game. Just as the relational investments were an incentive for the customer not to cut orders to the suppliers. Guarantee of orders, mutual interest in long-lasting relations, and numerous human interrelations created trust. Therefore, contractual arrangements were not very important and problems were generally solved through relational achievements. Also, the trust in long lasting relations (continuous transactions) was making possible for suppliers to dedicate their investment strategies to the customer needs, creating a broad synergy between them. This system was quite efficient until the late 80s, as long as growth could be sustained.

The system was so efficient that Western countries learned from Japanese transplants for example and tried to implement some of the elements in the 80s precisely. Adapting these elements to the national conditions, industrial partnership was born in Western countries, making the Western purchasing system more relational than in the past without integrating the notion of main customer for example (Lecler 1993).

8.4.2 The traditional principles challenged by customer diversification and capability increase

Japanese big customers being more global, they are reviewing their purchasing behaviour, including suppliers' selection criteria, and their division of labour. The repercussions on suppliers/subcontractors are many-fold, but as we have seen, the main problem for them is to secure orders. For the Japanese suppliers in Japan, the question is first of all to compensate the loss in volume of orders. For suppliers/subcontractors that relocate production abroad, the problem is to have enough orders to make the production unit profitable. In both cases, the orders from the main customer are not sufficient anymore to survive. Buyers' diversification is therefore on the agenda. Though customer diversification is not a new process for suppliers, the present dynamics is happening on a larger scale than ever. It is precisely because it happens on a large scale that it constitutes a new issue. The more the number of customers increases, and especially the more the rate of turnover realised through a single customer decreases, the weaker the dependence towards him is.

Furthermore, to secure orders, the suppliers have to undertake more value-added production to sustain competition from Asian countries. They have to move up in the production chain: imposing more design capabilities, R&D, etc. Technological improvement, knowledge accumulation (design, prototypes, etc.), learning how to work in different socio-economic contexts through relocation of production abroad, learning how to work with more diversified buyers, etc., all this is consolidating the dynamics of loosening the dependence towards the main customer. The suppliers who achieved such an evolution tend to become more autonomous from their main customer and from any customer in fact as they become increasingly efficient and globalised and take charge of more and more overall design activities for more and more complex products. In some cases, a technological dependence for the customer towards his suppliers may appear. This situation, experienced in Europe, is for Japan quite new and constitutes a reversal in the balance of power.

8.4.3 The structural implication of recent changes and the convergence issue

Let us come back to our findings on how the Japanese system is presently moving and compare the consequences with the traditional principles of the Japanese purchasing system we just introduced briefly.

Now, in Japan and abroad, suppliers are taking orders from several buyers. In car industry, cross-keiretsu orders are increasing not only abroad but in Japan too. The dependence towards the main customer is declining in the car industry and became quite loose in the electric/electronic industry. The suppliers had to increase their capabilities making technology and information transfer useless. On the contrary, for sophisticated components, buyers are now preferring suppliers that can make innovation or design proposal whatever their affiliated keiretsu is and even whatever their nationality is. For simple parts, they intend to benefit from market opportunity, turning to the supplier making the best offer. Suppliers for their part do not have any guarantee of orders anymore, they are asked to share the risks. They also intend to benefit from market opportunities, supplying all firms possible, whatever their nationality. In the car industry for example, as soon as GM and Ford announced the opening of plants in Thailand, located Japanese parts makers started preparing to supply these plants. They had already experienced working with GM or Ford in the US; they can do it in Thailand.

In such a context, the traditional Japanese system is shaking. To sum up, all the main characteristics of the system are blurring. The dependence is loosening, the technology and information transfer is not felt necessary anymore; the orders are not guaranteed anymore; why should the suppliers continue to dedicate their production process to the customer needs. But in that case, the synergy between a customer and his supplier will disappear too. The mutual trust-making contract will also become weaker. The risk for the customer to lose part of the control on the production chain will become higher. This could lead to re-integration of some strategic processes or production that were delegated to suppliers before.

If we consider the implications of these changes, comparing with the purchasing system of Western firms, especially of the firms that introduced industrial partnership in the 80s, it clearly appears that differences are getting smaller. Japanese firms still continue to consider transaction on a long lasting basis for sophisticated components. So do Western firms since they introduced partnership. Japanese firms are now putting orders to the best performing firm whatever its nationality or keiretsu is. Western firms are also doing so. Japanese firms' production is less integrated than Western firms'. In the 80s, Western firms disintegrated production a lot while Japanese firms seem to be integrating a little more. Japanese suppliers are taking their autonomy; they deliver products to several buyers with whom they entertain the same kind of relation. The Western suppliers who never referred to a main customer also do. Japanese suppliers now have to develop by themselves, to find buyers by themselves, to compete with other keiretsu suppliers or foreign firms for market share. Western suppliers always had to do so. In fact, in the 80s, Western firms introduced some relational practices of the Japanese system, giving some guarantee on the transaction duration to the suppliers to permit them to invest and modernise, introducing just in time or project management and concurrent engineering. They had to adapt their practices to introduce these new concepts or production principles making the system evolve to a more relational type than in the past. But they did not reproduce the Japanese organisational structure. Western workers are not hired directly from school; suppliers could become partners without making 60% of their turnover with a single customer, and so on.

196

8.5 CONCLUSION: FURTHER EVOLUTION FOR THE 2000s

Facing new constraints in the 90s led Japanese firms to introduce practices of Western firms or practices experienced in the transplants. This 'boomerang effect' led Japanese firm to eliminate some of the relational elements of its system, giving more weight to the transaction itself. While the Western purchasing system became more relational in the 80s, converging to some extent to the Japanese system, it is the Japanese purchasing system that is becoming more transactional in the 90s, converging to some extent to the Western one.

The increasing number of mergers and acquisitions that are taking place in Japan thanks to the easing of procedures through changes of corporate law since the Yamaichi failure, will bring Japanese and Western firms even closer. While the acquisition of Japanese firms by foreign ones in Japan was limited to 20–30 cases a year (2.5 % of the total in 1990) in the first half of the 90s, the number grew to 86 (12.2%) of the total in 1999. Japanese firms are also merging together to a larger extent than before: 429 cases in 1999, representing 60.7% of the total instead of 35.5% in 1990 (Etienne 1999). Most of these mergers concern the financial sector, but mergers of industrial firms are also on the agenda, and not only between firms in difficulties. For example, Bosch took control of Zexel, Delphi acquired 6% of Akebono assets. Two of the main suppliers of Nissan (Calsonic and Kansei) merged to better compete on the globalised market. The Alliance between Renault and Nissan, will probably results in more mergers or agreements involving former Nissan suppliers fearing that orders might be turned towards Renault suppliers.

Mergers are not the only present trend that could bring some new changes in the 2000s, for example in the car industry. Suppliers tend to specialise on their most performing components, progressively stopping production of less performing ones. They are also starting to concentrate their production in some units while closing other plants in Japan. For example, Akebono announced it would concentrate production of both drum braking and disk braking systems in the same unit in Saitama prefecture in the coming two years. Futaba is gathering the production of exhaust pipes in its Fukushima unit and will close its Nagoya plant in 2004 (Grasland 1999).

The impact of mergers in Japan, of unit concentration, is not yet measurable, but there is no doubt that further restructuring of purchasing networks are still to come at least in the car industry. Nowadays, the converging process is beyond doubt, but it is still too early to say how far it will go.

For example, the recovery process in the ASEAN and the lessons issued from the crisis could challenge the present convergence trend. The crisis showed how important the development of supporting industries in emerging countries was. If firms really want to increase their local procurement in the future, they will have to focus more than before on technology transfer. The past relational principles that disappeared or are disappearing in Japan could be activated again by Japanese suppliers to increase the technical capabilities of their local subcontractors/partners leading to an international networks structuring that would reproduce in Asian emerging countries part of the former Japanese organisation (Lecler 1999).

Analysing the changes in the firms' behaviour in terms of purchasing strategies in Japan and abroad have shown that Japanese and Western systems were presently converging. Whether these changes proceed in a converging direction or after a transition period there is a hybridisation, is still an open question.

REFERENCES

Chushokigyo cho, *chushokigyo hakusho 8 nenpan* [White paper on SMEs], Tokyo 1996.

Chushokigyo cho, *chushokigyo hakusho 11 nenpan* [White paper on SMEs], Tokyo 1999.

Etienne G., *Notes Economiques Japon*, Ambassade de France, Poste d'Expansion Economique de Tokyo, Nř 14, October 1999.

Fourin (ed.), *Nihon jidosha buhinsangyo no sekai jigyo tenkai* [The transfer of production units in the world by Japanese car and parts makers], Nagoya 1997.

Fourin (ed.), *Sekai jidosha sangyo* [World car industry], vol. 9 nř 1, March, Nagoya 1999.

Grasland E., 'Les équipementiers japonais se restructurent à pas comptés' (Japanese parts makers are restructuring progressively), in *l'Usine Nouvelle*, Nř 2705, 14 October (1999), pp. 34–38.

Guiheux G., Y. Lecler, 'Japanese car manufacturers and parts makers in the ASEAN Region: A case of expatriation under duress – or regionally integrated production?', in Humphrey J., Lecler Y., Salerno M. (eds.), *Global Strategies and Local Realities: the Auto Industry in Emerging Markets*, London 2000, pp. 207–233.

Lecler Y., *Partenariat industriel: la référence japonaise* (Industrial partnership, Japan as a reference), Limonest: l'interdisciplinaire, collection technologies, 1993.

Lecler Y., 'Recession and Globalisation: What Future for Japanese Industrial Keiretsu', in Dirks, Huchet, Ribault (eds.), *Japanese Management in the Low Growth Era: Between External Shocks and Internal Evolution*, Springer Verlag, 1999, pp. 183–205.

Lecler Y., Perrin J., M.C. Villeval, 'Concurrent engineering and institutional learning: a comparison between French and Japanese auto-parts makers', in Lung, Chanaron, Fujimoto, Raff (eds.), *Coping with Variety. Flexible productive systems for product variety in the Auto Industry*, London 1999, pp. 314–334.

Legewie J., 'Driving industrial integration: Japanese firms and the automobile industry in Southeast Asia', Paper presented at the DIJ-Conference, Regional Co-operation in Asia. *Will Japan Stand up to a Leadership Role*, Tokyo October 1998.

Maruyama Y., *Ajiano jidoshasangyo* [The Asian car industry], Tokyo 1997.

Nakagawa Y., *Prototypes in the Automobile Industry: the Japanese System*, Research Papers No. 1, The Institute of Economic Research, Chuo University 1992, 24 p.

Takeishi A., T. Fujimoto, S. Sei, *Nihonjidoshasangyo no sapuraya shisutemu no zentaizo to sono tamensei* [General portrait and multiplicity of the facets of the suppliers' network of the automobile industry], Discussion Paper Series 93-J-5, Faculty of Economics, University of Tokyo 1993, 29 p.

Discussant: Friederike Bosse

The purchasing system of Japanese manufacturing firms has been widely recognized as one of the core elements of Japanese industrial organization, structuring the firms into hierarchical networks with large customer firms at the top and medium- to small-sized suppliers/subcontractors below. The same system however is changing quite rapidly, which is mostly attributed to the new environment of a globalised economy. The changes did become apparent first outside of Japan, where (and when) Japanese manufacturers became increasingly active. But the changes have been increasing in speed and in the range of their impact in the second half of the 1990s and reach as far as the inter-firm relations and market organization in Japan itself.

However, although there are some converging trends between Japanese and European/American firms in the way they organize their purchasing system, it is far from certain, that there will be a complete convergence in the end. As of now, the system is in a period of transition and the evolution has not been finished yet. The developments in the electronic and automobile industries, where the subcontracting system is most elaborated and where the internationalization is most advanced, are a useful model to deploy the mechanism of changes and persistence and evaluate their respective chances.

When the Japanese manufacturers began establishing production facilities in Asia, they also continued using their specific purchasing system. Most of the parts and materials for their production were delivered from Japan and also a large number of suppliers were induced to follow their customers abroad. By transferring the familiar subcontracting system, they also transferred its merits: mainly a high reliability of quality and delivery. For the manufacturers this equalled a high degree of control and low risk – even if it came at the expense of the most efficient purchasing price. Since the Japanese firms were the first foreign manufacturers to serve the local markets with cars produced in the region (which was mainly a market of luxury goods first), they could at the same time realize high prices, thereby compensating for higher purchasing costs.

But then the environment changed: 1) The governments in the Asian countries introduced policies that favored local procurements, 2) the local market developed a new demand for middle-class consumer products, 3) the technological level of the Asian suppliers increased, 4) new strong competitors came up and lastly the value of the Yen increased dramatically, making products from Japan less competitive. In this context the focus on low risk and control lost its potential merits and cost became the top priority instead. Procurements were made rather in an opportunistic selection mode and new suppliers accepted simultaneously.

The cost orientation went along with a change in perspective that began integrating the whole Asian region. Integrated networks were established with regional headquarters as well as concentrated procurement and production systems, which are necessary to achieve economies of scale. Thus a new division of labor is established at the same time. Since Western firms pursue the same approach in Asia, one could speak of a converging trend here.

However, there is a conspicuous difference, since there seems to be a limit to this organizational restructuring and to the converging development. The Japanese firms are much less likely to shift authority to the regional headquarters than their Western counterparts. Instead they focus on a cost-efficient production network, including an optimal purchasing system. But the centre of control for the network is the company headquarters in Tokyo or Osaka. Also the most advanced technologies and products remain in Japan, as well as sensitive design work and F&E. The Japanese firms are not building up a horizontal network, but again a hierarchical cooperation as the well-known subcontracting system.

In the new context of extreme cost orientation and related opening of the suppliers' group, the domestic subcontracting system cannot be maintained unchanged. Firstly the pressure in the global competition to cut cost applies for production in Japan as well, and secondly the manufacturers bring back their experiences of opportunistic, market-based decisions from abroad and are likely to make use of them. Both developments should lead to an opening and loosening of the existing subcontracting structures in Japan. Empirical data show that this is already taking place.

The growing presence of foreign firms in Japan, which are founding own subsidiaries, concluding mergers and acquisitions or become major share-holders, are also part of the changing environment that Japanese firms have to act in – even at home. The foreign firms are bringing their own strategies and experiences, which is likely to enhance the development for more open procurement systems. This in turn could make it easier for Japanese suppliers to secure compensating business for the reduced subcontracting-orders, as it is creating an alternative platform to the rather closed *keiretsu*-organizations. Some suppliers thus might make use of the new 'opportunis-tic' business behavior themselves. Others are trying to strengthen the relation to their existing customers by increasing the benefit they represent for the manufacturer through innovation potential or higher value added production. Which way they will chose will depend on their technological and innovation potential as well as on the degree their products are customer-specific or widely usable and also on their ability to find access to the customers' market.

Depending on their future strategy the relation between customers and (some) suppliers might become less asymmetric than before, enhancing the power of the supplier. But a completely symmetric power relation is very unlikely or at least restricted to a small number of suppliers. The vast majority will have to adjust within the changed structures, that are less rigid than before – and less predictable.

Applied to the regional level, a similar evolution is feasible: a purchasing system, that integrates features of the old *shitauke*-system and adjustments to the respective necessities of the environment. Thus the transformation might develop from the strict hierarchical subcontracting system to a more open and expanded purchasing network with, in the end again, a vertically organized system.

9

IMPLEMENTATION OF STANDARDS: WHAT ABOUT THE POSSIBILITY OF A CONVERGENCE PRODUCTION SYSTEM BY INTERNATIONAL RULES?

Cornelia Storz

9.1 QUESTIONS AND RESEARCH DESIGN

Globalisation puts an increasing adaptation pressure on national systems and their economic actors, the companies. This pressure leads – as is one point of view – to an increasing convergence on a "global model", which maybe a result of a "race-to-the-bottom" or "race-to-the-top"-process, or just an Anglo-American model. The opposing view states that because of path dependencies national idiosyncrasies continue to exist and that national characteristics for example in business organisation and industrial organisation do not converge on an international pattern. This raises the question in what way economic actors have to adapt to global rules or if they are left with some scope to act.

This contribution tries to find an answer to this question within a specific area. The question of convergence and scope will be discussed in relation to international standards in Japan and Germany. The empirical part of this contribution aims at the investigation of the development of the product and work organisation[1] in Japan and Germany after the introduction of the global standard ISO 9000.

---

[1] Product organisation includes all the areas of the organisation of production; the shaping of organisational structure (i.e. hierarchical structure) or the shaping of the organisational processes; work organisation includes the organisation of all elements of work (operational procedure, shaping of work, job enrichment/enlargement, partly autonomous teams) and the design of working conditions (relation of employee to workplace, relation of employee to superiors and colleagues).

ISO 9000 determines in an extensive catalogue requirements for the quality management of a company. The regulations of the standards refer to in-plant and inter-firm processes, e.g. by determining the responsibilities and authorizations of the employees who influence quality. ISO 9000 standardizes therefore the implementation that means the process and not the outcome, the product. Divergences in the implementation processes in Japanese and German companies, which can be observed empirically, raise the question of theoretical clarification. This cannot be explained sufficiently by conventional standardisation economics, because standardisation economics are basically restricted to the focus on the conditions of setting efficient standards and on the conditions under which inefficient standards can survive (Arthur 1990; David 1987; Farrell and Saloner 1985 / 1987; Foray 1994, Katz and Shapiro 1986; Kindleberger 1983; Knieps 1994; Konrad and Thum 1993). All approaches have in common that they imply identical standards between senders and receivers and that they exclude the implementation process on the part of the receiver. As a consequence the divergences between senders and receivers as well as between receivers cannot be explained sufficiently and probable inefficiencies of a standard implementation are not taken into account.

This contribution considers these implicit assumptions to be unsatisfactory. Here the theory is supported that the convergence of product and work organisation as a consequence of implementing the standard ISO 9000 on a global "quality management model" is not to be expected. The central argument is that *one* standard is not *one* standard, because in order to make it effective receivers have to interpret it. In the following contribution, the formulation of a standard, its sending and its implementation is – as opposed to conventional standardisation economics – regarded as a communication process. Receivers interpret standards differently so that the "original standard" of the sender differs from the implementation process of receiver A and this again differs from the implementation standard of receiver B. With regard to ISO 9000 and its implementation process I will show that the global standard results in certain assimilation and alignment with the product and work organisation, but this does not mean that specific patterns of the product and work organisation are lost. The fact that divergences in the product and work organisation continue – even after introducing ISO 9000 – cannot only be explained by the scope existing within the standard. With the specific example ISO 9000 it will be shown, that only on the basis of conventional economics can a convergence of product and work organisation in different countries – in this case in Germany and Japan – be expected.

9.2 TERMINOLOGICAL ASPECTS: EXPLICATION OF THE TERM *STANDARD*, RELATED TERMS, SUBCLASSES

The term *standard* is used differently in the standardisation economics and in the New Institutional Economics partly because of the differences in Anglo-Saxon and German/French linguistic usage but also because of a lack of distinction of the terms *standard – rule – institution*. Without going into detail standards will be defined as follows:

A standard is a formal, explicit rule[2], which is employed by companies for production that includes all rules, which are applied in connection with production in companies. Here production includes both material and immaterial products. Formalisation means that a standard is presented on a document, so that interaction processes regarding this rule relate to a document. This does not necessarily have to come from the sender of the rule – for example the operation system from Microsoft designed for production could be called a standard, because this standard (by way of determining interfaces, etc.) can be reconstructed. All formal rules, which are applied in production, are called standard. Even formal business and financial rules, which are employed in production like CAD/CAM – standards for optimising processes belong by this definition to standards[3].

Unlike the category of norms standards do not have moral implications. A standard may be "better" from an economic-technical point of view, but that does not mean that those breaking the rules (=those not following the standards) are to be condemned morally. (Nevertheless, a dyadic classification is always somewhat simplifying: Standards – e.g. quality standards – imply *normatively* what is "good" (which quality process, which kind of technical education) and it can be easily imagined that there can be a moral pressure towards suppliers to imply a "new", "better" quality standard – if the subcontractor does not do this, he may be regarded as a transaction partner who is probably not (only) not able to introduce the new standard, but as someone who cannot be relied upon. This may be especially valid for the Japanese case, where relationships are strongly personalised but may exist in Western countries too, e.g. in industry agglomerations.)

---

[2]Rules, here defined as "behaviour regularity", create order which again reduces insecurity and makes coordination easier. In this sense rules increase efficiency. Likewise standards reduce insecurity and make coordination easier, but only with regard to specific functions (quality, compatibility, internalisation of external effects). Institutions are understood as a summary definition of rules.

[3]When applying rules this contribution follows the common classification of formal and informal rules, knowing that this dyadic distinction is problematic – many rules have two dimensions. Formalisation often establishes an informal actual state. Yet this kind of classification appears reasonable because the term "code" which will be introduced later differs depending on formality/informality.

According to the definition applied here standards belong to the class of conventions (=rules without added moral value) as distinct from the class of norms (=rules with added moral value). The emphasis of this contribution is on standards of processes. They differ from standards of products in having management processes and not the outcome as their object.[4]

As opposed to other uses both international and private standards are called standards. Neither the process of setting (market, consent), nor the range of a standard (in an enterprise, beyond an enterprise), nor its nature of agreement (consent, authority) are relevant for the work definition applied here.[5].

Figure 17 Standards – Rules – Institutions

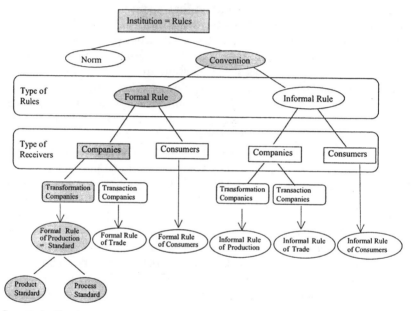

Source Author.

9.3 THE RECEIVER'S ROLE: EFFECTS ON THE QUESTION OF CONVERGENCE

In conventional standardisation economics the implementation of standards is considered to be uniform. This point of view can be simplified as follows:

---

[4] Regarding the introduction of international quality standards in China, it can be questioned, whether those technical standards do not have any value implications.
[5] The main focus is centred on process standards.

Figure 18 Standards in the economics of standardisation

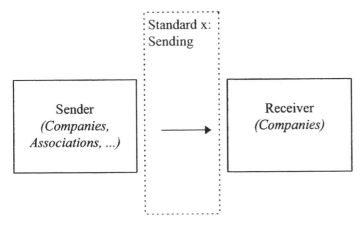

Source Author.

Thus the process of sending and implementing is not regarded as a communication process with its possibility of failure; it is assumed that the sent standard is identical with the implemented standard.

Opposed to that the following model will question the uniformity of the implemented standard: A standard is considered to be a code that needs decoding and therefore a creative interpretation on the part of the receiver:[6]

Figure 19 Standards in a model of communication[1]

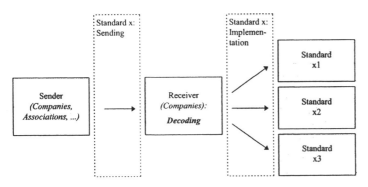

1 In further research, feedback processes should be integrated in the model.

Source Author.

[6]For the sake of simplicity it is assumed that (a) the sender sends unambiguous meaning and (b) the sender is not identical with the receiver (in practice there are occasional overlappings, i.e. with members of standardisation committees who then – after the joint formulation – apply the standard. Obviously this does not mean that those members of a company who have formulated the standard are identical with those who implement the standard).

In order to investigate the convergence of the product and work organisation the following contribution will focus on the receiver.

9.3.1 Who is the receiver of standards? Embeddedness of individuals and companies

Before dealing with the question of implementation processes in different countries two questions should be answered:

- How does the understanding and learning individual relate to the company, here defined as the receiver?

- How does the company relate to its respective culture, which is here defined on a national level?

This contribution will only touch on these two questions by combining the aspects in a – fairly simple – "embeddedness approach":[7]

Ad (a):

Basically different receivers of a standard are possible, like companies and private households. According to the definition above only those formal rules are standards, which are being implemented in transformation companies. The following is based on the assumption that – regarding a standard implementation – the individuals in such a company can be described as interindividually similar types. This is because companies are considered to be (partially) closed networks of communication processes (i.e. cognition, learning, implementation), while functional and hierarchical structures create similarities in their behavioural commitment.

Ad (b):

Companies are embedded in natural cultural contexts. Therefore the specific culture of a country influences the respective company. This is proved by differences for example in the organisation culture (product and work organisation) or in different transaction processes (long-term vs. short-term orientation). The author is aware that this kind of concept rather simplifies the matter but here is not the place to go into details. Just some remarks upon the complex concept of culture: Both individuals and companies are subject to different referential systems, so that Herrmann-Pillath (1999) – in clear distinction from Huntington et al. – considers each individual/each company to be a "crossing point of different cultures". Culture can not be related to a single, absolute level of reference (also cf. Wimmer 1996). The fact that national cultures influence company cultures does not mean that the national culture is to be considered an absolute and that there are no other relevant reference groups for a company – Sony obviously is a good example for that. As opposed to company cultures national cultures have limited possibilities to sanction, which facilitates deviant behaviour. On the

---

[7] With Baecker culture is understood as a difference (Baecker 2000).

basis of cumulative observations, it will be tried to identify some Japanese cultural characteristics (comp. 4.1.1), but it should be mentioned, that they should not be understood as "static" attributes, and they should be understood as characteristics stated by namely Western observers (while in some cases this "Japanese image" has been used by Japanese scholars too).

9.3.2 The step after the game – the implementation process of new standards

The following sections deal with the implementation of new standards. To simplify matters a "new" standard is a standard that deviates from an old one, including variations of an old standard. The focus on new standards is based on the assumption that old existing standards are repeated consistently because the receivers are interested in stability. It is conceivable that old standards are not repeated consistently either, which would offer a new possibility of divergence; but this will not be the subject of discussion here.

Here two interdependent questions are central. They are as follows:

• Processes of cognition and learning and
• Structuring of these processes by interaction.

Processes of cognition and learning

As explained earlier the standard reaches the company in a coded form. The code is presented in a document, in technical descriptions and other forms of storage. This kind of code is stored knowledge. The decoding of the stored knowledge requires action of an individual. This rather simple fact is essential because a code calls for interpretation in order to have an actual effect. This also means that codes can be interpreted differently in different contexts. A standard therefore does not follow natural laws; its "meaning" is only acquired by unconscious/conscious interpretation on the part of the receiver. Thus a standard is an "object of culture" (and not an "object of nature"; Busse 1975: 211). Although the sender sends the code, he does not send the meaning which can result in "reception errors" and in a "failure" in setting standards: the effect intended by the sender does not have to correspond to the desired effect (cf. Braun 1996: 228; Schulz von Thun 1994: 63). So a standard is not a given, but a created reality. A certification of companies according to international standards helps to compare companies; but it does not mean that neither company understands a code in an identical way nor that an implemented standard in company A is identical with the implemented standard in company B.

Interestingly, the dualistic structure of "code" and "decoding" is valid for all areas in the application of rules: thus it is in language (langue/parole or denotation/connotation), in technology (infrastructure/application) or in structural linguistics (significant/signifié; cf. Saussure and Chomsky; cf. Braun 1996: 45). Schulz von Thun's (1994: 61) in a continuation of Watzlawick distinguishes four levels of meaning in the communication process:

Besides the level of content ("Sachebene") levels of self-revelation, relationship and/or appeal. So a reaction on the part of the receiver is possible on different meta-levels, namely on the levels of content ("Sachebene"), self revelation, relationship and/or appeal: Concerning the process of implementation of international standards, there exists an interesting parallel: When ISO 9000 was introduced in Japanese firms there seemed to have been a particular sensitivity on the "level of relationship", because the foreign standard – at first quite independent of an assessment of its content – had been understood as a "dictate" since European companies made the standards as one prerequisite of transaction. The arriving message can therefore be understood as a "creation of the receiver", as Schulz von Thun correctly stated (1994: 61).

Cognition and learning in interaction processes

Until now it has been neglected that a standard implementation is not an individual but a social act within groups. Here groups are defined as socially coherent units in which group members agree on a consistent behaviour. Therefore the uniformity of rules, the similarity of age, the similarity of communication patterns are a result of social coherence.

Individuals/companies face a number of different groups. More recent studies (cf. Goyal 1996) point out that in situations of decision making not all groups have the same relevance but that respective reference groups influence decisions. "Small" subgroups like companies, families and friends can function as such reference groups, as well as "metagroups" like (international) occupational groups or (national) groups of countries. Because of the existence of reference groups there are structures of interaction, which can be distinguished from (uniform) interactions, which again are implied by the conventional standardisation economics (for the following cf. Goyal 1996). The readiness to change and to adapt to a new standard depends on the question whether in the reference group one is related most to, a new standard has already been implemented.

What does that mean for the process of standardization and the implementation of standards? Standards co-ordinate transactions; they co-ordinate the internal co-operation in a company as well as between companies. Only since standards are regular, can they work: Only the regularity makes it possible that expectations can be formed. A changing of these regularities in the patterns of communication – who communicates with whom, how is communication carried out[8] – is costly since new rules how to communicate have to been learned. One example for this interdependence is the implementation of the international standard EDI (Electronic Data Interchange) which causes in the American countries investigated enormous difficulties because the implementation of standards requires – neglected by

---

[8]Since standards define the "how" of communication, there is a strong interdependence between standards and processes in the enterprise.

economists analysing the "efficiency" of international standards – changes in the organisational process which has been learned by people acting in those processes (Brousseau 1994). In other words: there is not only a path dependency in the standard itself but a path dependency by the interdependence of *certain* standards with *certain* processes in the enterprise since people are used to *certain* patterns how to communicate, how to learn, how to work; and again this "how to" is coined by *certain* standards. Because of these learning processes of *certain* standards and *certain* processes, there exist "islands of standards" with a strong stability.

Recent approaches in game theory (Goyal 1996) prove that learning processes and the introduction of new standards are easier the more closed and smaller the group is. This is because (1) if there are fewer participants in a negotiation process the negotiation establishing the meaning of a standard is shorter[9] and small groups make it easier to build trust. Empirically, these deliberations are confirmed by the fact that, in Japan, small groups are preferred: Not only the average size of enterprises is lower, but too "small group activities" are central for the organisation of production and the way of learning, as e.g. by the system of guest engineers in research and development activities, or by quality circles in quality improvement processes. (And, the closer the groups the stronger the path dependency since there is no possibility to develop new communication patterns with other actors.) In the context of standard-setting, in Japan exclusive standards (standards in one business group) have been the dominant way of standard-setting and standard-implementation; fairly small groups between one assembler and one subcontractor were formed in order to enforce learning processes. In the above-mentioned self-enforcing processes it seems plausible that these "islands of standards" do persist. This explains why even today a standard architecture different from Western countries can be identified.

Standards seem to have an additional function, which can only be touched on here: one can assume that an established new standard creates identity because (a) the standard itself and even more (b) the communication about standards, the negotiation of their validity provides orientation. At the same time a dividing line is drawn between the in- and out-group by a standard. Each standard therefore has two functions: on the outside standards increase transaction costs (i.e. exclusive non-negotiated standards or design standards), on the inside standards decrease transaction costs (i.e. when increasing learning effects). Thus the "efficiency" of a standard changes according to the (physical) point of view of the observer. By the creation of identity and credibility, standards help to build-up trust. In this sense, they even fulfil an emotional function. If economic actors judge this function of standards as a central one it seems to be plausible that this kind of standard will be kept.

---

[9] Or it is revealed at an earlier stage that consent is not possible. Goyal does not refer to this possibility.

9.4 EXAMPLE: THE IMPLEMENTATION OF THE ISO-STANDARD IN JAPAN AND GERMANY

In the following, the standard ISO 9000 will be defined as a code which is sent by the ISO, the International Standard Organisation, and which is implemented by companies.[10]

9.4.1 Culture as difference: Is there a culture specific to Japan?

We are always liable to oversimplify the identification of differences between Japan and the Western industrialized countries. Culture is not a static phenomenon, deviations of national cultures are possible and, especially, the role of the observer is often neglected: Culture is not a characteristic of the analysed object, but its analysing reflects more the relationship between the observer and the observed. Bearing this problem in mind, culture is identified as an observable regularity of behaviour (compare Baecker 2000; Herrmann-Pillath 2000). Two levels are identified, namely:

A national culture specific to Japan on the meta level and a company culture specific to Japan; focused on the shaping of the product and work organisation.

Differences in national cultures

Contrasting to the American ideal type model Murakami and Rohlen, in Germany Pascha, have coined the term "generalized relationships of exchange" to define the Japanese rules of interaction that result from informal rules. Their goal is to describe a different short (USA) or long (Japan) term orientation of transactions (Pascha 1999). Germany moves in between both poles. Empirical research supports these findings (Möhwald 1996). To simplify the following empirical analysis, two differences between the Japanese culture and the American and, in a more moderate form, the German model, are assumed. These are:

• The preference of group-related decisions

• The existence of generalized relationships of exchange which cause a preference of long-term orientation, cooperation and personal relationships.

Differences in national cultures may – even though it is difficult to prove the individual case – influence the shaping of company cultures. This may happen within the individual company, which, for example, prefers group decisions as can be found in quality control circles. Or it may happen between companies on the level of long-term transaction relationships. (Here

---

[10]In reality, this process is more complex since standards have to be recognised as a national standard first. In the case of Japan this would be JISZ 9000; Nihon Kagaku Kyôkai 1992.

too the author is aware of simplification: according to the results of Sey (1999), e.g. none of the present studies concerning groups differentiate between group sizes nor do they question decision processes within groups – ; and most of research does not keep in mind the heterogeneity of enterprises.) The following model of culture is, indeed, a very stylised one, but cumulative analyses make it plausible that there is some difference. In this perspective, the following model is used as an "ideal type" design for comparison.

Differences in country-specific company cultures

In the respective literature, differences in "ideal type" product and work organisation on the company level in Japan and Western countries are identified. These differences are especially strongly discussed in the management literature. Therefore the characteristics will only be outlined.

The ideal type of product and work organisation of the 60s and 70s in Japan is defined by a long-term exchange of services, long-term personal relationships and a tight cooperation between client and subcontractor on the inter-firm level. On the in-plant level it is marked by the high importance of quality circles which are organised on the operative level, by the preference of team work and flexible division of labour sharing (troubleshooting, improvement of products, specification of responsibility) as well as participation of all staff members (suggestions, *kaizen* as permanent self rationalization, trainings). In the 80s and 90s transformations on the company level targeted the improvement of error analysis which had been considered as too little systematic as well as the acceleration of the decision making process. Outside of the companies the reforms on behalf of the producers are aimed at a stronger participation of the subcontractors in the producer's system of control ("system subcontractors") with clearer structures of management (for example evaluation, improvement, cost). The subcontractors aim at an increasing diversification of buyers as well as the development and sale of their own products.

The transformations outlined above, however, have not caused the loss of "distinctiveness", to follow Dore (Dore 1997), of the Japanese of product and work organisation.

On the in-plant level, decentralised processes of information and decision form the basis for flexibility and thus the development of the firm ("organisational learning"). Decentralized structures of organisation, especially the importance attributed to groups in information and decision making processes, create flexibility. These group dynamics are in contrast with formal, hierarchical relationships of authority with a clear sharing of tasks and standardized plans and rules, as we find them in the American ideal type model. Thus, the Japanese understanding of process orientation means the realisation of an incremental trial-and-error process, which is based on an unclear definition of roles and its (necessary) appreciation of personal relationships in and between groups.[11] On the inter-firm level, clear differences can be detected too: There is a much stronger differentiation of vertical division of labour: in Japan, the cooperation with – clearly fewer – buyers is tighter and more long-term oriented. Even today, the advantages of long-term relationships are valued: more than half of the subcontractors sustain relationships as old as twenty years with a buyer, only 6% have relationships of less than five years (Asanuma 1985 a,b; Clark 1989; Cusumano/Takeishi 1991; Dirks 1995: 130–145; Dirks/Otto 1998; Jürgens 1992; Kawasaki/McMillan 1987; Nakakita 1997; Piacentini 1996: 304; Storz forthcoming).

In the following, the "Japanese" product and work organisation will be used in reference to this ideal type of product and work organisation.

9.4.2 Implementation of the new standard: The decoding process

In this chapter German and Japanese differences and similarities in the implementation process will be demonstrated.[12] It will be argued that standards and processes in the company and between companies are interdependent. A change will occur if there is a change in one of the two dimensions. Indeed, it can be observed that the introduction of the new, global standard ISO 9000 changes processes in the enterprise. But that does not lead to convergence: The following examples demonstrate how the new standard is embedded in "well-known" structures. The embedding in established company structures is enforced by cultural characteristics which support an interpretation of standards in a certain, well-known-pattern. The result is an in-between of persistence and change.

How standards change processes in and between enterprises

Global standards have the possibility to change company structures. This point will be touched here only shortly since it has been discussed elsewhere. In the case of ISO 9000, two changes can be stated: First, documentation becomes necessary which requires a considerable amount of resources and at least a formal structure in the company analogous to the requirements of the standard. After the introduction of ISO 9000, the quality management process has become more transparent; especially it became easier to identify and eliminate the sources of errors. It was used as an instrument to counteract against the diffuse responsibility in the production process. Moreover,

---

[11] Cf. more recent results in organisational theory which desribe organisations as chaotic constructions.

[12] The basis of the following are first case studies conducted in Japan in 1999 and secondly, for the German part, a study of the German Science Centre, Berlin (Wissenschaftszentrum Berlin; Hancke and Casper 1996). Due to the limited amount of data for Germany, a complete comparison at this point in time cannot be made.

it helped to identify tasks connected with single positions more clearly. Through the identification of core competence, the diffuse area of responsibility especially of leading positions has been made much more clear. Intra-company-processes are touched too in the sense that subcontractors use the standard in order to break up vertical transaction processes. ISO 9000 is directly implemented by the subcontractor's own marketing. Apparently the atmosphere of transaction is perceived as no longer intact so that the ISO 9000 takes on an additional meaning, namely that of a signal function as regards the reputation of the subcontractor.

The degree to which firm- and inter-firm-processes are changed varies very much between companies. It depends very clearly of the aim for introducing the standard. It seems to be optional to the actors to which degree processes are changed. Therefore, depending on the motivation why the standard has been introduced (requirements from transaction partners; intention to improve the quality management process) the scope and depth of a new shaping of processes is influenced. Convergence does not happen "automatically" but is – if it comes to this point – intended by actors. This even stresses the scope of action for economic actors.

How different processes lead to a different adaptation of standards

First of all, there is a noticeable difference in the reference groups in which Japanese and German companies operate. In Germany, associations play an important role in the implementation of new standards.[13] In Japan, companies of the same business group (*keiretsu*) carry out that function: many of the Japanese subcontractors which were interviewed, started to implement ISO 9000 only after their parent company had asked them to. Other process standards where this behaviour can be observed can be found in the data transmission (Okamuro 1992; Storz 2000). The standard was implemented either after the respective buyer had asked for it – thus only few subcontractors implemented it as a result of their own initiative –, or the subcontractors implemented the standard in "anticipating obedience" in order to maintain transaction relationships by improving their reputation. It can be concluded from this that different patterns of communication in the creation and implementation of standards exist: in Germany we can detect a strong influence of associations and in Japan of the *keiretsu*.[14]

If the companies have decided to implement the new standard, the implementation in Japan is conducted on the operative level. The preliminaries for the implementation of the standard, namely the transformation

---

[13] Here: data transmission.

[14] For example it was reported that especially in the area of basic research, cooperation of a company was achieved only if the costs of setting a standard would have been paid by the government. In this association only one internationalized company took active part in the formulation of standards without additional financial support by the government.

of the abstract standard to the real situation in the company, was thus delegated to the staff, often experienced in quality control activities, who prepared the adaptation process through discussion: a necessary prerequisite is the above mentioned polyvalence of staff. Even though committees for the standard implementation were formed on the executive level (named *iinkai)*, the actual adaptation was carried out by subordinate committees (named *wâkingu grûpu)*. These, compiled from members of the operative level (named *hira shain; kakarichô*), worked under the direction of division or subdivision managers and adopted the demands of the ISO standard to the company. Since those staff members have often participated in the quality control circles before and thus had acquired specialist knowledge in quality management the formal implementation (in contrast to informal elements, see below) is not considered to be problematic. Thus, a characteristic of the "ideal type" product and work organisation – quality control, team work, flexible division of tasks and participation of all members of staff in the decision making process – can be found in the implementation of the ISO 9000 standard. The company sticks to the existing bottom-up principle. The operative level also develops mechanisms of correction, which complement the standard implemented. Leading electronic companies developed their own instruments of evaluation to complement the ISO standard. The companies respond to deficits with deviations from the original standard. This corresponds with a nationally and internationally obvious marketing strategy: so called "transparent", that is negotiated standards are complemented with company-specific standards which allow differentiation as regards competition.[15]

Additionally, the reinterpretation of the ISO standard can be, as far as organisation structure is concerned, detected in the attempt to reach an integration of the standard with the existing *kaizen*-movement. A typical example is the implementation of the standard ISO 14000 which parallels ISO 9000 in its attempt to standardize processes within the company: The standards have been integrated into the existing quality control movement. Thus the existing QCD (QC Delivery) movement is transformed to a QCD+E (E=ecology)-movement.[16] With other words: New task are integrated in well-known, established structures.

The process of implementation appears to have taken a similar course in Germany:[17] Mainly the positions of workers and foremen were responsible

---

[15] In this respect the classification in old and new standards is, as mentioned before, problematic, because it suggests a static picture.

[16] Cf. the similarity in the area of exclusive product standards: the reduction of "superfluous" (muda) inhouse standards which show a doubling of national or international standards is the task of shanai kaizen, the "permanent in-plant improvement"; from a linguistic point of view the term muda – meaning "superfluous" – also reflects one of the central kaizen-aims, namely the reduction of dissipation (muda).

[17] According to the results of the German Science Centre Berlin (Hancke/Caspar 1996).

for the implementation of the new standards. Thus Germany and Japan can apparently be distinguished from countries such as France, which tend to have more hierarchical company structures in which specialists are responsible for the implementation of the new standard. All three countries have thus used familiar patterns of communication and not developed new ones (for example use of specialist groups in Japan or Germany). Apparently new ones do not replace old standards but new ones are reinterpreted on the basis of familiar models in the communication process between old and new standards. New standards are integrated into existing company processes.

Japanese companies describe the current flexible definition of competence as an advantage for competition since it necessitates an improved information flow.[18] A further characteristic of the Japanese product and work organisation was thus the lack of an integrated "general standard" which determined for example (similar to ISO 9000) the process of standardisation. Also, only a small part was documented in order to maintain flexibility (about 1/10 of the documented volume in comparison to ISO 9000; cf. also Hinshitsu Kanri 1998, 49: 11: 64; Karatsu 1999; Nihon Kagaku Kôgyôkai 1992: 59). Some Japanese authors explain the differences in the documentation behaviour with a different management philosophy: The current system is considered as "management by people" (*hito ni yoru kanri*), ISO 9000 is "management by system" (*shisutemu ni yoru kanri*: Sakai 1996b: 46–7). This means that standardisation would make employees replaceable; personalized knowledge ("tacit knowledge") would be transformed to transferable knowledge. This is partly considered as an advantage, for example as far as training of new employees or error analysis are concerned (cf. Sakai 1996b: 49; Takada 1997: 61). However, about half of the certified companies are very critical of the high amount of documentation necessary for the ISO standard: in their eyes flexibility would be prevented in the case of the implementation of a standardized work process. Also an adaptation to fast changing environmental demands would be impeded. This possibly explains the preference of non-Western, especially Asian certifiers: according to various interviewees non-Western certifiers are considered to be more "lenient" towards a lack of clearness as far as responsibility is concerned. (This raises again the question whether one standard can be regarded as one standard. It raises moreover the question, which function quality standards like ISO 9000 can fulfil, why different certifiers are used whereas their judgement about the conformity to the standard seems to be different and, last, whether the "lemon"-phenomena does exist.)

---

[18]Several authors point out that this is one of the central differences between Japanese and non-Japanese product and work organisations: so far the extensive responsibility of the management for assessment or design has not been specified to such a degree (Maruyama 1998: 70–71).

ISO 9000 meets existing inter- and intra-firm-processes, which are different in the sense that they pronounce flexibility and diffusivity whereas the standard, by the documentation of processes, stresses rigidity by which the production process becomes transparent. Since an overall change of processes becomes too costly and since there is often a restricted interest in changing the structures (and would weaken in the perspective of Japanese interview partners the Japanese organisation of production), ISO 9000 is used like a "driving licence". Therefore, the implementation is described as "formally" simple; this explains the relatively short duration of the implementation process of 6 months on the average in Japan in comparison to the international average of about 12–18 months. This pattern can be detected very often and puts, beside the cost aspect, the meaningfulness of international standards into question.[19]

The adaptation of the abstract standard to the real company situation can be described as the first step of interpretation. This step, which leads to a persistence of existing production organisation, is enforced by a second step of interpretation, namely the decoding of the standards on the basis of well-known cultural patterns.

First, there is a tendency to avoid individual responsibility, even though the standard may demand it. Flexibility and lack of clarity are characteristics of the Japanese in-plant product and work organisation. One reason why Toyota does not introduce the standard is its rejection of a clear definition of responsibility. The critical overall evaluation of individual responsibility may have two reasons: on the one hand companies may be afraid of a loss of their strengths, as mentioned above. Secondly, there may be a possible contradiction between the lacking culture of individual responsibility and a "Japanese culture" – key word: preference of group relationships. It is striking that various interviewees call the standards clear demand for individual responsibility as not applicable and *tatemae* ("superficial"), even though they are certified to ISO 9000. In practice the attitude towards the adoption of individual responsibility has hardly changed. There is still a certain "shyness" to take over individual responsibility in conflict situations. Teamwork is still preferred when it comes to problem solving. Apparently "responsibility for mistakes" is often equated with individual responsibility meaning that a distinction between responsibility as employee and responsibility as individual is not made.

On the inter-firm level, too, generalised relationships of exchange, namely long-term orientation, cooperation and personal relationships are preferred: Many producers still conduct a bilateral audit (*kōjō kensa*)[20]

---

[19] If an international process standard is implemented, the adaptation to certain characteristics of an industry, a single company or of an overall national framework requires an adaptation to the individual situation so that the aim of the standard, e.g. the international exchange of data, becomes questionable (Reimers 1995: 166ff.)

[20] Though one subcontractor reported that now audits are being dropped.

instead of (or at the same time with) the recognition of an ISO certification. Before ISO 9000 has been introduced as an "objective criterion", "soft" information as e.g. the kind of education system, innovation potential, information concerning strengths and weaknesses in the production system has to be collected which meant a considerable burden of costs. By ISO 9000, transparency has – the aim of the standard – raised. The continuation of bilateral audits proves that trust can apparently not be acquired via "third" persons. In other words: personal trust is valued more than trust that can be acquired on the market (cf. Zucker, quoted in Lane/Bachmann 1996: 379).[21] Here, as far as the case studies allow such a conclusion, differences with Germany can be detected where the number of audits has clearly decreased and bilateral audits, compared with certified subcontractors, have lost their importance.[22] For this reason, too, numerous buyers in Japan will still rely on the subcontractor's own quality management: therefore very often a certification according to ISO 9000 is not required. Mutual knowledge renders an "objective" measure unnecessary.

Furthermore the implementation of the standard does not cause a – theoretically possible, even though costly as regards transaction costs – obvious strong diversification of subcontractors (for example of all subcontractors of the same branch which are certified to ISO 9000). This is especially astonishing since the goal of such a standard is of course to make companies more "tradable". Standards have, as defined above, the goal to increase competition for quality and price to be able to choose, in the case of ISO 9000 "better" subcontractors, namely those that can fulfil the standard. In Germany, VW has reduced as a consequence of having introduced quality assurance systems (one of it ISO 9000) the number of national subcontractors from 55% (1992) to 45% (1995; cf. Hancké 1997: 226) In Japan, by contrast, the social norms of "long term orientation", "personal relationships" and "group orientation" function as stabilizing factors. It appears that the ISO 9000 standard causes standardisation only where it is "desired" on the receiver's part, for example when in-plant deficits are perceived. In other areas, mechanisms of correction are introduced, in which deficits of standards are either replaced with own standards or in an at least informal continuation of traditional structures.

[21] Another explanation would be that costs are high but that the exactness of information about the transaction partner because of a long-term relationship and, in consequence, the minor number of failures (in a very general sense) would over-compensate the high(er) costs of screening.

[22] This does not mean that the balance of power is to be ignored: through this producers still define the range of their "territory" towards – de iure – independent subcontractors (concerning the strategic choosing behaviour cf. Child 1972: 8–14; also cf. Lane/Bachmann 1996: 365).

9.5 CONCLUSION

One standard is definitely not *one* standard. That means that a convergence of different product and work organisations is not to be expected, according to the result: First, there is scope within the standard given by the "abstract" – "concrete" dimension (not mentioned here were problems in the translation of international standards; a much discussed subject in Japan). Because of this (abstract–concrete) dimension, it depends on the strategy, on the aim, on the intention of introduction how a standard is implemented. This explains why obviously other international process standards like ISO 14000 have been introduced in more depth – the standard was introduced by own initiative in order to improve environmental quality. Moreover, non-negotiated company-specific standards are added to negotiated and transparent standards in order to counteract comparability (*sabetsuka*). Secondly, it is too costly to implement a new standard in depth, especially a process standard, since standards and company processes are interdependent: The implementation of a new standard is accompanied by immense implementation costs since a new standard and, by this, new regularities, have to be learned, which reduces strongly the "efficiency" of transparent standards. Actors decide to which degree they want to introduce the new standard, which again raises their scope for action. Receivers interpret codes differently and develop different solutions for "identical" codes. As a second step of interpretation, not only existing company structures but also culture plays a role in the way standards are interpreted. Terms like "responsibility" bear a different meaning in different cultural contexts, which again questions the possibility of convergence. That does not mean that processes are not open, as demonstrated by the diversification of subcontractors in Germany (on behalf of the assembler) and Japan (on behalf of the subcontractor), but possibly the aim to achieve comparability by standardisation of management processes is more restricted as has been perceived by the standardisation economics.

If we suppose first that the implementation process of a standard is considered to be a technical communication process and second that a standard can be regarded as a part of a rule, the above drawn conclusions may be valid for rules in general. If this is accepted, it may be really questioned whether the growing importance of international rules will lead to a convergence of different economic orders.

REFERENCES

Akerlof, G., 'The Economics of Caste and of the Rat Race and Other Woeful Tales', in *Quarterly Journal of Economics*, 90 (1976), pp. 599–617.

Albers, Willi, *Handwörterbuch der Wirtschaftswissenschaft (HdWW)*, Stuttgart 1988.

Arthur, W. Brian, 'Positive Feedbacks in the Economy', in *Scientific American*, Feb. (1990), pp. 80–85.

Asanuma, 'The organization parts purchases in the Japanese automotive industry', in *Japanese Economic Studies*, 13 (1985a) pp. 32–53.

Asanuma, 'The contractual framework for parts supply in the Japanese automotive industry', in *Japanese Economic Studies*, 13 (1985b) pp. 54–78.

Baecker, Dirk, 'Gesellschaft als Kultur oder Warum wir beschreiben müssen, wenn wir erkennen wollen', in Priddat, Birger P. (ed.), *Kapitalismus, Krisen, Kultur*, Marburg 2000, pp. 9–22.

Blankart, Charles B., Günther Knieps, 'Kommunikationsgüter ökonomisch betrachtet', in *Homo oeconomicus*, München 1994, Vol. XI, 3, pp. 449–463.

Blankart, Charles B., Günther Knieps, *State and Standards*, Berlin 1993 (Discussion paper / Humboldt-Universität zu Berlin, FB Wirtschaftswissenschaften : Economics series ; 2).

Braun, Edmund (ed.), *Der Paradigmenwechsel in der Sprachphilosophie: Studien und Texte*, Darmstadt 1996.

Brendel, Herwig, 'Wettbewerbspolitische Konzeptionen', in Von Delhaes, Karl, Ulrich Fehl (ed.), *Dimensionen des Wettbewerbs: Seine Rolle in der Entstehung und Ausgestaltung von Wirtschaftsordnungen*, Stuttgart 1997 (Schriften zu Ordnungsfragen der Wirtschaft; vol. 52), pp. 79–102.

Brennan, Geoffrey, James B. Buchanan, *Die Begründung von Regeln. Konstitutionelle Politische Ökonomie*, Tübingen 1993.

Brousseau, Eric, 'EDI and inter-firm relationships: toward a standardization of coordination processes?', in *Information Economics and Policy*, 6 (1994), pp. 319–347.

Busse, Winfried, 'Funktionen und Funktion der Sprache', in Brigitte Schlieben-Lange (ed.), *Sprachtheorie*, Hamburg 1975, pp. 207–240.

Child, John, 'Organizational Structure, Environment and Performance: The Role of Strategic Choice', in *Sociology (The Journal of the British Sociological Association)*, vol. 6 (1972), pp. 1–22.

Clark, K.B., 'Project scope and project performance: The effect of parts, strategy and supplier involvement on product development', in *Management Science*, 35 (1989), pp. 1247–1263.

Cusumano, M., A. Takeishi, 'Supplier relations and management: A survey of Japanese, Japanese-transplant, and US auto plants', in *Strategic Management Journal*, 12 (1991), pp. 563–588.

David, Paul A, 'Some New Standards for the Economics of Standardization in the Information Age', in Partha Dasgupta/Paul Stoneman (ed.), *Economic Policy and Technological Performance*, Cambridge 1987, pp. 206–239.

Dirks, Daniel, *Japanisches Management in internationalen Unternehmen: Methodik interkultureller Organisation*, Wiesbaden 1995.

Dirks, Daniel, Silke-Susann Otto, 'Das "japanische Unternehmen"', in Deutsches Institut für Japanstudien (ed.), *Die Wirtschaft Japans*, Heidelberg, New York et al. 1998, pp. 211–244.

Dore, Ronald, 'The Distinctiveness of Japan', in Crouch, Colin; Streeck, Wolfgang (ed.), *Political Economy of Modern Capitalism. Mapping Convergence and Diversity*, London, Thousand Oaks, New Delhi 1997, pp. 19–33.

Elster, Jon, *The Cement of Society: A Study of Social Order*, Cambridge 1995.

Farrell, Joseph, Garth Saloner, 'Standardization, compatibility, and innovation', in *The RAND Journal of Economics*, 16 (1985) 1, pp. 70–83.

Farrell, Joseph, Garth Saloner, 'Competition, Compatibility and Standards: The Economics of Horses, Penguins and Lemmings', in Gabel, Landis H. (ed.), *Product Standardization and Competitive Strategy*, Amsterdam, et al. 1987.

Bensoussan, A., P. A. Naert (ed.), *Advanced Studies in Management*, vol. 11 (1987), pp. 1–21.

Farrell, Joseph, Garth Saloner, 'Coordination through committees and markets', in *The RAND Journal of Economics* 19 (1988) 2, pp. 235–252.

Foray, Dominique, 'Users, standards and the economics of coalitions and committees', in *Information Economics and Policy* 6 (1994), pp. 269–293.

Goyal, Sanjeev, 'Interaction Structure and Social Change', in *JITE (Journal of Institutional and Theoretical Economics)*, 152:3 (1996), pp. 472–494.

Hancké, Bob, 'Vorsprung, aber nicht länger/(nur) durch Technik', in *WZB Jahrbuch*, Wissenschaftszentrum Berlin für Sozialforschung (ed.), Berlin 1997, pp. 213–234.

Hancké, Bob, Steven Caspar, *ISO 9000 in the French and German Car Industry. How international quality standards support varieties of capitalism* (discussion paper, WZB FS I 96–313. Forschungsschwerpunkt: Arbeitsmarkt und Beschäftigung, Abteilung: Wirtschaftswandel und Beschäftigung), 1996.

Hawkins, Richard W., 'Introduction: addressing the problématique of standards and standardization', in R. Hawkins, R. Mansell, J. Skea (ed.), *Standards, Innovation and Competitiveness. The Politics and Economics of Standards in Natural and Technical Environment*, Aldershot, Brookfield 1995, pp. 1–6.

Herrmann-Pillath, Carsten, *Was ist und wie betreibt man wirtschaft-skulturelle Transformationsforschung?* (Heft Nr. 40, Universität Witten/Herdecke; Fakultät für Wirtschaftswissenschaft, Institut für kulturvergleichende Wirtschaftsforschung, Lehrstuhl für gesamtwirtschaftliche und institutionelle Entwicklung) (discussion paper), 1999.

Herrmann-Pillath, Carsten, *Culture and Oberservation in the Study of Economic Systems* (Heft Nr. 52, Universität Witten/Herdecke, Fakultät für Wirtschaftswissenschat, Institut für kulturvergleichende Wirtschafsforschung, Lehrstuhl für gesamtwirtschaftliche und institutionelle Entwicklung) (discussion paper), März 2000.

Hinshitsu kanri, *ISO 9001 no yôso o TQM ni torikomu mono no hôhô (teian)* [Vorschläge zur Integration der Elemente von ISO 9001 in TQM], 49:11(1998), pp. 63–75.

Jürgens, Ulrich, 'Industriepolitische Gesichtspunkte: Die Bedeutung neuer Produktions- und Logistikkonzepte', in *AK-Beiträge (Arbeitskammer der Saarlandes)*, 5:1(1992) , pp. 29–49.

Karatsu, Hajime, 'Nihon fûdo ni najimanai' [Unpassend zum japanischen Kontext], in *Mainichi Shimbun*, 1999, p. 3.

Katz, Michael L. und Shapiro, Carl, 'Technology Adoption in the Presence of Network Externalities', in *Journal of Political Economy*, 94 (1986) 4, pp. 822–841.

Kawasaki, S., J. McMillan, 'The design of contracts: Evidence from Japanese subcontracting', in *Journal of the Japanese and International Economies* 1 (1987), pp. 327–349.

Kerber, Wolfgang, 'Wettbewerb als Hypothesentest', in Von Delhaes, Karl, Ulrich Fehl (ed.), *Dimensionen des Wettbewerbs: Seine Rolle in der Entstehung und Ausgestaltung von Wirtschaftsordnungen*, Stuttgart 1997 (Schriften zu Ordnungsfragen der Wirtschaft; vol. 52), pp. 29–78.

Kindleberger, Charles P., 'Standards as Public, Collective and Private Goods', in *Kyklos*, Vol. 36, Fasc. 3 (1983), pp. 377–396.

Kiwit, Daniel, Stefan Voigt, 'Überlegungen zum institutionellen Wandel unter Berücksichtigung des Verhältnisses interner und externer Institutionen', in *ORDO. Jahrbuch für die Ordnung von Wirtschaft und Gesellschaft*, Stuttgart 1995 (Band 46), pp. 117–148.

Knieps, Günter, 'Standards und die Grenzen der unsichtbaren Hand', in *ORDO. Jahrbuch für die Ordnung von Wirtschaft und Gesellschaft*, Stuttgart 1994 (Band 45), pp. 51–62.

Knorr, Henning, *Ökonomische Probleme von Kompatibilitätsstandards. Eine Effizienzanalyse unter besonderer Berücksichtigung des Telekommunikationsbereiches*, Baden-Baden 1993.

Konrad, Kai A., Marcel Thum, 'Fundamental Standards and Time Consistency', in *Kyklos,* 46 (1993) 4, pp. 545–568.

Lane, Christel, Reinhard Bachmann, 'The Social Constitution of Trust: Supplier Relations in Britain and Germany', in *Organization Studies*, 17:3 (1996), pp. 365–395.

Leipold, Helmut, 'Zur Pfadabhängigkeit der institutionellen Entwicklung. Erklärungsansätze des Wandels von Ordnungen', in Cassel, Dieter (ed.), *Entstehung und Wettbewerb von Systemen,* Berlin 1996, pp. 93–115.

Maruyama, Noboru, 'ISO kikaku no sekinin to kengen ni kansuru mono' [Zur Fragen von Verantwortung und Befugnissen im ISO-Standards], in: *Hinshitsu Kanri,* 49: 7, July 1998, pp. 70–76.

Möhwald, Ulrich, 'Wertewandel in Japan: Einige Aspekte der Ergebnisse des Forschungsprojektes des Deutschen Instituts für Japanstudien', in Trommsdorff, G., H.-J. Kornadt (ed.), *Gesellschaftliche und individuelle Entwicklung in Japan und Deutschland,* UVK, Konstanz 1996, pp. 169–188.

Nihon Kagaku Kyôkai, *ISO 9000. Kokusai hinshitsu hoshô to kigyô no taiô* [ISO 9000: Der internationale Qualitätssicherheitsstandard und die Antwort der Unternehmen], Tokyo 1992.

North, Douglass C., *Institutionen, institutioneller Wandel und Wirtschaftsleistung,* Tübingen 1992.

North, Douglass C., *The Contribution of the New Institutional Economics to an Understanding of the Transition Problem,* Helsinki 1997 (b) (WIDER Annual Lectures 1).

Okamuro, Hiroyuki, *Entwicklung des Abhängigkeitsverhältnisses im Zulieferer-Abnehmer-Netzwerk mit besonderer Berücksichtigung der neune Kommunikationstechnologie in der deutschen Automobilbranche,* Inauguraldissertation, Bonn, 1992.

Okruch, Stefan, *Innovation und Diffusion von Normen. Grundlagen und Elemente einer evolutorischen Theorie des Institutionenwandels,* Berlin 1999 (Heft 491).

Pascha, Werner, 'Theoretische Reflexionen zur Evolution von Interfirmenbeziehungen', in Pascha, Werner, Cornelia Storz: *Workshop KMU IV,* 1998 (Duisburger Arbeitspapiere Ostasienwissenschaften), 1999, pp. 35–36.

Piacentini, Paolo M., 'Future of "Toyotism": Preliminary Reflections on the Critical Points of a Japanese Model of Production', in Metzger-Court, Sarah, Werner Pascha (ed.), *Japan's Socio-Economic Evolution. Continuity and Change,* Japan Library: Kent/Folkestone, 1996, pp. 301–320.

Reimers, Kai, *Normungsprozesse. Eine transaktionsostentheoretische Analyse,* Wiesbaden 1995, pp. 7–33.

Sakai Ichirô, 'Gurôbaruka suru hinshitsu kikaku to kyôso yûi (ue)' [Zum Zusammenhang von sich globalisierenden Qualitätsstandards und Wettbewerbsvorteilen; Teil 1], in: *Seikai Keizai Hyôron,* August 1998a, pp. 55–59.

Sakai Ichirô, 'Gurôbaruka suru hinshitsu kikaku to kyôso yûi (shita)' [Zum Zusammenhang von sich globalisierenden Qualitätsstandards und Wettbewerbsvorteilen; Teil 2], in: *Seikai Keizai Hyôron,* September 1996b: 46–51.

Schulz von Thun, Friedemann, *Miteinander Reden*, Reinbek bei Hamburg 1994.

Sey, Anne, *Team Work in Japan. Evolution as Fact or Fiction*. Paper presented at the 7th GERPISA International Colloquium "Globalizaton Strategies for Automobile Firms and Growth Moves in New Automobile Areas: Torn between Confrontation and Hybridation", June 18–20, 1999, Paris, France.

Storz, Cornelia, 'Standardisierung als Kommunikationsprozeß: Konvergenz und Divergenz am Beispiel technischer Kommunikation', in Lageman, B., C. Storz (ed.), *Konvergenz oder Divergenz? Wandel der Unternehmensstrukturen in Japan und Deutschland* (forthcoming).

Storz, Cornelia, 'Venture Businesses in Japan. Protagonists of a new Economic Order?', in Institute for World Economics and International Management (IWIM)(ed.), *Schumpeter and the Dynamics of Asian Development*, Bremen [fortcoming].

Takada, Ryôji, 'Kigyôkan torihiki bungyô kankei to kankeizai' [Arbeitsteilung in der Transaktion zwischen Unternehmen und das "Beziehungsgut"], in *Ryûtsûkagaku Daigaku Ronshû – Ryûtsuu Keieihen –*, 9:2, 1997 (March; Ryûtsûkagaku Daigaku Gakujutsu Kenkyûkai).

Werle, Raimund, 'Staat und Standards', in Mayntz, Renate, Fritz W. Scharpf (ed.), *Gesellschaftliche Selbstregelung und politische Steuerung*, Max-Planck-Institut für Gesellschaftsforschung, vol. 23, Frankfurt/Main 1995, pp. 266–298.

Wessling, Ewald, *Individuum und Information: die Erfassung von Information und Wissen in ökonomischen Handlungstheorien*, Tübingen 1991 (Die Einheit der Gesellschaftswissenschaften; Bc. 71).

Wimmer, Andreas, 'Kultur, Zur Reformulierung eines sozialantropologischen Grundbegriffs', in *Kölner Zeitschrift für Soziologie und Sozialpsychologie*, Jg. 48 (1996), H 3, pp. 401–425.

Yano Tomosaburô, *Sekai hyôjun ISO Manejimento* [Das Management des globalen ISO-Standards], Nikka Giren Shuppansha, 1998.

Discussant: Christian Wey

In her paper Cornelia Storz (2000) offers interesting conceptual clarifications concerning the cognitive and cultural embeddedness of technical standards. Based on the adoption of the ISO 9000 quality management standard in Japanese firms the paper argues that both cultural embeddedness and cognitive constraints lead to different adaptations of the same standard, and hence, to a non-convergence of production systems. The paper also demonstrates convincingly that existing governance structures, as e.g., quality circles and long-term inter-firm relations, can be adversely affected by a one-to-one implementation of the ISO 9000, and thereby, add to the inertia in adopting the standard literally. Since I do not see any reason to criticize this paper, I will simply take the opportunity to add some remarks from the perspective of Industrial Economics, which relate to the subject matter of Cornelia Storz's paper.

The ISO 9000 Standard and its Adoption by Japanese Firms

The International Organization for Standardization (ISO) is a non-governmental standardization committee that serves as a consensus platform for international standards. While ISO standards are voluntary and adoptions by national authorities remain sovereign decisions, the consensus-based process assures widespread diffusion of ISO standards. Currently, ISO has some 130 member organizations on the basis of one member per country (ISO 2000a: 4). One of the main goals of the organization is to formulate and promote international standards to reduce technical barriers to trade (see Sykes 1995). Of course, since national quality standards usually differ significantly, they are one of the main threats to free international trade. Accordingly, ISO has built together with other standardization committees a partnership with the World Trade Organization (WTO) to reduce "technical barriers to trade" (for more information visit http://www.iso.ch/wtotbt/wtotbt.htm).

While the vast majority of ISO standards are highly specific to a particular product or process, ISO 9000 is a complex guide for a company's internal quality management; it includes, for instance, the allocation of responsibilities, auditing procedures, statistical methods, and training. According to ISO, "quality" is defined by all those features of a product or service, which are required by the customer (ISO 2000b: 1). Therefore, quality management is a means of organizing the production process such that a firm's products meet the consumers' requirements. While it is the ultimate goal of the ISO 9000 standard to assure that quality standards of the final products are met, the ISO 9000 certified label is not a guarantee for product quality. However, the ISO 9000 certificate informs the buyer that an independent auditor has checked that the supplier's production process influencing quality conforms to the relevant ISO 9000 standard's requirements (ISO 2000b: 1).

Since 1993 the worldwide adoption of the ISO 9000 standard is increasing rapidly over time. According to figures taken form ISO (2000b), up to the end of December 1999, at least 343,643 ISO 9000 certificates had been awarded in 150 countries worldwide. This is an increase of 26.40 per cent over a period of one year. International diffusion measured by the number of countries adopting ISO 9000 also increased sharply from 48 in 1993 to 150 in 1999. Adoption by non-European firms and in particular Japanese firms is also increasing and, more importantly, their share has been increasing over time. In 1993 only 2.46 per cent of worldwide certifications went to Far Eastern countries while in 1999 their share has increased to 16.48 per cent. This dramatic evolution is also mirrored in the total number of adoptions by Japanese firms.

Figure 20 ISO 9000 in Japan

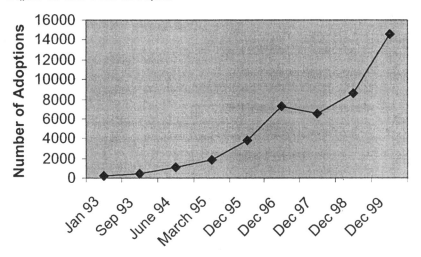

Source ISO (2000b).

Figure 20 depicts the diffusion of the ISO 9000 standard in Japan, which is increasing over time. In 1993 only 165 certificates had been awarded to Japanese firms while in 1998 14,564 firms got certified to an ISO 9000 standard. A similar pattern can be found in North America and the USA, where the number of certifications increased form 893 in 1993 up to 33,054 in 1999.

All in all, these certification figures provide some evidence that the adoption process of ISO 9000 has surpassed the critical mass and has gained momentum not only in Europe but in particular in Far East countries and, in particular Japan (see Figure 17), which experienced in 1999 the fifth highest annual growth with 5,951 new ISO 9000 certificates.

The industrial economics of ISO 9000

By inspection of the evolution of total adoptions of ISO 9000 in Japan and many other countries we can observe a non-linear diffusion process which will result in the S-shaped, or "logistic," pattern of growth common to positive feedback processes. In 1993 the adoption of ISO 9000 started slowly while in the following years the number of additional certificates increased steadily. This non-linearity can be interpreted as evidence for ISO 9000 having the property of a systems standard (also called compatibility standard). In this case, users' preferences exhibit positive network externalities, meaning that the utility of each user increases with the number of users adopting the same standard. As a result, the adoption process of a system standard is characterized by positive feedback leading to a non-linear diffusion process of the ISO 9000 standard. As is well known from the economics of standardization, the resulting outcome can be inefficient, because variety of systems or the adoption of a different industry-wide standard may be preferable. Both positive network externalities and specific investments, however, may keep society locked-in to an inferior system (for an overview see Wey 1999).

It is interesting to notice at this point that the ISO 9000 standard is – at a first glance – a pure quality standard. Thus, there seems to be no a priori reason to expect positive network effects shaping the adoption process of the ISO 9000 standard. However, since ISO 9000 formulates standards for an organization's internal quality management it is not just simply a product standard, but can be regarded as a "language" for making quality management internationally compatible. Of course, a language is a compatibility standard par excellence and its adoption clearly exhibits positive network externalities (see Lazear 1999). Sticking to the "language" analogy, the different interpretations of the ISO 9000 identified in Cornelia Storz's paper can be interpreted as "dialects". As in the case of "English" – the current lingua franca – we should expect that people speaking with different dialects in their home businesses should nevertheless understand each other, as long as there is continuous interaction over time. Because the ISO 9000 standard has been formulated exactly for that purpose (namely, to promote international trade flows and cross-country economic activities) we can expect compatibility among the various dialects evolving in different cultures and businesses. This supposition is confirmed by the adoption figures of the ISO 9000 standard that seem to support the existence of network effects. If the dialects were incompatible, those network effects would be absent. Hence, there is some reason to assume that the various dialects of the ISO 9000 standard remain compatible with each other and that, therefore, variety in dialects does not threatens the main purpose of the standard; namely, to achieve a framework for compatible technology worldwide.

Besides the "language" property of ISO 9000, we are clearly confronted with a minimum quality standard which can be interpreted as an efficiency enhancing regulatory device to avoid market failure when buyers cannot inspect a product's quality ex ante; i.e., before purchasing the product. In the absence of enforceable guarantees or effective signaling mechanisms, buyers are unable to distinguish high quality from low quality. Thus, buyers ex ante view all products as perfect substitutes, and the market may fail to deliver high quality products as Akerlof (1970) has shown in his seminal paper on the used car market ("The Market for 'Lemons'"). As is well known this kind of market failure can be mitigated by explicit, enforceable contracts such as licensing arrangements or guarantees. Further, even when explicit contractual solutions are ruled out, boycott and reputation mechanisms can assure high quality products as has been shown by Klein and Leffler (1981). Under incomplete information, introductory prices and, in particular, advertising expenditures may signal high quality production (Milgrom and Roberts 1986). Finally, in an international setting firms can also signal their product quality by locating at high-cost locations, and thereby, franchising a well-established country-of-origin label, as e.g. "Made-in Germany" (Haucap, Wey, and Barmbold 2000).

Under this "informational" perspective, the ISO 9000 certificate can be interpreted as a means to reduce informational asymmetries directly as well as a costly signaling device. ISO 9000 might be superior to purely dissipative signals as, e.g., advertising because it also offers valuable technological guidance and verifiable auditing. However, as has been shown by Leland (1989), quality standards which are determined in an industry profits maximizing fashion can be too restrictive. High quality standards may deter low quality entry, reduce industry output, and thereby, can secure monopoly rents.

In the case of supplier-manufacturer relations bilateral governances of auditing, inspection and long-term relations can reinforce high quality production. As described in Cornelia Storz's paper and, for example, in Waldenberger (1999) Japanese subcontractor relations offer various institutional arrangements for governing exchange in the vertical production chain. More importantly, those vertical governances are embedded in production, design and engineering practices, the vertical *keiretsu*, employment relations and seniority based payment schemes that are strongly complementary to each other. In the words of Milgrom and Roberts (1990: 526) we might regard the Japanese model as a "coherent business strategy" that exploits organizational complementarities. As a result of those complementarities, relatively small organizational changes can reduce the overall performance dramatically and a successful implementation of the ISO 9000 quality management system requires a coordinated adjustment of all decision variables that recognizes the prevailing complementarities. Of course, such a "large scale" coordination of single businesses and inter-firm relations is costly to achieve, and imposes a binding constraint on firms' willingness to implement ISO 9000 literally.

At this stage, I think it is not too bold to hope that Cornelia Storz's finding that "*one* standard is not *one* standard" is the result of an efficient adaptation process in which the emergence of "ISO 9000 dialects" does not threatens the compatibility (or "language") property of ISO 9000 while at the same time allowing for firm-specific adjustments which protect organizational complementarities.

REFERENCES

Akerlof, George A., 'The Market for "Lemons": Quality Uncertainty and the Market Mechanism', in *Quarterly Journal of Economics*, Vol. 84 (1970), pp. 488–500.

Haucap, Justus; Wey, Christian, and Barmbold, Jens, 'Location Costs, Product Quality and Implicit Franchise Contracts', in *Journal of International Economics*, Vol. 52 (2000), pp. 69–87.

ISO, *Introduction to ISO*, International Organization for Standardization, Geneva, http://www.iso.ch/infoe/intro.htm, 2000a.

ISO, *ISO in Brief*, International Organization for Standardization, Geneva, http://www.iso.ch, 2000b.

Klein, B. and Leffler, K., 'The Role of Market Forces in Assuring Contractual Performance', in *Journal of Political Economy*, Vol. 89 (1981), pp. 615–641.

Lazear, Edward P., 'Culture and Language', in *Journal of Political Economy*, Vol. 107 (1999), pp. S95–126.

Leland, Hayne E., 'Quacks, Lemons, and Licensing: A Theory of Minimum Quality Standards', in *Journal of Political Economy*, Vol. 87 (1989), pp. 1328–1346.

Milgrom, Paul and Roberts, John, 'Price and Advertising Signals of Product Quality', in *Journal of Political Economy*, Vol. 94 (1986), pp. 796–821.

Milgrom, Paul and Roberts, John, 'The Economics of Modern Manufacturing: Technology, Strategy, and Organization', in *American Economic Review*, Vol. 80 (1990), pp. 511–528.

Storz, Cornelia, *Implementation of Standards: What About the Possibility of a Convergence of Production Systems by International Rules*, 2000.

Sykes, Alan O., *Product Standards for Internationally Integrated Goods Markets*, Washington, D.C. 1995.

Waldenberger, Franz, *Organisation und Evolution arbeitsteiliger Systeme: Erkenntnisse aus der japanischen Wirtschaftsentwicklung*, München 1999.

Wey, Christian, *Marktorganisation durch Standardisierung. Ein Beitrag zur Neuen Institutionenökonomik des Marktes*, Berlin 1999.

10

FLEXIBLE RIGIDITIES AND REDUNDANT CAPACITIES: LIBERALIZATION OF EMPLOYMENT IN JAPAN AND GERMANY

Karen A. Shire and Jun Imai[1]

10.1 INTRODUCTION

In the 1980s, the strength of regulated and institutionally dense capitalist economies such as the German and Japanese economies highlighted the importance of institutions and market coordination in organizing and embedding economic activities. A decade later, the relative decline of these economies, counterposed against the strong performance of the more liberal US economy posed an important cognitive challenge to embedded capitalism (Crouch and Streeck 1997). Both the German and Japanese employment systems are under pressure to liberalize and in some respects are *liberalizing*. Scholarship on comparative models of embedded capitalism "in crisis" strongly suggests however, that liberalization does not permeate national level systems in anything like a unified way (Boyer and Drache 1996, Hollingsworth and Boyer 1997). Especially the adaptation of employment and labor markets involve re-regulation as well as de-regulation and recent indications are that divergence between national regulatory regimes and practices is both narrowing and persisting (OECD 1999a, Regini 2000). How are we to understand the sources of employment liberalization?

The present transformation in employment is more than a process of dismantling regulations and activating external labor markets. Work transformations, which span new working styles, new types of workers, new

[1] The authors would like to acknowledge and thank Mehmet Gunsür for research support and the construction of statistical tables published in this paper.

occupations, new industries, and the so-called new economy are changing the nature of work. These transformations exert another set of pressures on existing employment institutions which in some respects parallel the policy directions of deregulation, but in other respects create the need for institutional reconstruction. Work transformation and liberalization do not necessarily launch the same repertoire of employment changes.

In the study of employment changes, sociologists of work make a basic distinction between numerical flexibility and functional flexibility. Increasing numerical flexibility in employment involves removing restrictions on the employment contract in order to allow for quick and frequent adjustments (hiring, firing and transfers) in employment levels. This is the usual sense of liberalizing employment relations, and implies the returning of labor from a fixed to a variable cost through employment deregulation. Functional flexibility is achieved where workers are trained and developed in a way that allows for their effective deployment in a range of organizational tasks and functions. The development of a functionally flexible workforce typically rules out numerical flexibility, since training investments on the part of firms are best realized through employment commitments.

From a sociological point of view, the strong performance of the Japanese and German economies in the 1980s was linked to the emphasis on functional flexibility. The employment commitments which underlay these functionally flexible employment systems are now being called into question by policy makers for a number of reasons. First of all, the industrial transition from manufacturing-based to service-based economies is slow in Germany and Japan because employment in the industrial sectors remains protected through traditional practices, which insure long-term job security. Employment liberalization in the form of removing these protections is viewed by its proponents as a mechanism for speeding up this transition and dealing with relatively high unemployment. While employment commitments in the traditional sectors of employment in Germany and Japan are weakening, it is too soon to assume that job security or new types of regulations are inappropriate for the range of new activities and occupations related to the information and service sectors where employment is in high demand. Precisely this assumption however, is often made. The question which needs to be asked is whether functional flexibility might not continue to contribute important sources of competitive strength within the new forms and processes of information and high skilled service work.

The strengths of German and Japanese employment institutions were best elaborated in the social institutional approaches of Streeck and Dore, both of whom emphasized the importance of rigid employment commitments and the acceptance of employment redundancies, contrary to neoliberal labor market logic. Sluggish employment adjustment, resistance against the dismantling of traditional employment regulations, and continuing normative commitments to existing employment institutions all signal continuities in the commitment to a functionally flexible (rather than numerically flexible) work force. Despite this continuity, an important change in Germany and Japan is the declining numbers of employees covered by traditional employment relations (regular and long-term employment). Though slow, the shift out of industrial employment is taking place. The persistence of high unemployment on the one hand, and labor shortages in information services on the other, make clear that the shift into new areas of employment is also slow.

Because of slow adjustment, regulatory regimes which had governed employment relations so well up through the 1980s in Germany and Japan are now the subject of national debate. In both countries, these national debates take the form of calls for and against the liberalization of labor markets and employment relations. Looking at these debates, the idea of a less regulated labor market has become an imaginable alternative to the traditional institutions of employment regulation. Yet the turn to the market involves enough of the same regulatory legacy of the traditional systems to suggest considerable divergence from the model of a liberal labor market. Changes which are evident are in part a sign of "giving in to liberalization pressures", but this is not the whole story. Debates and even what appear, as deregulation is also part of the changing social orientation toward working life and the emergence of new working styles in Germany and Japan. We conclude by arguing that sociological work on the convergence or divergence of employment institutions should focus less on liberalization pressures, and more on the nature of work transformation, working values and orientations in order to better map out the contours of likely and desired institutional changes.

10.2 THE STRENGTHS OF EMPLOYMENT COMMITMENTS

10.2.1 Flexible rigidities in Japan

The traditional strengths of the Japanese employment system lie in employee commitment, functional flexibility and incentives for skilling generated by the system of long-term employment. Taking labor out of market competition through long-term employment introduces rigidity against industrial adjustments to new activities and sectors. In *Flexible Rigidities* Dore (1986) argues the contrary. Long-term employment commitments in Japan generated labor consent in the process of automating production and diversifying into new production areas in the 1980s.

What is often remarked on as a disability under which Japanese companies labor – the lifetime commitment and the fact that the wage bill thereby becomes a quasi-fixed cost – can paradoxically be seen as an advantageous stimulus to diversification. Where workers can be dismissed at will, a firm faced with shrinkage in its traditional markets can be tempted to solve its problems in the short term by cutting costs to get back to profitability. Where that option is not available – or involves heavy once-for-all payments as inducements to early retirement – there is likely to be a stronger incentive to diversify into some new product line in order to get the best out of workers who have to be employed anyway. (p. 72)

While cutting employment, especially through *voluntary* early retirement and reduced recruitment was not uncommon in the recessions of the 1970s, employment reductions were treated as last resort adjustments following wage cuts and reduced working hours. State policies underwrote long-term employment despite economic downturn primarily by providing further incentives for employers to retain employment. By the end of the 1970s, the lifetime employment system was strengthened rather than weakened, by an "institutional repertoire of a whole set of new conventions about how to deal with severe recession" (p. 249). Employment security measures continue to be important in the current wave of high unemployment in Japan (rôdôshô 1999).

Further, this pattern of employment security based on labor's consent in diversifying production was based in a particular pattern of skill-formation which while firm-centered, was most importantly developed through the high internal mobility of employees between firm functions and work activities, and even between related firms and customer organizations. The regular rotation of employees is a matter of managerial prerogative in large Japanese organizations (Shire and Ota 1998), and yields a particular type of skill mix. First, rotations tend to concentrate in a particular area of firm business, and the skills which are developed can be best characterized as "specialized generalization" (Nakamura 1995). Second, on-the-job training is the focus of skill acquisition which occurs through experiential learning and depends on coworker and supervisor communities of practice. A proclivity to learn is the fundamental capacity of employees, and learning to adjust to new situations, as well as to problem solve (Koike 1987) form as much of the skill repertoire of individual employees as specific aspects of manual and analytical skills. Finally, rotations and communities of practice bring employers in contact with each other, and coworker relations play an important role in on-the-job learning as well as in the facilitation of cooperative work practices. Orientation programs for new firm recruits focus specifically on community building, and provide an initial socialization of young employees (Shire 1999a). The subsequent years of rotations and experiential learning *in situ* result in the development of relational networks among coworkers which socially underlie inter-organizational work processes, and transform inter-functional relations into coworker network relations. The result of this pattern of skill formation and working is a functionally flexible, personally adaptable workforce with high coworking capacities. Long-term employment is an essential precondition for the development of such working and coworking capacities.

10.2.2 Redundant capacities in Germany

German workforce skills are developed out of a dual vocational training system codetermined by employers' association and trade-unions, and with an emphasis on occupational knowledge as well as technique learned through direct workplace experience. Employment patterns in key industries in Germany (e.g. metalworking) have also been long-term and internal labor mobility is also common. The social regulation of vocational training together with institutions of workplace codetermination which constrain the extent to which firms may lay off workers greatly limit the capacity of managers to unilaterally make decisions about training and employment levels (Streeck 1992). Skill (and employment) redundancies inevitably recur with recessions and downward swings in the business cycle.

In the wake of the 1970s recessions, exactly these redundancies were strengthened in the context of unions and works councils demands for using "training as a way of maintaining employment in internal labor markets and reducing youth unemployment" (Streeck 1992, p. 182). A pattern of purposive overskilling developed whereby apprentices were taken on even where no further skilled workers were needed, and recruited instead to production jobs until a position opened for a skilled worker. It was in the context of rapid technological changes in the 1980s that these redundancies became capacities for "absorbing technical change without disruption" (p. 184).

A crucial resource for firms in technologically and economically volatile markets are high skills that are at the same time broad enough to allow for application to a wide range of rapidly changing, as yet unknown tasks (Streeck 1992, p. 16).

Similar to Japanese firm-specific skills, German occupationally based training also resulted in polyvalent skills which were "not functionally dedicated to any specific purpose or activity" and which included the "general capacity to acquire more skills"(Streeck 1992, p. 16). Further, occupational communities rooted in the common socialization of vocational training and firm-internal apprentice programs formed the basis for coworker cooperation and informal learning through experience beyond the apprentice stage.

10.3 FROM STRENGTHS TO WEAKNESSES?

Similar patterns of long-term employment, high commitments to train young workers and maintain employment of skilled workers posed constraints on Japanese and German employers, especially in times of economic downturn. Yet the shared response to the last serious economic crises of the 1970s strengthened rather than weakened "rigid and redundant" employment practices. In the 1980s these employment patterns were celebrated as enabling work transformations through the introduction of new technology in response to internationalization and increasing competition. The lesson of robust employment institutions, adaptable to new economic and industrial developments, defied the model of flexible employment structures in more liberal, less-embedded economies like the U.S. and the U.K.

Since 1992 and 1993 respectively, the Japanese and German economies have been experiencing their worst recessions in the post-WWII period. For Japan, the liberalization and internationalization of capital markets have exerted profound pressures, not least of all due to the archaic regulation of the finance industry, the absence of transparency and high levels of irresponsible lending (Pempel 1998). For Germany, the dual-unification, ongoing in the case of the European Union, and a shock to the economy, in the case of the integration of East Germany into the *Bundesrepublik* have added enormous pressures for change on the German model. The shock of unification with the East alone, may have been enough to end the German model, though problems were already evident in the 1980s (Streeck 1997).

Nonetheless, one of the remarkable features of employment in Germany and Japan at the end of the 1990s is the persistence of employment protections which limit dismissals as a response to economic pressures. The continuation, certainly against all recent OECD recommendations, of active labor market measures for dealing with unemployment (OECD 1999a, OECD 1999b, OECD 1999c) is a second, related continuity. German and Japanese employment institutions are resisting liberalizing. Can or should this continue?

By the late 1990s in both Japan and Germany, record high unemployment, and the slowing down of the shift from manufacturing to service employment were evident. While the continuities with past employment practices remain important, debates and discussion within Japan and Germany about employment restructuring now seriously consider (numerically flexible) market alternatives for dealing with unemployment which would expand employment in growing sectors. Ironically however, liberalization is not aimed at the protected core of skilled industrial workers. Still, these workers remain well protected in Germany and Japan. In the next section we review major changes in employment, especially in the late 1990s.

10.4 CHANGE IN THE GERMAN AND JAPANESE EMPLOYMENT STRUCTURES IN THE LATE 1990s

Employment has stopped growing in both Germany and Japan. The German trend is in part a factor of "parking" several million potential employees in various forms of education and training, the relatively low female labor participation rate, and overall, a relatively low employment rate (71.7% in 1998, compared to 78.2% in Japan; Table 17). In Japan, for the first time in the post-war period, the number of employees declined over the previous year in 1998, and continued to decline in 1999 (rôdôsho 1999, www.mol.go.jp). High unemployment (discussed below) and demographic factors are dimensions of the problem, but inadequate employment adjustment is also clearly a factor.

Table 17 Labor force participation rates, Germany and Japan,
1990–1999

Year	Germany	Japan
1985	67.6	72.2
1990	69.1	74.1
1995	71.2	76.4
1996	71.4	77.0
1997	71.1	78.0
1998	71.7	78.2
1999	–	78.1

Sources: For 1985 - 1999, OECD Labor Force Statistics 1977-1997, publication year, 1998. Rates for Japan in 1998 and 1999 based on self-calculations from the following sources: working age population from Management and Coordination Agency Statistics Bureau home page tables (www.stat.go.jp), and employed labor force statistics from telephone reports from the Ministry of Labor, Tokyo. German rates for 1998 as reported in a telephone inquiry with the Statistisches Bundesamt. German rates for 1999 still not available as of 12/2000.

Table 18 Average yearly change in selected sectors of employment
1990 – 1997 (thousands and percents)

GERMANY

	Change in Employment Numbers and % Change 1985–1990	Change in Employment Numbers and % Change 1991–1995	Change in Employment Numbers and % Change 1995–1998
Total	+1926 1.4%	-1018 -0.7%	+812 0.8%
Manufac-turing	+435 1.0%	-2,491 -5.8%	-535 -2.0%
Wholesale and Retail Trade	+409 1.9%	+848 3.9%	+122 0.7%
Finance, Insurance, Real Estate and Business Services	+495 4.8%	+801 6.6%	+237 2.2%
Services	686 2.0%	-126 -0.3%	+560 1.9%

Sources: OECD (1999d).

JAPAN

	Change in Employment Numbers and % Change 1985–1990	Change in Employment Numbers and % Change 1991–1995	Change in Employment Numbers and % Change 1995–1998
Total Employment	+4420 1.5%	+2080 0.7%	+330 0.2%
Manufacturing	+520 0.7%	-490 -0.6%	-740 -1.7%
Wholesale and Retail Trade	+970 1.4%	+340 0.5%	+340 0.8%
Finance, Insurance, Real Estate, and Business Services	+1,240 5.7%	+390 1.5%	-2980 -17.2%
Services	+1,350 2.2%	+1590 2.3%	+3870 8.4%

Sources: OECD (1999d).

Throughout the early 90s, employment in manufacturing declined in both countries (Table 18). Employment grew in various parts of the service sector up until the early 1990s, but then variations by sector and country are evident. Employment growth in all service sectors slowed between 1995 and 1997 in Germany to an average of 1–2 %. Financial and business services employment declined sharply in Japan during the late 1990s while growth in personal and social services boomed (8.4% from 1995–1998). Female part-time employment grew while regular employment declined with 380,000 such jobs added to the Japanese labor market in 1998 (Japan Institute of Labor 1999).[2] Current German debates about the liberalization of labor markets focus in part, on expanding a similar low-wage and part-time sector of employment.

Unemployment (Table 19) remained high in Germany, not least of all because of the above average rates in the new German states in eastern Germany. Despite large budget allocation to various old and new employment security and labor market adjustment measures, unemployment in Japan has continued its upward climb.

---

[2] The expansion cannot simply be credited to an increase in the female employment rate however, since female "regular" employment decreased by 4.5% between 1992 and 1997 and female unemployment remained in sync with the national and male rates (Shire and Imai 2000).

Table 19 Unemployment rates 1990 - 1999

Year	Germany	Japan
1985	9.3	2.6
1990	7.2	2.1
1995	10.4	3.2
1996	11.5	3.4
1997	12.7	3.4
1998	12.3	4.1
1999	11.7*	4.7

*Reported in a telephone inquiry with the Statistisches Bundesamt

Sources: For Germany, Statistisches Bundesamt (1987 and 1996) and Bundesanstalt für Arbeit (2000) for various years; for Japan 1995-1999 Japan Institute of Labor at www.jil.go.jp. Japan rates for 1985 and 1990 from Japan Statistical Yearbook on-line at www.stat.go.jp.

The decline in manufacturing and growth in various service sectors was evident in occupational terms too. In Table 20, the selected occupations are reported by country due to differences in the construction and reporting of occupational categories. In both Germany and Japan, the numbers of skilled craft and production workers declined, though the decline was sharper in Germany (Craft and trades -4%, Plant and machine operators -3.8%). A clear difference was in the employment of unskilled workers; a decline of 3.9% in Germany, but an increase of 7.9% in Japan. The same trend was evident in white-collar work, where clerical employment declined in Germany (-2.4%), but grew in Japan (+3.3%). Occupational growth in both countries was evident in service and sales occupations (5% in Germany; 3.4% in Japan) and in professional and technical occupations (the largest category of growth in Germany with 7.4% and second to unskilled work in Japan with 6.5%).

Over the last two decades, both Germany and Japan have retained a relatively large share of employment in manufacturing and have kept it longer than the American "service economy model" (Castells 1996). The analysis of changes over the last five years shows that the shift from manufacturing to service employment has continued, with high unemployment and stronger growth in professional and technical work. In the more deregulated employment context of Japan, growth was also strong in low-wage sectors of employment (clerical work and unskilled work).

Growth in the category of professional and technical workers in both countries is qualified by very acute labor shortages, especially in high skilled information and knowledge services. The German government has prepared a "green card" immigration program and has begun to recruit foreign IT specialists for limited contract employment. In Japan, the category "professional and technical" is the only one, where employers report labor shortages (see Shire and Imai 2000, Figure 1). Nikkeiren (the management association representing mainly large employers' interests in policy negotiations) plans

Table 20 Change in employment by selected occupations 1995 - 1999 (thousands and percents)

German Occupations	Germany Change in Employment and % Change	Japanese Occupations	Japan Change in Employment and % Change
Legislators, senior officials and managers	-48 -2.3%	Managers	-150 -6.5%
Professional and technical and associate professions	+801 7.4%	Professional and technical	450 6.5%
Clerks	-111 -2.4%	Office workers	390 3.3%
Service and sales workers	194 5%	Service and sales workers	410 3.4%
Craft and related trade workers	-260 -4%	Skilled workers	-300 -2.2%
Plant and machine operators and assemblers	-107 -3.8%		
Unskilled workers	-111 -3.9%	Unskilled workers	220 7.9%

Sources: German data compiled from ILO Labor Statistics Database on-line, Japanese data compiled from Ministry of Labor sources, 1998 and 1999 data in Japan obtained through personal correspondence with the Ministry of Labor, Tokyo. The category "plant and machine operators and assemblers" is not reported in Japan, and spread instead among skilled and unskilled workers. Other categories provide reasonable matches, but we report these by country due to inexact matching.

to use relaxed temporary work regulations to recruit technical specialists from worker dispatching services (Nikkeiren 1995, Shire and Imai 2000). As response to the shortage of knowledge workers, the German plan to recruit foreigners, and the Japanese plan to recruit non-regular workers are in fact, quite traditional. In Germany, foreign guest workers were recruited in the past to industrial employment during times of labor shortage, especially to fill less skilled assembly jobs. This time the shortage is in areas like software engineering, and part of the policy response is to recruit foreign computer specialists with non-permanent residence status. In Japan, the demand for low wage and numerically flexible workers in the 1970s was met by expanding part-time work, typically taken up by women. At present, the composition of new forms of temporary work is nearly 75% female, and the new "professional temporary" employment category proposed by Nikkeiren can be understood as a way of channeling educated women into non-regular jobs while preserving regular jobs for men (Shire and Imai 2000). Foreign software engineers with limited working visas, and female professional workers temporarily dispatched to work assignments are forms of employment with important precedents in Germany and Japan (guest workers and part-timers respectively). New is the targeting of foreign and women workers for high skill jobs in the information and knowledge service sectors, and in both cases employment is not with long-term possibilities. Thus a precarious sector of high-skill employment is emerging alongside a protected sector of regular employment.

The steady, though slow, decline of regular employment in Germany and Japan has been achieved without any fundamental change in the protection and status of the core industrial workforce. Nonetheless, the scope of coverage of traditional employment institutions is clearly affected, with growing proportions of the working population falling outside the realm of employment commitments and protections. Both the ranks of the core regular employees (*seishain*) in Japan and those of the German skilled industrial worker (*Facharbeiter*) paid at the collectively bargained rate have thinned in the 1990s (Thelen and Kume 1999). In Germany, the exit of employers from employers' associations is one mechanism decreasing the coverage of collectively bargained contracts. In Japan, downsizing of large firms is the main cause of decreased coverage. In both cases, labor is shed through forms of early retirement. Some have interpreted the phenomena of declining coverage without deregulation as evidence of the persistence and continuity in employment institutions (Thelen and Kume 1999). The development could also be interpreted as one of increasing irrelevance of existing employment regulations, as greater proportions of the labor market in both countries are found outside the regulated sector of employment (see Hassel 1999 for Germany).

In this context, a debate has unfolded in both countries about the limits of industrial employment institutions for regulating employment in a transforming German and Japanese economy. In both countries, the market as an alternative to regulation has become an imaginable alternative for expanding employment in low skill (and low wage) services. When new forms of employment for new types of work are addressed, policy directions are less clear, but nonetheless aim at re-regulation rather than de-regulation.

10.5 MARKETS OR REGULATIONS?

The concepts of *flexible rigidities* and *redundant capacities* point to the unexpected strengths that may derive from regulations, which contribute to generating a functionally flexible workforce. Rigidities and redundancies are exactly the qualities, which the free exchange of labor, according to the rule of supply and demand, are meant to eliminate. Yet in both Germany and Japan, employment regulations were shown to achieve other desirable economic goals, namely flexible labor deployment and the capacity to adapt quickly to technological change, as well as broader social goals such as relatively low inequality and social integration. As such, the German and Japanese models of employment pose formidable alternatives to the liberal model of labor markets.

So far the similarities between Germany and Japan have been emphasized, but several differences are also key in understanding the possible directions of future changes. In Germany more than Japan, employment regulations were economy-wide on the basis of labor law and industrial relations practices. In contrast, the Japanese labor market has always been a segmented labor market, with employment protections covering about one-fifth of the total labor force in large firms. In an important sense, a periphery of numerically flexible workers has always counterbalanced the core of functionally flexible workers in Japan. This difference is proving to have an impact on the pace and direction of change in Japan, and contrasts with a more solidaristic approach in Germany.

As suggested above, employment commitments are most obviously loosening for foreign and female workers in Germany and Japan respectively. Most recently however, public debates about employment adjustment have called for more liberalization in employment, and discussions in both countries center around the principle of "more market and less regulation" characteristic of Anglo-American economies. In the present situation of employment stagnation and labor shortages, the strengths of "rigid and redundant" employment alternatives to a liberal labor market are no longer beyond a doubt, (though outcomes like relative equality and social cohesion continue to be defensible outcomes). In response, there is a greater willingness among social as well as economic actors to consider at least loosening regulations (if not outright deregulation) in order to reintroduce *more market*. We can date this shift in discourse in both countries to the late 1990s.

According to Streeck and Heinze, writing about the German case, "(t)he most important instrument of a new labor market policy in the transition to a service society is – the market" (1999, p. 44). The statement is all the more dramatic in that the authors are not business leaders or neoclassical economists, but rather two scholars close to the social-democratic party in Germany, one of whom is responsible for the original formulation of the strengths of the German model. In Japan the major shift came with the inclusion of labor market regulations in the deregulation efforts of the Japanese government. Up until the mid-1990s, labor market regulations were considered an element of social policy (Araki 1999, p. 5). The traditional set of measures guaranteeing employment security for core workforces during recessions were supplemented with programs to "activate the external labor market" in order to increase labor "mobility" from the declining sectors of the economy to growth sectors such as services and medium size firms (rôdôshô 1999).

Traditionally restricting dismissals was the employees' safety net. In the era of restructuring where dismissals are inevitable, an active labor market which can provide the unemployed with suitable new employment opportunities swiftly and smoothly functions as a new safety net (Araki 1999, p. 6).

In both the German and Japanese discussions there are two separate justifications for a turn to the market in employment policy debates. The first concerns the alleviation of record high unemployment levels. The German version of the new market rhetoric is partly aimed at addressing long-term unemployment and relatively low labor force participation rates, especially among women. In the words of Streeck and Heinze "(almost) every job is better than none" (1999, p. 44), and controlled deregulation of sectors such as low-wage employment would create more job opportunities. The Japanese turn to the market is justified with a similar logic. The external labor market is seen as a new "safety net" in exchange for the old guarantees of long-term employment (Araki 1999) for redundant workers and the growing ranks of the long-term unemployed.

On closer examination, the concrete *market oriented* employment proposals do deviate in important respects from a liberal model of relatively unregulated labor markets. In the German policy debates, the concept of a subsidized low wage sector where state transfers would replace the social contributions deducted from the lowest categories of wage-earners represents an important continuity in as far as all wage-earners would continue to be included in the system of social insurance. Another concrete proposal which would extend the coverage of collectively bargained wages would have the state subsidize the wage bill of temporary work agencies when they hire unemployed workers at the collectively bargained employment conditions. Streeck and Heinze argue that "(W)age subsidies should be paid to those temporary work firms which hire the unemployed at the collectively bargained conditions. Collectively regulated employment in temporary work firms is an ideal way to tie together social security with flexibility" (1999, p. 45). The new Japanese measures to "activate the external labor market" also involve a range of state subsidies for wages offered to firms which employ the unemployed or accept redundant workers from other companies. The aim of these policies is "reemployment without unemployment". One could also interpret these new measures as skipping the labor market altogether, by encouraging direct labor mobility and transfers between firms and sectors. Labor transfers have long been a feature of inter-firm relations and labor adjustment in Japan. The new element lies in the fact that the firms involved are not necessarily in the same business groups, and state subsidies rather than inter-firm links provide the mechanisms for the transfers.

Despite the relatively limited nature of the *market* element in these new policy proposals and measures, they are the subject of considerable debate in both national contexts. One area of debate concerns whether the measures will have their intended effects at all, or whether they might well lead to unintended and undesirable effects. Yoji Tatsui, Director of Labor Policy for RENGO argues that the "shift in emphasis from maintaining long-term employment practices to encouraging labor mobility" will not solve the unemployment problem. "(S)imply increasing 'labor mobility' will put job-searching workers into a labor market with few stable jobs and will serve only to increase the number of workers who feel uncertain about their employment prospects" (1999, p. 13). The debates in Germany are even fiercer with claims that measures like a subsidized low wage threaten to change "our whole institutional framework" including creating disincentives for employers to train workers, increasing income inequality and longer working hours (Bosch 1999; Bosch 2000). In both Germany and Japan, the new market discourse is mainly aimed at dealing with unemployment (and labor force participation in the German case). Very little of the liberalization rhetoric addresses the sorts of employment institutions which might promote effective working relations in the information and knowledge economy. The question might be put as follows: Does functional flexibility contribute to effective working relations in high skill information and knowledge services? If so, what sorts of adjustments to traditional employment regulations (i.e. what re-regulations) are necessary for effective working relations in the new areas of work?

Re-regulation evident in Germany and Japan so far follows the path of traditional institutional developments. In both cases, responses to labor shortages in information and knowledge services fall back on traditional sources of numerically flexible labor on the periphery of these employment systems (foreign workers in Germany and women in Japan). The Japanese employment structure is traditionally more segmented between an employment core and periphery, and regulatory attempts to expand the periphery are stronger in the Japanese case. Thus, in Germany, where shortages in IT employment are also addressed by adding four new IT related occupational courses to the vocational employment system, in Japan, the response is to relax temporary work regulations in order to expand non-regular employment into high skill job areas. Nikkeiren proposes adding a new employment type – temporary professionals – alongside long-term employed core workers and numberically flexible part-time workers – to the large-firm employment structure (1995, Shire and Imai 2000). German discussions about non-regular employment expansion, in contrast, aim at integrating part-time and temporary work into the social insurance systems and extending professional development schemes, which at present apply only to the full-time employees, to new forms of employment (Baethge 1999). This is the opposite current of Japanese regulations, and more in line with the traditional concern for solidarity through "normalizing" employment conditions economy-wide.

10.6 EMPLOYMENT POLICIES FOR KNOWLEDGE WORK

In closing our analysis, we wish to speculate on the possible strengths of an amended German and Japanese model of employment. We begin with the assumption that increasing numbers of professional and technical workers will be employed in large organizations in the future (Abbott 1992). Organizational professionals are likely to form the rank-and-file of the new expanding sectors of information- and knowledge-intensive work, and current shortages in professional and technical workers may be a more important employment problem than unemployment and low-wage service sector expansion. What types of work do organizational professionals engage in?

Information- and knowledge-intensive work is most often project-based, involves an expanding range of knowledge gained from working experience (contextual knowledge), and is often extremely complex, thus requiring cooperative working between professionals with quite different areas of expertise (Frenkel et al. 1999). The nature of information- and knowledge-intensive work points to the continuing importance of employment commitments in generating the on-the-job learning and coworking networks required of complex forms of service work. Do present employment policy responses in Germany and Japan promise to generate employment practices, which are based on employment commitments for organizational professionals in the information and knowledge work sectors? The temporary professional employment scheme proposed by Nikkeiren, and in part realized in the 1999 reform of the dispatched workers law in Japan is unlikely in our estimate, to facilitate either the contextual knowledge or coworking capacities demanded in knowledge and information intensive forms of service work. In the German case where the reform discussions move more in the direction of integrating new forms of employment into traditional labor market policy goals, we see a greater possible alignment with the requirements of information- and knowledge-intensive service work.

For knowledge professionals, long-term employment within an organization may remain an important form of employment. Organizational communities facilitate the development of coworking relationships which early research has shown is important to complex project-based forms of work organization. Organizational communities also facilitate the communities of practice central to experiential learning and knowledge development, both for individuals and for organizational learning. From the point of view of the *nature* of information- and knowledge-intensive work, we argue that strengths are evident in employment systems predicated on employment commitments and the facilitation of communities of practice.

10.7 CONVERGENCE OR DIVERGENCE?

High unemployment and stagnation in the shift of employment from manufacturing to services have encouraged social actors in Germany and Japan to turn to the market as an alternative to the regulatory repertoire of industrial employment. The market alternatives, upon closer examination, reveal a greater resemblance to traditional employment policy directions than to a more liberal model of labor market regulation. In both countries this is true especially for new policies and proposals aimed at alleviating unemployment ("reemployment without unemployment" in Japan and "subsidized low wages" in Germany). In discussions concerning new forms of employment and the problem of shortages in new professional and technical occupations we see a turn to the traditional labor periphery (guest workers, though highly qualified ones in Germany, and women, though highly educated ones in Japan).

There is also a continuation of the old divergence between the German and Japanese employment systems evident especially in relation to the new professional occupations. Both the Nikkeiren proposals as well as the revision to the Japanese dispatched workers law in 1999 point to the re-institutionalization of a dual labor-market structure. For the secondary sector of temporary and flexible, (primarily female) labor, the labor market remains relatively deregulated. In contrast, the primary sector of regular and regulated, primarily male labor, remains relatively secure and protected. German debates and developments, in contrast to the Japanese case, and despite the recent discussions about foreign computer specialists, show more concern with integrating new forms of employment into the traditional aspects of the German model, such as the training system, social insurance coverage and collectively bargained employment conditions. The impact of a low wage sector on social equality remains an area of controversial political and academic debate, precisely because of some claims that a low wage sector will create a dual labor market. This is not the desired effect of those who back the subsidized low wage proposal, which from the beginning is being conceptualized as a regulated deviation from a solidaristic wage structure.

The analyses in this paper point to continuities in the Japanese and German employment systems in the face of structural adjustments and the rising importance of new forms and types of work. We hypothesize that these employment systems may continue to provide strengths, if they stress the traditional strengths of employment commitments for new sectors of information- and knowledge-intensive work rather than expanding old or new peripheral workforces. Rather than the emphasis on (numerical) flexibility propagated by the OECD among others, we attempt to shift the focus to the changing *nature* of work and the possible continuing benefits of an emphasis on functional flexibility.

REFERENCES

Abbott, Andrew, *The System of Professions: An Essay on the Division of Expert Labor*, Chicago and London 1992.

Araki, Takashi, *Revisions of Employment Security Law and Worker Dispatching Law: Drastic Reforms of Japanese Labor Market Regulations*, Japan Labor Bulletin. Vol. 38, No. 9, September, (1999), pp. 5–12.

Baethge, Martin, 'Transformation des Industrialismus – Konturen der Dienstleistungsbeschäftigung im 21. Jahrhundert', in Fricke, Werner (Hrsg.). *1999/2000 Jahrbuch Arbeit and Technik.*, 1999.

Bosch, G., 'Was tun, wenn einfache Arbeit in der Industrie abnimmt? Niedriglöhne oder Innovation: Überlegungen zur Zukunft der Erwerbsarbeit', in *Frankfurter Rundschau*, 9. Februar, Nr. 33, (2000), p. 21.

Bosch, G., 'In der Globalisierungsfalle? Tendenzen wirtschaftlicher und sozialer Entwicklungen im Ländervergleich', in *Gewerkschaftliche Monatshefte*, 50. Jahrgang, April, (1999), pp. 210 – 220.

Boyer, Robert and Drache, Daniel, *The Future of Nations and the Limits of Markets,* London 1996.

Bundesanstalt für Arbeit, *Arbeitslose, Arbeitslosenquote, Kurzarbeiter und offene Stellen,* Nürnberg 2000.

Castells, Manuel, *The Rise of the Network Society. The Information Age: Economy, Society and Culture Volume 1*, Massachusetts 1996.

Crouch, Colin and Streeck, Wolfgang (eds.), *Political Economy of Modern Capitalism: Mapping Convergence & Diversity*, London 1997.

Dore, Ronald, *Flexible Rigidities: Industrial Policy and Structural Adjustment in the Japanese Economy 1970–80*, Stanford 1986.

Frenkel, Stephen. Korczynski, Marek, Shire, Karen and Tam, May, *On the Front Line: Organization of Work in the Information Economy*, Ithaca 1999.

Hassel, Anke, 'The Erosion of the German System of Industrial Relations', in *British Journal of Industrial Relations.* September, Vol. 37, No. 3, (1999), pp. 483–505.

Hollingsworth, Roger and Boyer, Robert, *Contemporary Capitalism: The Embeddedness of Institutions*, Cambridge 1997.

Japan Institute of Labor, 'Working conditions and the labor market: fewer regular employees, longer periods of unemployment', in *Japan Labor Bulletin.* August, Vol. 38, No. 8, (1999), p.1.

Koike, Kazuo, 'Human Resource Development and Labor-Management Relations', in Yamamura, Kozo and Yasuba, Yasukichi (eds.), *The Political Economy of Japan*, Vol. I: The Domestic Transformation, Stanford 1987, pp. 289–330.

Nakamura, M, 'Breadth of Careers of Japanese White-Collar Workers', in *White-collar workers in Contemporary Japan* [Gendai nihon no howaito karaa]. Annals of the Society for the Study of Social Policy, No. 39, May, (1995), pp. 35–56.

Nikkeiren, *Shin-jidai no "nihon-teki keiei"* (New age Japanese Style Management), Nikkeiren Publishing 1995.

OECD, *OECD Employment Outlook*, Paris 1999a.

OECD, *OECD Economic Surveys: 1998—1999*, Germany, Paris 1999b.

OECD, *OECD Economic Surveys: 1998-1999*, Japan, Paris 1999c.

OECD, *OECD Labor Force Statistics 1978-1998*, Paris 1999d.

OECD, *Labor Force Statistics 1977-1997*, Paris 1998.

OECD, *Labor Force Statistics 1974-1994*, Paris 1995.

Pempel, T.J, *Regime Shift: Comparative Dynamics of the Japanese Political Economy*, Ithaca 1998.

Regini, Marino, 'Between Deregulation and Social Pacts: The Responses of European Economies to Globalization', in *Politics & Society*. Vol 28, No. 1, (2000), pp. 5–33.

Rôdôshô (Japanese Ministry of Labor), 1998 *Rôdôhakusho (1998 Labor White Paper)*, Tokyo 1999.

Shire, Karen, 'Sozialization and Work in Japan: The Meaning of Adulthood of Men and Women in a Business Context', in *International Journal of Japanese Sociology*, Number 8, (1999a), pp. 77–92.

Shire, Karen, *The Comparative Organization of Knowledge Work*, Paper prepared for the autumn meetings of the Industrial Sociology Section of the German Sociological Association, Duisburg, Germany, November, 1999b.

Shire, Karen and Imai, Jun, 'Gender and the Diversification of Employment in Japan', in Hanns-Georg Brose (ed.), *Die Reorganisation der Arbeitsgesellschaft*, Frankfurt a. M. 2000.

Shire, Karen and Ota, Nobuyuki, *Relational Networks in Japanese White-Collar Workplaces*, unpublished manuscript, 1998.

Statistisches Bundesamt, Statisches Jahrbuch für die Bundesrepublik Deutschland, Wiesbaden 1996.

Statistisches Bundesamt, Statistisches Jahrbuch für die Bundesrepublik Deutschland, Wiesbaden 1987.

Streeck, Wolfgang, *Social Institutions and Economic Performance: Studies of Industrial Relations in Advanced Capitalist Economies*, London 1992.

Streeck, Wolfgang, 'German Capitalism: Does It Exist? Can It Survive?', in Crouch, Colin and Streeck, Wolfgang (eds.), *Political Economy of Modern Capitalism: Mapping Convergence & Diversity*, London 1997.

Streeck, Wolfgang and Heinze, Rolf, 'An Arbeit fehlt es nicht', in *Der Spiegel*. Nr. 19, May, (1999), pp. 38–45.

Tatsui, Yoji. 'Adjustment of Policies Seen in the White Paper on Labour', in *Japan Labor Bulletin*, Vol. 38, No. 12, December, (1999), p. 13.

Thelen, Kathleen and Kume, Ikuo, *The Future of Nationally Embedded Capitalism: Industrial Relations in Germany and Japan*, Germany-Japan Project Meeting, Max Planck Institute for Social Research, June, (1999).

Internet Sources:

ILO Labor Statistics Database. URL: http:
   www.ilo.org
Japan Institute of Labor. URL: http:
   www.jil.go.jp
Ministry of Labor Japan. URL: http:
   www.mol.go.jp
Statistics Bureau & Statistics Center Japan. URL: http:
   www.stat.go.jp

Discussant: Uwe Hunger

Why is it that the German and Japanese labor market systems are so resistant to change? Why is it that the view generally prevailing in the USA and the UK on the advantages that derive from a liberal labor market is evidently not able to assert itself in Germany and Japan? As Karen Shire and Jun Imai impressively demonstrate in their article, despite all the "new market rhetoric" of the last few years, there have been virtually no changes in the employment market regime in these two countries. Both the German system of employment with its compulsory social security contributions and high level of security and the Japanese model of lifetime employment in the core segment of the dual labor market have continued in place. Reforms – even when proclaimed as liberalization and flexibilization along US lines – seem to be more an expression for the constancy of the systems. In view of the new recipes of a state-subsidized low wage sector in Germany and the effects of the reform of temporary work in Japan, Shire and Imai also speak of a "new solidarism" in Germany and a "new dualism" in Japan.

The reasons for this adherence to old structures can be found in the countries' cultural history and political institutions. The roots of the employment and security traditions in both countries go back a long way. The institutions were already well-established even before the two countries were refounded after the end of the Second World War, and are therefore deeply anchored in the public sense of justice and fairness (Seeleib-Kaiser 1996). In Germany, the party system and the electoral laws make it difficult for a clear majority to be gained by any one party who would then be able to make radical changes unhindered, as the Conservatives under Margaret Thatcher did in Britain. Moreover, with the Christian Democrats (CDU) and the Social Democrats (SPD), Germany has no fewer than two "welfare state parties", who each support the solidaristic labor market model (Heinze, Schmid, Strünck 1999). Nevertheless, there are also political initiatives that call for radical changes to German structures along the lines of the Anglo-American employment market system. One such driving force in Germany are the Free Democrats (FDP), who call for abolition of what they see as obsolescent structures, like the "cartel between the two sides of industry" (e.g. Lambsdorff in: Handelsblatt, 7.7.1996). A typical example of this conflict in Germany was that in the 1990s over regulation of the labor market in the building industry, which in essence was about the introduction of minimum employment conditions for all workers (Hunger 2000).

In the early 1990s, the German building industry had become the object of a new type of labor migration. Because, due to the nature of the building business, it was not possible to transfer production abroad, an increasing number of low-wage workers were imported into Germany from other countries. Initially, building workers were recruited from the former Eastern Bloc countries of Central and Eastern Europe (Faist, Sieveking, Reim u.a. 1999). Today, there are more than 200,000 people from other countries of the European Union (EU) working on building sites in Germany, sent to Germany under the freedom of movement and services within the EU (Hunger 1998). This new form of employment of foreigners, working under contracts for the provision of work and labor, formed the background against which the conflict over abandonment of the principle that had been valid up to that time, namely of equal treatment between German and foreign workers ("same work for the same pay at the same place") was fought out. However, this was not only an attempt to abolish "consensus capitalism" in the building industry, with its dominant institutions of jointly organized social security bodies and jointly funded training systems, it was also a first step on the way to a hoped-for system change in German labor market relations as a whole.

Today, however, the labor market in the building sector does not so much resemble the Anglo-American model but rather the Japanese employment market structure, with a core labor market and a peripheral one. Despite the introduction of a minimum wage law ("*Entsendegesetz*", "labor dispatch law"), the labor market in the building sector continues to be divided into a high-wage sector, in which for the most part highly skilled domestic workers are employed, and a low-wage sector, where less well qualified workers from abroad are used to do the less skilled tasks. If the example of the building industry should be followed by other sectors, this could in time lead in Germany to some extent to a segmentation of the labor market along Japanese lines, with established employees from home on the one hand and foreign labor migrants on the other and, as Shire and Imai point out, with the segmentation line running in particular between the sexes. Today, other segmentation trends can also be seen in Germany, for example along the DM 630 job line or in terms of bogus self-employment. What began as "Americanization" of the labor market seems to be developing towards "Japanization" instead. While at the moment the German system can still be described as stable, the changes described above are nonetheless real, even though they are taking place only slowly and by encroaching from the margins (Streeck 1998).

This example also points to a new challenge for the "new world economy" (Reich 1993), to which so far only little attention has been paid by researchers but which could be leading to greater changes to the labor market structures in both countries. It should be remembered that as well as globalization of the market for goods and capital, there has also been internationalization of the labor market, with not only goods and capital being transferred across national boundaries, but workers as well. As leading economic nations and major global exporters, Japan and Germany will be unable to resist the logic of worldwide economic integration in this area. Although until recently, or even still today, both countries have seen themselves as non-immigration countries (Thränhardt 1988, 1999), an opening-up of their employment markets for foreign workers will be inevitable. How far they succeed in preserving their traditional structures, with their attendant strengths, will be just as crucial an aspect as the changes in the content of work which Shire and Imai have brought into the discussion.

REFERENCES

Faist, Thomas, Klaus Sieveking, Uwe Reim, Stefan Sandbrink, *Ausland im Inland. Die Beschäftigung von Werksvertragsarbeitnehmern in der Bundesrepublik Deutschland*, Baden-Baden 1999.

Heinze, Rolf G., Josef Schmid, Strünck, Christoph, *Vom Wohlfahrtsstaat zum Wettbewerbsstaat. Arbeitsmarkt- und Sozialpolitik in den 90er Jahren*, Opladen 1999.

Hunger, Uwe, 'Arbeitskräftewanderungen im Baugewerbe der Europäischen Union. Problemanzeigen, Lösungsmodelle und Schlu"sfolgerungen für die zukünftige Beschäftigung von Ausländern in Deutschland', in Dietrich Thränhardt (ed.), *Einwanderung und Einbürgerung in Deutschland. Jahrbuch Migration 1997/98*, Münster, London 1998, pp. 65–103.

Hunger, Uwe, *Der 'rheinische Kapitalismus in der Defensive. Eine komparative Policy-Analyse zum Paradigmenwechsel in den Arbeitsmarktbeziehungen am Beispiel der Bauwirtschaft*, Baden-Baden 2000.

Reich, Robert, *Die neue Weltwirtschaft. Das Ende der nationalen Ökonomie*, Frankfurt 1993.

Seeleib-Kaiser, Martin, 'Sozialhilfe und Arbeitslosenversicherung im deutsch-japanischen Vergleich', in Dietrich Thränhardt (Ed.), *Japan und Deutschland in der Welt nach dem Kalten Krieg*, Münster, London 1996.

Streeck, Wolfgang, 'Industrielle Beziehungen in einer internationalen Wirtschaft', in Ulrich Beck (Ed.), *Politik der Globalisierung*, Frankfurt 1998, pp. 169–202.

Thränhardt, Dietrich, 'Abschottung und Globalisierung. Die japanische Nichteinwanderungspolitik und ihre sozialen und politischen Kosten', in *IMIS-Beiträge*, No. 11 (1999), pp. 17–38.

Thränhardt, Dietrich, 'Die Bundesrepublik Deutschland – ein unerklärtes Einwanderungsland', in *Aus Politik und Zeitgeschichte*, No. B 24 (1988), pp. 3–13.

Section D:

Consequences for
Public Policy

11

COPING WITH MARKET RIGIDITIES IN GERMANY AND JAPAN

Mark Tilton and Patricia Boling

11.1 INTRODUCTION

Germany and Japan have both brought about the remarkable achievement of combining rapid growth and high per capita incomes with high levels of income equality.[1] Important differences notwithstanding, each has attained economic success by nurturing market rigidities and long-term relationships that encourage investment in skills, technology and equipment. Based on an intense development of craft skills, Germany has developed a specialization in high-quality engineered products, while Japan's forte at close relations between firms has given it a specialization in products that involve complex assembly (Lehrer/Darbishire 1997; Streeck 1997; Kitschelt 1991).

Yet in the 1990s this system has faltered in both countries. Growth rates have dropped and unemployment has increased, due to several factors. First, the high costs of rigid markets have been an increasingly large burden, as markets for end-product engineering goods have become more competitive and commoditized. Second, the stable labor markets that were so good a basis for industries such as autos are poor at adjusting quickly enough to keep up in software and IT markets. Third, the high prices that market rigidities tend to produce have stifled innovation in downstream industries, particularly those related to the internet. Market rigidities in both Germany

---

[1]The authors would like to thank Mark Lehner and to the Midwest Japan Seminar for reading and commenting on the paper and to Mindy Kotler of the Japan Information Access Project for help in identifying sources.

and Japan look likely to produce even bigger problems in the future because of the way in which rigid employment systems, combined with conservative social policies, appear to be depressing childbearing and thus responsible for a projected sharp drop in the size of the workforce. The stark trade-offs that rigid labor markets pose between careers and childbearing appear to be an important reason for fertility rates in Japan and Germany that are one-third below replacement levels. Both countries are trying to solve these problems in ways that reflect their particular political patterns and economic institutions.

11.2 TELECOMMUNICATIONS: THE PROBLEMS OF ADJUSTING QUICKLY TO NEW TECHNOLOGIES

Telecommunications is a good case for seeing how the strengths and weaknesses of different national industrial systems have affected the success of new technologies. One key dimension of national policy is whether a state chooses to promote tough competition and low prices, or weak competition and higher prices. Tough competition pressures providers to find innovative solutions to problems, while low prices stimulate the development of downstream industries, such as internet services. Lax competition and high prices may encourage waste, but can also give firms deep pockets to fund industrial development. Both Germany and Japan have been slow to promote telecommunications competition and telecommunications services have been more expensive than in the US or the UK.

Telecommunications was regulated as a monopoly in all countries until 1982, when the U.S. forced AT&T to divest itself of its local telephone service (Crandall/Waverman 1995). Germany and Japan have moved more slowly than the U.S. to encourage competition. Promoting competition in the telecommunications industry is not a one-time decision, but an ongoing process. The key is for regulatory authorities to decide that the benefits of competition outweigh the benefits of protecting national champions. In all nations, dominant firms oppose regulations that would force them to cede opportunities to newcomers and regulatory institutions must have considerable independence to impose such regulations. In the United States several factors have paved the way for vigorous pro-competitive policy. First, the fact that the U.S. was the world's economic superpower meant that debates over competition concerned benefits to domestic consumers rather than the standing of the American telecommunications industry relative to other countries. Second, pro-competitive, antitrust philosophy was influential and made policymakers receptive to new arguments from academics that were critical of existing monopoly arrangements. Third, the Federal Communications Commission, the Justice Department and the courts all had some autonomy from vested interest pressure (Aufderheide 1999).

Pro-competitive reforms have come more slowly to Germany and Japan. In both countries the lateness of pro-competitive reform reflects strong union opposition and a weaker consensus in favor of market competition than in the U.S.. In the case of Germany, the European Commission has taken the lead in promoting telecommunications competition. While telecommunications deregulation came later than in the U.S., the European Commission has moved aggressively to promote competition. In contrast, in the regulatory authority for telecommunications in Japan, the Ministry of Posts and Telecommunications (MPT), has been much more hesitant in pushing competition (Vogel 1996). Notably, it has not adopted the European and American concept of a "dominant telecommunications carrier" that should be subject to special regulation to force it to make its facilities available to its competitors. The MPT has been weak in promoting competition and standing up to the NTT union and to diet members who support NTT. Aggressive regulatory pressure has instead come from the United States Trade Representative, in alliance with Japanese firms attempting to expand market share.

Slower and weaker pro-competitive policies have had a direct impact on economies' ability to innovate in the new internet economy. Weaker competition has meant higher service charges in Germany than in the U.S. and much higher charges in Japan. An OECD survey of the combined charges by telephone service and internet service providers found that forty hours of internet use in Japan cost $78, while in Germany they cost $49 and in the U.S. $23 (OECD, "Internet Price Comparison"). The OECD found that cheaper rates seemed to stimulate internet use and innovation in the use of the internet. In September 1999 the U.S. had 160 internet hosts per 1,000 inhabitants while Germany had 20 and Japan had 18 (OECD, "Internet and Electronic Commerce Indicators Update").

Pro-competitive regulatory reform has brought large benefits to the American telecommunications industry. Competition has pushed rates down, and low phone rates have helped make the U.S. the leader in the internet revolution. Pro-competitive reforms have also supported the development of new services. Although local telecom companies resisted being forced to unbundle their networks in the mid-1990s, unbundling led to the development of broadband telecommunications networks. Germany is currently considering proposals to force national telecommunications monopolies to unbundle their networks (*Financial Times*, February 24, 2000). Japan has as yet made little progress on unbundling.

Japan's regulatory system has produced high telecommunications prices, and these high prices have encouraged waste and inefficiency. Japanese telecommunications equipment is expensive by world standards, and Japan has lagged at developing certain technologies, such as wave division multiplexing, which enables fibers to double their carrying capacity. But the monopoly rents have not been completely wasted. Though economists would object that cross-subsidies are distorting, in Japan's case cross-subsidies from high telecommunications rates have helped the electronics firms that supply NTT to successfully develop computers and semiconductors. NTT's subsidiary, DoCoMo, has funded the development of mobile telephone technology. Currently data-transfer speeds are slow, but DoCoMo plans to introduce a "third-generation network" which will increase data transmission speeds 40 times, permitting high-quality streamed video and audio. According to *The Economist*, the Japanese wireless industry is 18 months ahead of Europe, which is in turn 18 months ahead of the U.S. In Europe and the U.S. the wireless industry spent a long time negotiating a standard before developing a wireless application protocol (WAP) for text-based services on the internet. DoCoMo, 67% owned by NTT, developed the technology much faster (*The Economist* March 11, 2000: 97–98).

Although Japan has been slower to move to aggressive pro-competitive regulation in telecommunications than Germany, the fact that labor unions are company-based and that labor training is done within the firm has given it some advantages over Germany in adapting to new technologies. This is in contrast to the German telecommunications industry, where strong labor unions and the rigidity of the apprenticeship system have slowed the move to new technologies. Job security has played an important role in nurturing the craft skills of German workers and enabling them to produce high-quality, internationally competitive products. Germany's system of co-determination has ensured that workers are well treated and given incentives to work with enthusiasm and it continues to function well in many industries (Thelen/Kume 1999). But Lehrer and Darbishire found that the German system of codetermination put Deutsche Telekom at a disadvantage compared to British Telecom. While job security and the codetermination had made German firms flexible enough to respond rapidly to new market opportunities in industries where technologies changed incrementally, such as machine tools or autos, in telecommunications this model has not worked because much of the work is no longer craft based, but instead uses software and clerical skills. As in most industries, German telecommunications work is organized along craft lines and workers have been reluctant to accept substantial work reorganization. Worker resistance to change has forced Deutsche Telekom to produce detailed and cumbersome plans for reorganization and has slowed adjustment (Lehrer/Darbishire 1997).

Also, Germany's system of labor training through apprenticeships is slower than Japan's at producing new skills. Federal Minister for Education, Science and Research Edelgard Bulmahn warned in February 2000 that some 250,000 information technology jobs would go unfilled in 2001 because of a shortage of skilled workers. According to the Federal Association of Information Technology, Telecommunication and New Media (BITKOM) in March 2000 computer firms have been unable to staff 75,000 jobs (*Interpress Service* 2000).

11.3 STEEL: HOW PROTECTIONISM AND CARTELS INHIBIT SHIFTS OUT OF UNCOMPETITIVE SECTORS

A general problem for the German and Japanese economies is that market rigidities often mean higher costs for downstream industries. Market rigidities, particularly barriers to international trade, may also prevent a nation from switching out of sectors in which it is uncompetitive and moving to more productive areas. A good example is the steel industry, an industry with enormous political importance in all industrialized nations. A key input for other manufacturing and munitions industries, steel has been synonymous with national strength and autonomy. The industry's large unionized workforces and gigantic firms wield great political power. Yet steel is an industry in which low labor costs give middle and low-income nations like South Korea and China a production cost advantage.

The steel industry is highly concentrated in all nations, creating the potential for cartels to hold back the tides of change. In the U.S. oligopolistic cooperation in the steel industry kept prices high and stable until the early 1960s. The oligopoly was overturned by steel minimills, imports and by pressure from American presidents to keep prices down (Scherrer 1991: 189; PaineWebber 1998: 116). In contrast, during the same period both the European Community and Japan explicitly encouraged firms to cooperate to support prices. In the late 1970s German firms, dismayed that European competitors were not abiding by production-reducing agreements under the Simonet Plan, joined with steel firms in the Netherlands and Luxemburg to form Denelux. Concerned about what appeared to be a German-centered cartel, E.C. authorities formed the Davignon system, under which the European Commission mandated production levels and prices and fined firms that produced too much or sold too cheaply. In 1980 an American antidumping action against European steelmakers cut European exports. The resulting excess stocks in Europe triggered cheating on the Davignon system. European commissioner Etienne Davignon criticized Europe's steelmakers for competing: "European steelmakers should be prepared to learn from Japan, where overproduction has been swiftly quashed by a close consensus of all parties involved. Rather than criticizing the Japanese Europe should imitate them" (Howell 1998: 80). The European steel cartel had some success in the 1980s due to agreements on capacity cuts, but German firms resented having to cut capacity to make room for government subsidized steel from Italy and other nations. German frustration with the system led the European Commission to end the official cartel in 1988. Soon after, the Commission investigated informal cartels in stainless steel sheets and steel beams. This reversal on the steel cartel was part of a broader move by the European Commission to reduce trade barriers between European nations by strengthening competition policy (Dumez/Jeunemaître 1996).

The withdrawal of official support for the cartel and anti-cartel action by the European Court of Justice has made it impossible for European steel makers to carry out oligopolistic pricing. According to *World Steel Dynamics*, "As we see it, the managements of the major (European) mills think oligopolistically; they believe that production restraints can limit price decline. However, there are so many E.U. producers, plus a high level of intra-E.U. trade and a high level of exports to third markets, that we don't see how prices can be sustained when demand weakens" (PaineWebber 1998).

The picture in Japan is quite different. There the Japanese government continues to support a strong cartel. The Ministry of International Trade and Industry meets quarterly with firms and issues "demand forecasts" which serve as a guide for individual firms' production. MITI officials claim that there is no cartel and that MITI plays no role in guiding one.[2] Yet Japan's integrated steel producers have been astoundingly successful at enforcing strict market sharing agreements since 1973 (see Figure 21). Industry insiders are frank about the existence of a cartel (Tilton 1998: 176).

Figure 21 Market share among Japan's 5 integrated steel producers

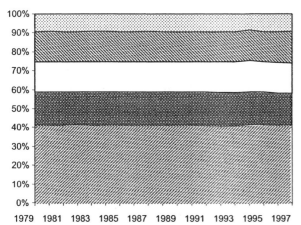

Source: Tekkô chôsa shûhô (Steelsurvey report) (Tokyo: Kinzoku kenkyû chôsa kai (Association for metals research and surveys, various years).

The steel cartel is successful at maintaining high prices. Japanese domestic contract prices for cold-rolled sheet steel averaged 47 percent higher than

[2] Mark Tilton, personal interview with head of iron and steel section, MITI, Tokyo, July 1999.

U.S. contract prices from 1993 to 1998. Even after the decline in the yen brought the domestic price of Japanese steel down in dollar terms the price was still 19 percent above the domestic American price in 1998. Japan's spot steel prices for 1993–98 for hot-rolled coil also averaged 19 percent above American spot prices in 1993–98 and stayed at this level through 1998.[3] Yet in 1996 Japan imported only 7% of its steel, compared to the 25 percent imported by the U.S. and 49 percent by Germany. How are Japanese steel firms able to keep prices high without attracting in imports? In part this is because major Japanese steel users voluntarily pay high prices in exchange for prompt delivery and high quality, and because of nationalist loyalty to the domestic steel industry (Tilton 1996: 169–189). Nevertheless, even firms that are less loyal or concerned with high levels of quality are prevented from buying cheaper imports because of pressure from steelmakers. The Japanese press reports that steel companies press trading companies and steel processing centers not to handle imports. (*Nihon Keizai Shimbun* 10 May, 1994).

The larger point of the steel story is that Japan's weak competition policy has economic consequences. In the case of steel, Japan has chosen to maintain high production capacity and employment at the cost of high prices and international trade disputes. This late-developer, catch-up strategy has enabled Japan to take money out of consumer pockets and put it into investment in plant, equipment and technology. Using competition policy to break up the steel cartel and drive down prices would help Japan shift from an investment to a consumer driven economy.

But unlike the European Commission, which has become quite aggressive on competition policy, the Japanese FTC is hemmed in by strong political opponents (Beeman 1997). There is intense pressure from within the ruling Liberal Democratic Party (LDP) to weaken Japan's anti-monopoly policy. 165 LDP diet members have formed the "Group to Revitalize the Japanese Economy". Muto Kabun, the head of the LDP group, warns against following the U.S. pattern of tough antitrust policy: "The law of the jungle, with the weak falling prey to the strong, will prevail if Japan follows the U.S. model" (*Nihon keizai shimbun*, February 28, 2000).

11.4 RIGID LABOR MARKETS AND DISINVESTMENT IN THE FUTURE WORKFORCE

At this point, we shift our focus away from the problems of flexibility and efficient allocation of goods and services that labor and product market rigidities have produced, to a discussion of the connection between labor

---

[3]Calculated from PaineWebber, World Steel Dynamicsÿ Price Track #59, September 30, 1998. Data used with permission.

market rigidities and long-term labor supplies. One of the key elements of what Michel Albert calls the Nippo-Rhine, communitarian capitalist model is that its job stability and capital markets foster long-term investment in skills, technologies and equipment (Albert 1993). Yet the German and Japanese varieties of communitarian capitalism also appear to encourage disinvestment in the most important resource of any economy, its future workforce. Although all of the advanced industrialized countries have had fertility rates below replacement since the early 1970s, Germany and Japan stand out. Their fertility rates of 1.3 lifetime expected births per woman are at least twice as far below replacement levels as the fertility rates of France and most of the Anglo-Saxon and Nordic countries.[4] These low fertility rates are closely linked to the bargains that capital has made with labor in Germany and Japan, the same bargains that have sustained these nations' rapid economic growth and income equality. The problem is that the long-term labor relations and seniority-based pay that characterize the Japanese and German economies greatly increase the opportunity costs for women or men who leave the workforce temporarily to raise children. The same labor movements that have so valiantly pushed for good breadwinner wages in both Germany and Japan have not pushed for modifications in workplace organization or, particularly in Germany, in the daycare and school systems to accommodate working mothers. Further, the egalitarian wages and tough labor regulations that promote social equality in these countries also make daycare prohibitively expensive. While both Germany and Japan have used income subsidies to promote childbearing, the amounts of these supplements pale in comparison to the income a woman (or man) in Germany or Japan foregoes if she (or he) steps off the career ladder. The pattern of employment which rewards predominantly male workers with job stability and high pay while relegating people who care for children, largely women, to lower status and lower pay, rests on a variety of public policies, company practices, and social attitudes. These "gender regimes" differ in Germany and Japan, but with similar results in terms of making childrearing less attractive than in the U.S., Britain, or France.

11.5 THE GENDER REGIME IN JAPAN

Japan's postwar economic system has rested on employers' promises of job security and high pay to lifelong workers in exchange for workers making such sacrifices as working long hours, accepting transfers, spending free time socializing with work mates at bars or on weekend outings, or not

---

[4]The total fertility rates of Canada and Sweden were until recently much higher than Germany and Japan's but have recently fallen to 1.5. In Sweden this appears to have been due to cuts in generous social benefits for families (Population Reference Bureau 2000).

taking vacation time. It has been assumed that these workers would be male breadwinners and that women would cheerfully accept the burdens and challenges of childrearing, elder care, and household management with little or no help from their husbands. Women's participation in the labor force would fit around these core familial obligations: working at an entry level job before marriage or birth of one's first child, and returning to work as a part timer once the kids were in school in order to earn money for "extras" like music lessons or cram school. Indeed, this pattern is still broadly accepted, reinforced by tax and spousal benefit policies that provide big financial incentives for dependent spouses not to earn more than about 1 million yen per year ($9,000 at an exchange rate of 110 yen to the dollar), effectively pushing women into low paid part time work (Gottfried/O'Reilly 2000: 24–5). Both Germany and Japan use tax policies to promote a socially conservative model of childrearing by a stay-at-home mother.

Opinion leaders and policy makers bemoan Japan's low fertility rate, which has fallen steadily since the early 1970s and reached a low of 1.34 in 1999. Low fertility means that in the future there will be fewer workers to keep the economy robust and to pay into pension and insurance programs to support a mushrooming population of physically frail retired people.

Explanations commonly given for Japan's low fertility range from the high cost of educating children, to the lack of open spaces for children to play in, to Japan's notoriously small houses and apartments. Though all of these are plausible, one of the biggest disincentives to women to marry and have children (and note that the two decisions usually go hand-and-hand, as few Japanese women have babies out of wedlock, and few married couples remain childless) is the high opportunity costs in terms of the potential earnings they forego if they quit good jobs to marry and have kids, then return in their middle years to work as a part-timer. Economist Yashiro Naohiro explains:

> "the largest cost of child-rearing is not necessarily the cost of education but the mother's opportunity cost incurred as a result of her suspending employment. This opportunity cost is pushed upward by Japanese employment practices such as long-term employment, long working hours, and promotion and wage systems based on seniority; it is further increased by the lack of child care services outside the family. The incompatibility of child care and employment is widely understood by women before marriage, and there is no doubt that women who are committed to their jobs will hesitate to marry because of this constraint" (Yashiro 1998: 142).

The traditional gender roles of male breadwinner and female care-giver are quietly coming under attack as women increasingly postpone or reject marriage and childbearing in order to continue working (Ueno 1998: 119). In Japan and in other states that make the tradeoffs between working outside the home and having children too steep, women are refusing to marry and have babies. Gøsta Esping-Andersen warns that countries that neglect the population issue are steering for trouble as low fertility threatens their basic financial viability (Esping-Andersen 1999: 69).

How can Japan address the problem of smaller numbers of children and working-age people? At present about 12% of children under age three and 32% of 3–6 year olds attend publicly regulated and subsidized day care centers (*hoikuen*); another 49% of 3–6 year olds attend kindergarten (*yôchien*) for half days. Current policy initiatives include plans to expand and marketize day care services, especially a big increase in spaces for infants (0–2 year olds) and extended hours day care (*Japan Times*, 12–19–99); a doubling of family allowances (*jidôteate*); and implementation of a long-term care insurance program to provide services to frail elderly people, which began in April 2000. These measures aim at relieving the burden on parents, especially working mothers, and are undertaken in the hope that the trade-offs between kids and career will not seem so stark to young women that they decide not to marry and have children. And indeed, Esping-Andersen believes that increasing day care is a good way to facilitate women's workforce participation rates; he argues that increasing the supply of daycare by 20% would increase the female employment rate about 10% (Esping-Andersen 1999: 59).

The fact that young women are deciding in droves not to marry or have babies is shaking the old consensus in Japan. Under fire are the gender ideology of complementarity and duties rooted in separate spheres, then the ideal of the professional housewife whose main satisfactions revolved around her caretaking role, who if she worked at all worked in a part-time job at low pay, forming collectively a female shock absorber for the vicissitudes of the labor market. Perhaps young women's avoidance of marriage and family will open the door to a new understanding of Japan's long-term political interests that will push family-friendly policies further along, and help a new consensus to emerge about women's role in the home and the marketplace, and the state's role in supporting working women.

11.6 THE GENDER REGIME IN GERMANY

In Germany, as well, cultural values, official policies, and labor practices reinforce the ideal of stay-at-home mothers and housewives who participate in the labor force episodically (if at all), and often as part-time workers. Yet there are significant differences between the two countries, especially with respect to gender ideologies, attitudes toward and support for childcare, and level of expressed concern about declining fertility.

In terms of the overall level of spending and notions of state responsibility for ensuring the welfare of citizens, Germany's family policies are generous. They include substantial family allowances, parental allowances for newborns, a 14 week paid maternity leave, job-protected parental leave, a law which provides long-term care insurance for the elderly passed in

1995, and the *Kindergartengesetz* (which Ilona Ostner translates as "Child-care Facility Act") of 1996, which guarantees spots in kindergarten for every child age three and older (Maier/Rapp 1995: 98). Ostner explains the passage of these two new statutory care provisions in the mid-1990s – a time when workers' employment rights were gradually being curtailed – in terms of concern about Germany's falling fertility and rapid aging. She thinks one must understand these new care policies in "the broader context of welfare restructuring and its objectives. Germany has been trying to get rid of its image of a 'pensioners' welfare state', a society with few jobs and few children, on the one hand, and soaring non-wage labour costs and pressures on insurance funds, on the other" (Ostner 1998: 114).

Policies of subsidizing mothers to stay home with their children are not always applauded by feminist scholars, who see them as a ploy for reducing the number of women on the unemployment rolls (Fagnani, 1998). Landenberger "shows the extent to which parental leave policies work as a flexible 'exit-and-part-time-reentry mechanism', turning structural constraints within the labour market into a female problem to be dealt with by different categories of women workers and non-workers" (Ostner, quoting and paraphrasing Landenberger 1993: 102). In Landenberger's judgment, "the German social policy tradition has promoted a policy which channels women with children towards a partial exit from the labour market but which does not take any positive action to promote the simultaneous performance of paid and unpaid work. It serves continuously to strengthen the German version of a strong male breadwinner welfare regime" (Ostner 1993: 103).

Germany's preference for mothers staying home with babies and children is evident not only in generous parental leave measures, but also in the absence of provisions for publicly funded day care. Recent figures show only 2% of infants under age three were cared for in publicly funded daycare centers in Germany, far fewer than for France, the Scandinavian countries, or Japan (Gornick et al., 1997, 56). Figures for children age three to five who are enrolled in publicly funded kindergartens jump to 78% (Gornick 1997: 56), but kindergarten is a useful form of day care only for those with part-time work schedules, as most kindergartens offer half day schedules (Maier/Rapp 1995: 107). It has been estimated that only twelve percent of kindergarten places are full-day slots, suggesting that only nine percent of children over age three are in full-time childcare (Ondrich/Spiess 1998: 36–7). Nor does the situation improve markedly when children begin to attend public school, as the German school day is very short. Schools do not have a lunch hour. Instead children spend a long morning in classes, with mid-morning snack breaks and early dismissal so they can come home to hot lunches made by their mothers.

There are several curiosities in reading scholarly work on the German childcare system. For example, many commentators are rather casual about differentiating between child care (intended to care for children while their parents work full time), and kindergarten (typically a half-day preschool educational program), even though this distinction is fundamental (see for examples Ondrich/Spiess 1998; Ostner 1998; Pfau-Effinger 1998). German writers frequently report that women who would put their children in full-time childcare are selfish or remiss for not spending more time at home with their children. Thus one scholarly article hypothesizes that there would be a "learning effect" whereby parents would discover when they sent their first child to an institutional childcare center that the care was substandard, and would decide not to send subsequent children to childcare (this was not however borne out by their data; Ondrich and Spiess, 1998). Pfau-Effinger discusses attitudes toward maternal employment, comparing West Germany with the Netherlands. Her work indicates that West German attitudes are consistently hostile to mothers working and to children being in full-time care, and that more West German than Dutch women would prefer to be stay-at-home housewives (Pfau-Effinger 1998: 185–6)

Such comments suggest that Germany is more hostile to institutional childcare and to women working outside the home than most of its peer countries in the OECD, and certainly much more so than the United States or even Japan. Ilona Ostner notes that West German parents' preference for part-time over full-time childcare is both shaped by and shapes supply (Ostner 1998: 130), a remark which suggests how values and long-term institutional patterns of provision and policy are interwoven.

Germany and Japan are likely to follow different trajectories in dealing with policies to support childrearing and women's role in the workforce. While both states up until now have treated women as a pool of unpaid caregivers and supported labor regimes that channel women into low-paid part time work, different cultural values and political and institutional capacities, and different demographic imperatives, seem likely to lead them along different courses in the coming decades.

Ondrich and Spiess note that expanding child care policy in Germany could help avoid long-run declines in population by reducing the overall cost of child care to parents (Ondrich/Spiess 1998: 35). Yet the level of awareness and discussion of fertility decline as a public issue in Germany is quite different than it is in Japan, and so is the level of legitimacy accorded population policies. Alison McIntosh claims that Germany's legacy of pronatalist and eugenicist policies associated with National Socialism made it so taboo to talk about population policies that Germany was unable to deal with its demographic problems, or even to train demographers and population specialists or undertake research on population issues until the 1960s (McIntosh 1983: 66). This is in stark contrast to the situation in Japan, where demographers and population policy experts have been prominent in public debates and policy making throughout the postwar period.

Institutionally, each country has rather different capacities for influencing the direction of future social welfare and labor policies. The Japanese state has a far more interventionist, respected, and effective national bureaucracy, while Germany has much more powerful and independent unions. It seems apparent that the bureaucrats in the Ministry of Health and Welfare and the National Institute for Population and Social Security Research are interested in developing family-friendly policies with a view toward stemming the plummeting fertility rate, and that they are not helpless bystanders, but likely to effect policy changes in the coming years as the public consensus crystallizes around the need to do something about the falling birth rate. Germany's corporatist government is more likely to respond to powerful unions which will probably push for policies that protect male breadwinner wages and relegate women to the household and to low-paid part time work. As Pfau-Effinger writes, "in terms of the social actors in the German system the trade unions have for a long time oriented their policies towards the security of the standard employment relationships of their male clients" (Pfau-Effinger 1998, 187).

Though some argue that Japan and Germany have similar constellations of social and cultural values that support women's responsibility for the household and care taking work, as well as wage systems and labor norms and regulations oriented toward the male breadwinner model, we think there are important differences here too. Japan has already begun to modernize its attitudes toward working mothers and institutionalized child care, and appears to have a more pragmatic, adaptive set of attitudes about nurturing work, children's health, well-being and educational development. Women aren't considered anti-mothers simply because they work outside the home. Increasingly people recognize that state-regulated, competent and well-trained childcare teachers can do a good job of raising children. In contrast, Germany seems to resist adopting such attitudes, and continues to define children's well-being in terms of stay-at-home mothers, and to harshly judge working mothers.

11.7 REPLENISHING LOW-FERTILITY POPULATIONS FROM ABROAD

One certainly might argue that Germany and Japan need not worry about their low fertility rates because they can simply import enough labor to make up for the shortfall. The United Nations reports that Germany's working age population is projected to drop from 56 million in 2000 to 43 million by 2050, Japan's from 87.2 to 57.1 million. The ratio of people of working age to those of retirement age is projected to fall from 4.4 down to 2.1 in Germany over that same period and from 4.8 down to 1.7 in Japan. To keep the working-age population stable Germany would require an average of 458,000 immigrants annually between 1995 and 2050. Japan would require 609,000 immigrants annually (United Nations Population Division 2000).

Germany currently brings in some 260,000 immigrants a year, including 100,000 asylum applicants, 60,000 relatives of residents of Germany, and 100,000 ethnic German immigrants (*Aussiedler*) (*Migration News* 2000). Yet Germany continues to not officially consider itself a country of immigration. The pool of ethnic German potential immigrants in Eastern Europe and the former Soviet Union is being rapidly drained. Non-German asylum seekers are only given temporary residency and are expected to return home eventually. In 2000 the Schröder government decided to admit a small number (20,000) of information technology specialists from outside the European Union. These technical guest workers would only be able to stay five years, but Schröder's new policy received prompt criticism from labor unions and from the Christian Democrats. Jürgen Rüttgers, the head of the CDU in North Rhine-Westphalia, made a centerpiece to his campaign for the premiership of the *Land* out of his slogan, "*Kinder statt Inder*" (children instead of Indians). Although Rüttgers's xenophobic slogan embarrassed many Germans, the opposition by both labor unions and the center right to Schröder's modest immigration policy suggests that Germany will have difficulty absorbing the large numbers of non-ethnic Germans, much less non-Europeans, it would need to make up for its low fertility.

Japan is far less receptive to immigrants than Germany. Japan constantly reminds the rest of the world (and itself?) that it is an island nation, and that cultural and racial homogeneity are central values. Foreigners currently make up only 1% of Japan's population, and public opinion in Japan is strongly against adopting easier immigration policies and introducing large numbers of poor Asians as permanent residents of Japan. Japan has difficulty accepting even tiny numbers of foreign scholars as permanent workers and residents (Hall 1998).

An alternative to either immigration or more effective pro-family policies would be to simply allow the populations and economies of Germany and Japan to decline. Declining populations would be an environmental boon, but the economic effects of such declines are difficult to predict, since capitalism has no experience with rapidly falling populations. It might be that labor scarcity would improve the bargaining power of workers and make societies more egalitarian, just as the bargaining power and status of peasants rose in the wake of the Black Death in the 14th century (North 1990). Or perhaps elderly, frail populations will simply be unable to do enough work to maintain living standards.

11.8 CONCLUSION

This paper has explored the ways in which Germany and Japan are seeking to either reduce market rigidities or cope with the undesirable consequences of them. The two types of market rigidities explored here have been restrictions on competition in product markets, and the rigidity of sharp distinctions between high pay for male, breadwinner career work, and lower pay for workers who interrupt their lives to take on the burdens of childrearing. In both the areas of product competition and the labor market for workers who take on childrearing duties, U.S. markets are more flexible. To a great extent this is because of government action to force flexibility. The U.S. government has carried out anti-trust policy in both steel and telecommunications that was both earlier and tougher than in Germany or Japan. And the U.S. government has leaned harder on employers not to discriminate against women than have the German or Japanese governments.

Is convergence by either Germany or Japan to American models inevitable or desirable? In the area of competition policy there has been considerable convergence between E.U. and U.S. policies due to powerful political pressures within Europe to integrate the E.U. by making national markets open to international trade and investment. Although the U.S. has pressed Japan to adopt stronger competition policy, this foreign pressure has not had the moral or legal force that E.U. policy has had in Germany or other European countries. Japan is likely to continue to experiment with pro-competitive regulatory reform, but domestic political pressures against such reforms, combined with the weakness of the JFTC, suggest that competition policy in Japan will remain only modestly effective relative to that of the E.U. or the U.S.

Is there some normative imperative to shift to more competitive markets? Both Germany and Japan are wealthy societies where more efficient markets are not a matter of life and death for many people. Japan may continue to decide it prefers somewhat less intense competition, higher prices, and greater job stability. Although shifting to more competitive and open markets would enable Japan to contribute to poorer countries' development by buying more of their manufactured goods, such as steel, this argument carries no real political weight in Japan.

Paradoxically, although Germany and Japan are more generous with direct subsidies to support families and parental leaves, the U.S. has higher female work force participation rates and total fertility rates that either Germany or Japan. Despite the pre-eminence of traditional gender roles and "family values" in Japan and Germany, both have structured the labor market and tax and other policies to be difficult for working mothers, discouraging childbearing far more than in the U.S. Although Japan has improved childcare policies to ease the situation of working mothers, it seems unable or unwilling to require employers to relax workplace expectations and create a workplace environment for fulltime workers that is compatible with childrearing responsibilities.

Should Japan and Germany make labor markets more flexible so as to enable women to both work and have children without being shunted into poorly paid jobs? Many in Germany and Japan consider the U.S. model of frenzied two-worker families undesirable. Perhaps both countries will choose to maintain job markets that are rigidly segregated between full-time, lifetime workers and workers with major caregiving responsibilities in the home. Even if neither adopts policies conducive to gender equality, it may be that both societies will make admirable contributions by shrinking their populations, and thus their burden on the global environment, and by absorbing tens of millions of immigrants from poorer countries to replace the children they choose to forego.

REFERENCES

Interpress Service, Germany Accepts that it Needs Foreign Labor, February 25, 2000.

Albert, Michel, *Capitalism vs. Capitalism: How America's Obsession with Individual Achievement and Short-term Profit has Led it to the Brink of Collapse*, New York 1993.

Aufderheide, Patricia, *Communications Policy and the Public Interest: The Telecommunications Act of 1996*, New York 1999.

Beeman, Michael L., *Public Policy and Economic Competition in Japan: The Rise of Antimonopoly Policy, 1963–1995*, Ph.D. Dissertation, Oxford University 1997.

Boling, Patricia, 'Family Policy in Japan', in *Journal of Social Policy*, 27(2), pp. 173–190 (1998).

Crandall, Robert W. and Leonard Waverman, *Talk Is Cheap: The Promise of Regulatory Reform in North American Telecommunications*, Washington, D.C. 1995.

Dumez, Hervé, Alain Jeunemaître, 'The Convergence of Competition Policies in Europe: Internal Dynamics and External Imposition', in Berger, Suzanne, Ronald Dore (eds.), *National Diversity And Global Capitalism*, New York 1996.

Esping-Andersen, Gøsta, *Social Foundations of Postindustrial Economies*, Oxford 1999.

Fagnani, Jeanne, 'Helping Mothers to combine paid and unpaid work – or fighting unemployment? The ambiguities of French family policy', in *Community, Work & Family*, Vol. 1, No 3, 1998, 297–312.

Gauthier, Anne Helene, *The State and the Family: A Comparative Analysis of Family Policies in Industrialized Countries*, Oxford 1996.

Gornick, Janet C., 'Gender Equality in the Labour Market', in Sainsbury, Diane (ed.), *Gender and Welfare State Regimes*, Oxford 1999.

Gornick, Janet C., Marcia K. Meyers, Katherine E. Ross, 'Supporting the Employment of Mothers: Policy Variation Across Fourteen Welfare States', in *Journal of European Social Policy* 7(1): 45–70 (1997).

Gottfried, Heidi, Jacqueline O'Reilly, *The Weakness of a Strong Breadwinner Model: Part-time Work and Female Labour Force Participation in Germany and Japan*, Wayne State University CULMA Occasional Paper Series, n. 3, January 2000.

Hall, Ivan, *Cartels of the Mind: Japan's Intellectual Closed Shop*, New York 1998.

Harney, Alexandra, 'Japan turns to dating agencies to lift births', in *Financial Times*, March 25, 2000.

Howell, Thomas R., William A. Noellert, Jesse G. Kreier, Alan Wm. Wolff, *Steel and the State: Government Intervention and Steel's Structural Crisis*, Economic Competition Among Nations Series, Boulder, Colorado 1988.

Japan Times, Initiative to ease child care: Dubbed 'New Angel Plan', Dec. 19, 1999.

Japanese Ministry of Health and Welfare, *Shôshi shakai to enzeru puran* [Few children society and the Angel Plan], 1999.

Kitschelt, Herbert, 'Industrial governance structures, innovation strategies, and the case of Japan: sectoral or cross-national comparative analysis?', in *International Organization*, Vol. 45, No. 4 (Autumn 1991).

Lehrer, Mark, Owen Darbishire, *The Performance of Economic Institutions in a Dynamic Environment: Air Transport and Telecommunications in Germany and Britain*, Discussion Paper, FS I 97-301, Wissenschaftszentrum Berlin für Sozialforschung, February 1997.

Maier, Friederike, Zorica Rapp in collaboration with Catherine Johnson (language editing), *Women and the Employment Rate: The Causes and Consequences of Variations in Female Activity and Employment Patterns in Germany*, German Report for the EC-Network 'Women and Employment', Equal Opportunities Unit, DG V, Commission of the European Union, Berlin, June 1995.

McIntosh, C. Alison, *Population Policy in Western Europe: Responses to Low Fertility in France, Sweden and West Germany*, New York 1983.

Migration News, Vol. 7, No. 4, April 2000.

North, Douglass, *Institutions, Institutional Change and Economic Performance*, Cambridge 1990.

OECD, 'Internet and Electronic Commerce Indicators Update', October 3, 2000, http://www.oecd.org/dsti/sti/it/cm/, 29 Oct. 2000.

OECD, 'Internet Price Comparison', October 23, 2000, http://www.oecd.org/dsti/sti/it/cm/, 29 Oct. 2000.

Ondrich, Jan, C. Katharina Spiess, 'Care of children in a low fertility setting: Transitions between home and market care for pre-school children in Germany', in *Population Studies* 52 (1998), 35–48.

Ostner, Ilona, 'Slow Motion: Women, Work and the Family in Germany', in Lewis, Jane (ed.), *Women and Social Policies in Europe: Work, Family and the State*, Aldershot, England: Edward Elgar, 1993.

Ostner, Ilona, 'The Politics of Care Policies in Germany', in Lewis, Jane (ed.), *Gender, Social Care, and Welfare State Restructuring in Europe*, Aldershot, England 1998.

PaineWebber, *World Steel Dynamics*, June 1998.

PaineWebber, *World Steel Dynamics*, Price Track #59, September 30, 1998.

Pfau-Effinger, Birgit, 'Culture or Structure as Explanations for Differences in Part-Time Work in Germany, Finland and the Netherlands?', in O'Reilly, Jacqueline, Colette Fagan (eds.), *Part-Time Prospects: An International Comparison of Part-Time Work in Europe, North America and the Pacific Rim*, New York 1998.

Sainsbury, Diane, 'Taxation, Family Responsibilities, and Employment', in Sainsbury, Diane (ed.), *Gender and Welfare State Regimes*, Oxford 1999.

Scherrer, Christoph, 'Governance of the Steel Industry: What Caused the Disintegration of the Oligopoly?', in Campbell, John L., J. Rogers Hollingsworth, Leon N. Lindberg, *Governance of the American Economy*, Cambridge 1991.

Schiersmann, Christiane, 'Germany: Recognizing the Value of Child Rearing', in Kamerman, Sheila B., Alfred J. Kahn (eds.), *Child Care, Parental Leave, and the Under 3s: Policy Innovation in Europe*, Westport, CT: Auburn House, 1991, pp. 51–79.

Schwartz, Felice N., 'Management Women and the New Facts of Life', in *Harvard Business Review*, 67: 1, January 1, 1989, pp. 65ff.

Streeck, Wolfgang, 'German Capitalism: Does It Exist? Can It Survive?', in *New Political Economy*, Vol. 2, No. 2 (1997).

The Economist, *I-modest Success*, March 11, 2000, pp. 97–98.

Thelen, Kathleen, Ikuo Kume, 'The Effects of Globalization on Labor Revisited: Lessons from Germany and Japan', in *Politics & Society*, Vol. 27, No. 4 (December 1999), pp. 477–505.

Tilton, Mark, *Restrained Trade: Cartels in Japan's Basic Materials Industries*, Ithaca, NY 1996.

Tilton, Mark, 'Regulatory Reform and Market Opening in Japan', in Carlile, Lonny E., Mark Tilton (eds.), *Is Japan Really Changing Its Ways? Market Reform and the Japanese Economy*, Washington, D.C. 1998.

Ueno, Chizuko, 'The Declining Birthrate: Whose Problem?', in *Review of Population and Social Policy* 7: 103–28 (1998).

United Nations Population Division, *Replacement Migration: Is It a Solution to Declining and Aging Populations?*, May 4, 2000.

Vogel, Steven K., *Freer Markets, More Rules: Regulatory Reform in Advanced Industrial Countries*, Ithaca, NY 1996.

Weiss, Linda, *The Myth of the Powerless State*, Ithaca, NY 1998.

Yashiro, Naohiro, 'The Economic Factors for the Declining Birthrate', in *Review of Population and Social Policy*, 7 (1998), pp. 129–44.

12

THE CHANGING ROLE OF HIGHER EDUCATION IN THE PROCESS OF INTERNATIONALISATION AND GLOBALISATION – A JAPAN–EUROPE COMPARISON

Ulrich Teichler

12.1 INTRODUCTION

12.1.1 New challenges for higher education

Experts tend to agree that the processes of internationalisation and globalisation might affect higher education substantially in various respects. Three directions of change deserve attention.

First, exchange of knowledge all over the world will be even more all-comprising and faster than ever before. It is generally assumed that Japan is well prepared for that – not the least because Japan as a late-coming country in the process of industralisation and the corresponding modernisation emphasized the need to collect information from all parts of the world more strongly (at a time when the first modern universities were established) than most other of today's most advanced societies (Nagai 1971).

Second, international cooperation between institutions of higher education and international mobility of students and staff grew, and higher education increased efforts to prepare their students for future international job roles. We know that Japanese programmes for exchange of scholars were substantially expanded in the 1990s. Also regulatory frameworks were changed in order to facilitate the employment of foreign academic staff. Finally, the Japanese government launched a programme which should stimulate the increase of foreign students in Japan from about 10,000 in early 1981 up to about 100,000 around the year 2000 (Ministry of Education, Science and Culture 1991). Actually, the figures remained below 60,000 (Teichler/Teichler-Urata 2000).

Internationalisation of the professional life of academics obviously takes different routes in the various major industrialized countries. On the one hand, academics in the U.S. and to some extent in the United Kingdom see little need for taking over international activities themselves, i.e. being active in international academic organisations, publishing abroad or even in other languages, seeking for information abroad which is not easily accessible at home, etc. In a survey on the academic profession in comparative perspective, I called this attitude "internationalisation by import". On the other hand, we note a "life-or-death-internationalisation" among some academics in smaller countries, e.g. Sweden or Israel, where academic achievement depends so much on international recognition that hardly any genuine national academic arena exists anymore. Japan and Germany still seem to be between these two extremes; they are "two-arena countries" where many academics believe that they can choose between primarily national visibility and primarily international visibility (Enders/Teichler 1995).

Third, it is widely assumed that, as a consequence of internationalisation and globalisation, the higher education institutions and their "products" will be in a more direct competition across countries in the future than they were in the past. Pressures for convergence of higher education might grow. At least, higher education institutions might be more strongly challenged in the past to compare their processes and outcomes and seek for the best possible solution.

12.1.2 The 12-country graduate survey

The aim of this contribution is to present the results of a recent survey of graduates from institutions of higher education in Japan and various European countries which might be salient for the challenges of internationalisation and globalisation. The study addressed some aspects of international learning of students and some international activities of graduates. However, the survey focused on the links between higher education and employment that Japanese and European graduates experienced within their national contexts. The differences between the findings in Japan and Europe might provide food for thought about changes required in the rapid process towards a global world.

In 1999, a survey was conducted of about 40,000 graduates from eleven European countries and Japan about four years after graduation. The study *Higher Education and Graduate Employment in Europe*, coordinated by the author of this contribution, initially was funded by the European Commission in the framework of the Targeted Socio-Economic Research Programme (TSER). Initially, nine European countries had prepared the research proposal jointly. Subsequently, two European countries and Japan joined the project. The European countries included are Austria, the Czech Republic, Finland, France, Germany, Italy, the Netherlands, Norway, Spain, Sweden, and the United Kingdom. The Japanese country study was funded by the Japan Institute of Labour and coordinated by Keiichi Yoshimoto, Kyushu University.

The study addressed the job search and transition period from higher education to employment as well as the employment situation during the first years after graduation. The study also examined the graduates' competences and their utilisation on the job, the extent to which the graduates consider their position and work tasks linked to higher education, graduates' expectations and the extent to which these expectations were fulfilled. Finally, questions were asked regarding further education and training and regarding the graduates' view of their long-term career prospects. Some questions on the socio-biographic background of the respondents, on the study conditions and provisions and on the study achievements and grades were asked as well in order to determine the extent to which these factors might explain varying employment and work paths of graduates. This analysis is based on a provisional data set available in August 2000.

12.2 INTERNATIONAL EXPERIENCES AND ACTIVITIES

For Japanese university graduates, international mobility prior to graduation and, after graduation, international experience have remained exceptions. This is true to all dimensions addressed in the survey.

Only two percent of the Japanese graduates had attended a school abroad or had worked abroad for some period before they enrolled at institutions of higher education. In the European countries included in the survey, the respective proportion ranged from four percent to 32 percent and was ten percent on average. Studying abroad for some period (the definition also might include the participation in summer courses) was more frequent: Eleven percent of the Japanese respondents had been abroad for some period during their course of study as compared to 23 percent of the European students.

It is well known that Japanese pupils have to prepare themselves thoroughly for entrance tests to higher education institutions. As English is a typical subject of the entrance examination, their knowledge of vocabulary and grammar tends to be high. However, only 20 percent of the Japanese graduates believe that they reached a high level of competence in English in order to read professional texts. In contrast, 69 percent of the European graduates believe that they can read well professional texts in English.

Given these conditions, it does not come as a surprise to note that few Japanese believe their employers have hired them because of their foreign experiences and foreign language proficiency. Actually, 13 percent of the Japanese graduates as compared to 26 percent of the European graduates stated that international experience was among the major employers' reasons for hiring them, and only eight percent of the Japanese graduates as compared to 14 percent of the European graduates believe that experience abroad was a major criterion.

Only a marginal number of Japanese graduates (less than one percent as compared to 8% of the European graduates) were employed abroad some time during the first four years after graduation. Three percent of the Japanese graduates had some assignment abroad by their employers. The respective figure was 13 percent for European graduates.

Finally, the proportion of Japanese graduates in charge of visible international tasks is small, as Table 21 shows. Only three percent embark frequently in professional communication in a foreign language (as compared to 23% of European graduates), and also only three percent communicate frequently with foreigners in the Japanese language (as compared to 18% of the European graduates who often communicate with foreigners in their home country language).

Table 21 International experiences and activities (percentage)

		Japan	Europe (range)	Europe (total)
(1)	Education/employment prior to study	2	4 – 32	10
(2)	Study abroad during study period	11	14 – 30	23
(3)	Reading professional English	20	30 – 100	69
(4)	Experience abroad as recruitment criterion	8	10 – 21	14
(5)	Foreign language proficiency as recruitment criterion	13	9 – 42	26
(6)	Professional communication in foreign language	3	11 – 32	23
(7)	Communication with foreigners in home language	3	5 – 61	18
(8)	Employment abroad since graduation	0	3 – 16	8
(9)	Assignment abroad by employer	3	7 – 26	13

Source: CHEERS.

For most of Japanese graduates, internationalisation and globalisation have little direct impact on their study and their career. One could have expected from the relatively low export quota and from the island situation of Japan that international mobility and international experiences play a much lesser role for Japanese graduates than for European graduates. The differences, though, are more striking than one could have expected. Globalisation affects study and professional roles of the Japanese graduates only to a limited extent.

12.3 EXPERIENCE ALONGSIDE STUDY

According to available statistics, Japanese higher education is more "efficient" than any other higher education system as far as students flows are concerned.[1] About 90 percent of those enrolling in a university programme eventually graduate, and among those graduating about 90 percent do so in the required period of study (i.e. mostly in four years).

Only few Japanese students undertake major activities outside the university during their course of study. Asked whether they were employed, acquired experiences through internships or spent major periods for child or family care, Japanese graduates stated that those kinds of activities comprised only three months on average during the course of study.

In contrast, the European graduates surveyed reported that they spent on average 20 months on those activities, ranging among eleven European countries from 14 to 28 months (see Table 22). Those periods could be viewed as interruption of study, as distraction from study, as frequent occurrence of part-time study, etc. As will be shown below, however, European graduates seem to believe that they have acquired a broader range of competence upon graduation than their Japanese counterparts, and certainly this was to some extent a consequence of their learning outside higher education.

Table 22 Other Activities During Study Period (months)

	Japan	Europe (range)	Europe (total)
Employment not related to study	0.1	6.0 – 9.5	7.6
Employment related to study	0.0	2.6 – 14.1	6.0
Internships, etc.	0.0	0.7 – 6.0	2.4
Child/family care	0.0	0.6 – 30	1.5
Others	0.1	–	2.5
Total	0.3	14.5 – 27.9	20.0

Source: CHEERS.

This does not mean that Japanese students spent most of their time during the study period on learning. The Japanese graduates reported that they spent only 20 hours on average on study activities during the lecture period. The corresponding figure was 33 hours for European students. Actually, Japanese graduates stated that they spent eleven hours per week during the lecture period and 20 hours outside the lecture period on *arubaito*, i.e. occasional jobs for earning money – about twice as much time as the European students (see Table 23).

The responses to the first questions are somehow misleading. Japanese students also acquire experience outside the organized teaching and learning processes, and this absorbs a considerable time span. However, the time devoted to work on the part of the Japanese students does not prolong, as

[1] Cf. various articles in Kaneko/Teichler 1997, OECD 2000.

Table 23 Weekly activities during study period (*hours*)

	Japan	Europe (range)	Europe (total)
(a) During lecture period			
Study activities	20.8	.	33.8
Extra-curricular activities	6.3	.	4.6
Employment/work	11.1	.	5.2
Other	.	.	0.8
Total	38.2	.	44.4
(b) Outside lecture period			
Study activities	4.6	0.7 – 13.4	3.8
Employment/work	20.3	3.7 – 23.0	12.5
Other	.	0.7 – 2.5	1.5
Total	24.8	11.0 – 26.9	17.4

Source: CHEERS.

a rule, the overall period of study, whereas such a prolongation is widespread in many European countries. In addition, the Japanese students hardly consider their *arubaito* as salient in any respect for their professionally-relevant competences whereas many European students believe that these activities outside study enrich their professionally-relevant competences.

12.4 TRANSITION TO EMPLOYMENT

Traditionally, analyses of the relationships between higher education and the world of work did not put much emphasis on the period of transition from study to employment. It was taken for granted that the labour market works more or less rationally in allocating the labour force as far as possibly according to job requirements. In recent years, however, more attention was paid to the transition process, which might operate smoothly or less smoothly (OECD 1999). Also, the transition period might be a stage with specific dynamics which, for example, possibly provide the smart ones of the less qualified students another chance and possibly cause problems for the highly qualified students not well prepared to handle the transition process.

Japan is known for the most smooth transition processes from education to employment (Teicher 1996; Yoshimoto 1996; Teicher/Teichler 2000). At least, until the early 1990s, the facts confirmed the conventional wisdom. Also, this survey of 1995 graduates by and large confirms this, even though employment problems of recent Japanese graduates increased since 1992.

According to the 12-country-study, 97 percent of Japanese graduates began their job search prior to graduation (most decisions are actually taken more than 6 months prior to graduation). In contrast, about one third of European graduates started the job search only around the time of graduation and more than one quarter only after graduation (see Table 24). Notably, many graduates from Southern European countries started the job search after graduation.

As far as the survey provides information, Japanese and European students and graduates spend a similar amount of time and energy on the job search. Both sought on average for a period of half a year and both contacted about 20 employers (see Table 24).

It is widely known that higher education institutions in Japan strongly assist their students' job search. Taking this into consideration it is surprising to note that "only" 30 percent of the Japanese graduates stated that help of their institution of higher education or of their teacher was actually instrumental for getting employed for the first time after graduation. But this figure clearly surpasses that of the European graduates where only five percent get employed through the help of their higher education institution or their teacher. About 30 percent each of the Japanese graduates get employed through responses to advertisements. In contrast, many European graduates found their job through contacting employers themselves (i.e. not in response to vacancies announced). The respective proportion was only three percent in Japan (see Table 24).

Table 24 Job search

	Japan	Europe (range)	Europe (total)
(a) Begin			
Prior to graduation	97%	16 – 63%	41%
Around graduation	2%	18 – 42%	32%
After graduation	1%	14 – 64%	27%
(b) Number of employers contacted	20.1	6 – 70	21.5
(c) Duration (months)	6.0	3.0 – 12.0	5.9
(d) Most important method			
- Response to advertisement	31%	12 – 55%	30%
- Help of HEI/teaching staff	30%	3 – 7%	5%
- Personal contacts/connections	13%	6 – 34%	15%
- Private employment agency	2%	0 – 21%	5%
- Self-application	3%	12 – 33%	20%
- Public employment agency	2%	1 – 6%	4%
- Others	16%	.	21%

Source: CHEERS.

The relatively smooth process of transition from higher education to employment in Japan is also underscored by the graduates' major activities during the first four years after graduation (see Table 25):

ULRICH TEICHLER

- Only one percent of the Japanese graduates, as compared to five percent of the European graduates, reported that they were unemployed most of the time.

- Only three percent of the Japanese, as compared to twelve percent in Europe, made their living predominantly with the help of temporary jobs.

- Four years after graduation, however, these differences have almost disappeared. 4 percent of the Japanese graduates compared to three percent of European graduates reported that they were unemployed (see Table 25).

Table 25 Employment of graduates (percentage)

	Japan	Europe (range)	Europe (total)
(a) Major activities since graduation			
- Regular employment/self employment	78	44 – 87	69
- Temporary jobs	3	2 – 23	12
- More than one job	1	0 – 14	6
- Unemployed most of the time	1	1 – 18	5
- Further study/training	14	5 – 60	22
- Child/family care	1	1 – 11	4
- Other	2	1 – 20	9
(b) Current activity - Employed	87	60 – 89	77
- Self employed	2	2 – 18	6
- Unemployed	4	1 – 10	3
- Training/study	5	1 – 14	7
- Child/family care	2	0 – 9	3
- Other	1	1 – 10	3

Source: CHEERS.

A smooth transition process is often seen as a favourable indicator of a desirable articulation between education and employment. In recent years, however, critical voices in Japan were more often heard than in the past. They ask whether the Japanese modes of transition create disadvantages for those not choosing the regular track of transition, do not work well if the labour constellation is shaken by economic problems, and discourage graduates to correct their choice of employment when they are disappointed, thus contributing to job dissatisfaction.

12.5 LINKS BETWEEN STUDY AND WORK

Students already get acquainted with their future job requirements in the transition process. They might collect information about possible assignments, and they get to know the employers' expectations. In the 12-country study, graduates were asked what aspects their employers appreciated when they recruited the respondents. As far as information on study is concerned, Japanese employers seem to take into consideration the reputation of the higher education institutions more strongly than their European counterparts, whereas the European employers more often see the field of study as crucial for employment.

These findings confirm the conventional wisdom that the higher education system in Japan is characterized by a steeper hierarchy of the institutions than the European systems and that Japanese employers more often expect graduates not to be specialists for certain occupational areas. There are differences among the European countries, but there is not a single European country among the eleven countries surveyed in which the reputation of the higher education institution plays such an important role and in which the field of study plays such a limited role as we observe in Japan.

Table 26 Importance of recruitment criteria (percentage)

	Japan	Europe (range)	Europe (total)
Field of study	37	54 – 85	72
Exam results	28	8 – 42	28
Practical/work experience	16	20 – 55	41
Reputation of HEI	41	15 – 26	20
Experience abroad	8	10 – 21	14
Foreign language proficiency	13	9 – 42	26
Computer skills	17	19 – 57	40
Recommendations, etc.	27	21 – 48	32
Personality	80	57 – 84	73

Source: CHEERS.

Table 26 shows, in addition, that European employers much more strongly emphasize additional competences which are not necessarily an integral part of the study programme: work experience, international experience, foreign language proficiency and computer skills. European graduates, in fact, believe that the acquisition of those additional competences turned out to be beneficial for them in the search for employment and desirable work assignments.

Japanese graduates rated their possibly professionally-relevant competences upon graduation not very favourably. In retrospect, Japanese graduates substantially less frequently than their European counterparts believe that they were prepared to work independently. But even as regards broad general knowledge their ratings were less positive than the Euopean graduates' ratings. Only with respect to competences such as adaptability, loyalty and leadership, were the responses of the Japanese and the European graduates similar on average (see Table 27).

Table 27 Select competence at time of graduation and job requirements
four years later (percentage)

	Japan	Europe (range)	Europe (total)	Japan	Europe (range)	Europe (total)
Broad general knowledge	44	47–71	60	77	432–78	58
Disciplinary theoretical knowledge	53	59–78	67	60	56–71	61
Planning, co-ordination, organising	18	18–51	39	67	59–88	78
Problem-solving ability	39	41–74	58	87	80–90	86
Creativity	29	34–62	47	60	45–72	63
Working under pressure	36	37–67	55	81	69–92	83
Working independently	31	50–83	72	81	69–92	83
Working in a team	46	50–86	61	81	73–93	81
Adaptability	59	50–82	64	83	65–88	79
Loyalty, integrity	70	45–89	68	75	63–80	75
Critical thinking	43	51–73	64	60	59–81	70
Leadership	28	15–42	28	56	44–68	57

Source: CHEERS.

According to the graduates, the job requirements for Japanese and European graduates four years after graduation are relatively similar. European graduates perceived somewhat higher demands for independent work and critical thinking, while Japanese graduates perceived a higher need for broad general knowledge. Otherwise, differences were marginal. This indicates that Japanese graduates feel much less prepared upon graduation for their work tasks than European graduates.

The data presented up to now still would allow one to assume that the higher discrepancy in Japan between competences upon graduation and job requirements could be a transient phenomenon, whereby Japanese graduates are less prepared for the work tasks upon graduation but catch up soon in a process of more intensive in-company training than their European counterparts. The subsequently presented data, however, do not confirm such a view.

In the 12-country study, graduates were also asked to characterize their job expectations and their real work situation. Responses suggest that Japanese graduates are similar in their expectations to their European counterparts. They are substantially more moderate in their hopes and expectations only as regards the opportunity of being assigned coordination and management tasks, and they harbour slightly more modest expectations regarding challenging work tasks and good career prospects. On the other hand, Japanese graduates hope more frequently than European graduates that their job provides them an opportunity to do something useful for society, and they also expect more frequently that their job will leave time for leisure activities.

Japanese graduates described their real work situation less favourably than their European counterparts. They less often were assigned coordination and management tasks, they less often had independent, varied and challenging assignments, and they could pursue their own ideas less frequently. They rated the social climate at work less favourably, and they were also less optimistic about their long-term career prospects and their opportunities of combining work and family tasks. Altogether, the Japanese graduates less often perceived their expectations as fulfilled than the European graduates (see Table 28).

Table 28 Desired and real work situation - select aspects (percentage)

	Japan	Europe (range)	Europe (total)	Japan	Europe (range)	Europe (total)
Independent work	70	51–88	76	50	43–88	66
Well-ordered tasks	60	29–78	56	34	31–69	43
Job security	38	39–66	48	55	50–77	62
Opportunity of pursuing own ideas	78	76–90	81	44	44–78	59
Good social climate	90	79–96	91	59	58–89	71
Chances of influence	32	6–92	29	25	6–83	22
Challenging tasks	64	49–90	78	40	42–81	66
Good career prospects	54	56–82	69	25	25–57	42
Time for leisure activity	83	55–84	73	47	31–67	45
Co-ordinating/ management activity	37	38–58	50	18	36–51	41
Chance of doing something useful for society	67	43–78	58	50	34–62	46
Variety	84	69–90	81	52	45–81	63
Good opportunity of combining employment and family tasks	60	51–84	67	30	37–75	45

Source: CHEERS.

Finally, the graduates were asked to assess the links between their study on the one hand and on the other employment and work in a general way. As Table 29 shows,

- only 22 percent of the Japanese graduates believe that they utilize their knowledge on the job to a considerable extent which they had acquired in the course of study. The respective proportion is higher in all eleven European countries surveyed. It varies from 28 percent to 74 percent and is 54 percent on average;

• similarly, only 43 percent of Japanese graduates consider their status and level of position as appropriate to their level of education; the respective proportion is 70 percent among European graduates whereby the country averages vary form 48 percent to 87 percent;

• 49 percent of Japanese graduates state that their work meets or even surpasses their expectation as compared to 81 percent of the European graduates (varying from 63% to 90%).

Table 29 Links between study and employment (percentage)

	Japan	Europe (range)	Europe (total)
Use of knowledge/skills	22	28 – 74	54
The only or best field of study	23	20 – 54	39
Appropriate level	43	48 – 87	70
Work meets expectations or better	49	63 – 90	81
Satisfaction with work	48	48 – 78	66
Utility of study for long-term career prospects	51	43 – 76	59
Utility of study for personal development	67	58 – 78	68
Would you choose the same field of study again	46	61 – 70	65
Would you study again	94	91 – 99	96

Source: CHEERS.

The differences are smaller with regards to overall satisfaction with their work (48% as compared to 66%). Almost as many Japanese as European graduates believe that their study will turn out to be useful for their long-term career (51% as compared to 59%).

It is not surprising to note that fewer Japanese graduates than European graduates believe that their field of study is the only one or the best one for their work assignments (23% as compared to 39%), because the links between area of knowledge and occupational field seem to be more flexible in Japan. However, substantially fewer Japanese graduates than European graduates state that they would choose the same field of study again (46% as compared to 65%).

The observed discrepancies and the stated disappointments notwithstanding, almost all Japanese graduates state that they would study again if they could choose again (94%). This is also true for European graduates (96% on average). Whatever the critical thoughts are, forgoing study is not viewed as a real choice.

12.6 CONCLUDING OBSERVATIONS

Japanese university graduates certainly live in an internationalised world. Knowledge is quickly spread over the globe. Many graduates work in globally active companies. Products and services from all parts of the world are at hand. Advertisements in Japan even might create the impression that there is hardly any other industrialized country so much in the heart of the globalised economy.

When asked, however, how much the trend towards internationalisation and globalisation affects their daily life of learning, other experience alongside their course of schooling and study and their professional life, the Japanese seem to be substantially less affected than the Europeans. Learning abroad and other concurrent experiences abroad are less frequent. Few feel really versatile in utilizing foreign languages. Few are commissioned abroad or work abroad, and few of those working at home have regularly visible international work assignments. The 12-country study is a snap-shot: it shows the differences between Japan and eleven European countries at a given point in time. The impact of internationalisation and globalisation on education and employment in Japan might have grown over time, but the differences between Japan and European countries is higher than one might have expected.

We currently discuss in Europe the possibility of the emergence of a real global market of higher education, whereby the institutions might put emphasis more and more on preparing students for a global labour market. Currently, only about two percent of European graduates are internationally mobile; so we might speculate about a distant future. If, in fact, a globalised labour market emerged soon, Japanese graduates would not be well prepared in respect to most of their competences. The 12-country survey suggests that the competences potentially relevant for work acquired upon graduation are substantially lower in Japan than in most European countries. Four years later, this is not made up for, and Japanese graduates note a higher discrepancy between their expectations and their real job situation. They note both that they are less prepared for the job and that they utilize their knowledge to a lesser extent on the job. Finally, Japanese graduates express more often dissatisfaction with their employment and work than their European counterparts.

A note of caution is in place. The 12-country study does not present any objective measure, and the ratings by the Japanese respondents might be more modest than those by the European respondents. However, the Japanese graduates express motives and expectations which are substantially more similar to their European counterparts than the statements about the job situation and the actual links between education and employment. Therefore, it seems unlikely that the yardsticks of Japanese and European students are completely different.

Altogether, the findings suggest that the higher education system and the employment system in Japan might come under an even stronger pressure for change than in Europe, if globalisation and internationalisation is going to have a stronger grip on the daily life of employment and work. But in concluding so, we should not overlook that the daily life of the U.S. graduates – not addressed in this study – is likely, at present, to be even less affected by internationalisation and globalisation than that of the Japanese graduates.

REFERENCES

Enders, Jürgen and Teichler, Ulrich, *Der Hochschullehrerberuf im internationalen Vergleich*, Bonn 1995.

Kaneko, Motohisa, Ulrich Teichler (eds.), 'Japanese Higher Education' (special issue), in: *Higher Education*, Vol. 34, no. 2 (1997).

Ministry of Education, Science and Culture, *Japanese Government Policies in Education, Science and Culture 1991: Scientific Research Contributing to the International Society*. Tokyo 1991.

Nagai, Michio, 'Westernization in Japanization: The Early Meiji Transformation of Education', in Shively, Donald H. (ed.), *Tradition and Modernization of Japanese Culture*, Princeton, NJ 1971, pp. 35–76.

OECD, ed. *Preparing Youth for the 21 Century*. Paris 1999.

OECD, *Education at a Glance: OECD Education Indicators 2000*. Paris 2000.

Teicher, Kerstin et al., *Bildung und Beschäftigung in der japanischen Forschungsliteratur*, München 1996.

Teicher, Kerstin and Teichler, Ulrich, *Der Übergang von der Hochschule in die Berufstätigkeit in Japan*, Opladen 2000.

Teichler, Ulrich, Yoko Teichler-Urata, 'Deutschland als Studienort für Japaner: Grenzen und Chancen', in Deutscher Akademischer Austauschdienst (ed.), *Mobilitätsstudien: Zur Attraktivität des Studienstandorts Deutschland in Asien*, Bielefeld 2000, pp. 5–106.

Yoshimoto, Keiichi, *Transition from School to Work in Japan*, Paris 1996, mimeo.